C000083617

The Welsh Rivers

For Clare, with whom I share my life.

THE WELSH RIVERS

**The Complete Guide to Canoeing and Kayaking
the Rivers of Wales**

Chris Sladden

Published by Chris Sladden Books

First published in Great Britain in 1998

by Chris Sladden Books

Copyright © 1998 Chris Sladden
ISBN 0-9516147-2-X

All trade enquiries to:
Cordee
3a De Montfort Street
Leicester LE1 7HD
U K
Fax [+44] 0 116 2471176

Warning: this book is printed using laser phobic ink and may degrade if scanned by photo-copiers.

Produced by The Ernest Press, Glasgow G44 3QD

Printed in China through Colorcraft Ltd.

Front Cover: gorge below Penmachno Woollen Mill.   Photo by Clare Jefferson.
Rear cover, top to bottom, left to right:

Stillness on the Lower Dee.   Photo Chris Sladden collection.
The first big hit on the Gain, photo taken by Grahame Burns.
Isolation in "The Hidden Gorge", located in N Wales and left for the paddler to discover. Photo by Clare Jefferson.

The Author

Chris Sladden has spent much of the last 17 years living and canoeing in Wales (though he is still an avid English rugby supporter). He spent four years at Bangor University where, in between rainfalls, he picked up a BSc and teaching diploma. After a brief spell teaching chemistry and outdoor education, he returned to university life in Cardiff, to read medicine. Here, placements at the various district general hospitals around the Principality coincidentally suited the exploration of the more out-lying of Wales' rivers.

He has kayaked in Europe, the Indian and Nepalese Himalaya, Mongolia, the Peruvian Andes, Africa, Australia, New Zealand, the USA, and Canada. In 1988, he completed a solo 1,400-mile descent of the River Danube, raising money for LATCH, a children's cancer appeal.

He is a general practitioner with various interests, including 'outdoor medicine'. Previous books include the *White Water Runs …* series.

Acknowledgments

I am extremely grateful to my sponsors who have assisted me during the research for this book:

Graham Mackereth of Pyranha Mouldings Ltd

For the past 16 years or so, I have been using *Pyranha* boats. During the research paddling for this book, I used a variety of *Pyranha* boats. These were mainly the *Stunt 300*, *Micro Bat 240*, *Acrobat 275* and a *Prospector* (Canadian canoe). The paddling of an estimated 5,000-plus kilometres of Welsh rivers has all been in *Pyranha* boats.

Lendal Paddles

For many of the later stages of the book, I used paddles specifically made for me by Alistair Wilson of *Lendal*. Always willing to be involved with a new project, Alistair and *Lendal* have been at the cutting edge of paddle technology for many years.

Dave Holloway of Euro Kayaks

I am extremely grateful for the supply of a selection of the *Cyclone* range of canoeing gear produced by *Euro Kayaks*.

Huw Evans of White Water Consultancy International Limited

Huw Evans runs *White Water Consultancy International Limited*, one of the country's foremost canoeing and kayaking traders. Based at Bronwydd Arms, on the banks of the Gwili, he supplies anything to do with the paddling world. Huw has faithfully supported me during the publication of all of my books and I am most grateful for his loyalty.

A project of this sort is rarely just one individual's efforts but, rather, represents the contributions and enthusiasms of many others. I am extremely grateful to the many people who have been involved in 'the book' in one way or another. If I have missed anyone out of this list, I apologise.

I would like to thank the 'Cryptic Irishman', who inspired a generation of paddlers - myself included. My mentor and life-long friend, Tim Palmer, is owed a special thanks; and my mother, Rosemary Sladden, for all kinds of support over the years.

I owe a particular debt of thanks to Phil Blain who not only provided me with photographs of some outrageous paddling, but was the main proofreader of the text. Without his knowledge and enthusiasm it would have been far more difficult to complete the project. Other proofreaders were Dave Proctor, Franco Ferrero, Carol Blain and Clare Jefferson who put in no less effort.

Trying to obtain photographs of Welsh paddling is a difficult task and I have relied on the goodwill and kind help of the following: Ian Walsh, Alan Fox (Foxy), Phil Blain, Shaun Baker, Heather Gunn and Loel Collins.

In addition, Ken Vickers of Cordee and Peter Hodgkiss of the Ernest Press were both extremely kind in steering me in the right direction regarding book publication.

Once again, I would like to thank Graham Mackereth, firstly, for agreeing to write the foreword and also, secondly, for his personal encouragement and faith in my canoeing projects over many years.

In addition to finding some excellent photographs for me to use, I would once again like to thank Alan Fox for dreaming up the chapter illustrations in the book.

In addition, to those people who have paddled with me, transported, fed and encouraged me, especially at times of low water - thank you. In particular, Fred Wondre, Paul and Jane Howells, Ambrose and Janice Hearne, Kimberley and Jane Jones, Neil and Carol Sweirs, Patrick and June Jefferson, Paul Jefferson, George Novak, Jel Coward, Piers Nesbit, Paul 'Wibbler' Ross, Mike Harrison, Andy Knight, John-Paul Eatock, Dave and Chrissie Evans. I would also like to thank Dick Renshaw, "climber turned paddler", who was willing to be led astray on a few of my more hare-brained ideas, and in doing so reflect some of his own enthusiasm back on me.

Finally, I would like, once again, to thank Clare Jefferson who not only has completed the huge task of typing but has, also, put up with my foul temper brought to the surface every time the PC crashed.

CONTENTS

FOREWORD

I feel particularly honoured to be asked to write a foreword for Chris and this guide to the rivers of Wales. Chris is the first person that I know who has attempted all the rivers in a country. Not only has he done this, but he has written a wonderful guide that will lead us all to the sections of exciting and stimulating rivers previously unknown.

Wales has so much to offer paddlers. An enormous diversity exists from the classic touring rivers of the Severn and Wye, the white water rivers of the Dee, Tryweryn and Usk and the fabled creeks such as the Fairy Glen. Wales also has a great number of unknown creeks, as I am beginning to find out, which are well worthy of further investigation. Wales is a land full of heritage, stories and folklore of King Arthur and the land of Dragons, of knights, castles and squires. A land of high peaks and peaceful places and easy or challenging travelling - the choice is yours.

Many British paddlers spend some time on the better known rivers and dream of trips to far away rivers in the Himalayas or the Americas. But in the right weather and with the right river conditions we have some fantastic water here, so accessible and ready for paddlers of all experience. Chris has done many of the technical rivers first but with the speed that rivers in Wales rise and fall, running these will not be like running the Tryweryn. Every time will be different, every time a new adventure.

This book that Chris has created will tell you more about Wales at its best and more about yourself.

Graham Mackereth

INTRODUCTION

Canoeing and kayaking are increasingly popular sports with tens of thousands of people trying their hand throughout the year. Adventure, challenge, days out with the family, exercise, nature-watching or simply messing about on the river are just a few of the reasons for participation in these fantastic sports.

Each of the reasons given above has contributed to the inception of this guide-book, over the past 17 years or so of my paddling in Wales. I clearly remember my first tentative strokes on the Menai Straits, and my words when I capsized and lost my glasses! From here, it was down the Llugwy and Dee and then ticking off rivers in Hargreaves and Storry's excellent first guide to North Wales. I still have my battered but precious copy. From these beginnings, I began to explore lesser-known streams during the exciting times of the early '80s, when many classic streams and falls were opened up. Unlike climbers, canoeists never really kept a proper record of first descents, though there are many of us who probably like to think we got some in. Who knows, really?

With ever changing water levels, the river is dynamic and always fresh. During a frantic period most rivers, streams and trickles were paddled. As someone once said, "if you spill your beer, someone will come along and paddle it"! By the early '90s, most stretches had been paddled and, by now, I would hazard a guess that nearly all the Welsh rivers have been paddled. This book details the rivers of Wales in their entirety (or as near as I can make it); with all of the information, unless stated otherwise, based entirely on personal experience.

Of course, claiming to have paddled all the Welsh rivers (in the region of 200 and over 2,500 kilometres of paddling) will cause a few raised eyebrows. I suspect it is nigh on impossible to paddle *all* stretches of moving water in a country - after all, a "once a year flood", makes even the unlikeliest of ditches a possibility. The dictionary definition of river is "a copious natural stream of water flowing in a channel to the sea or a lake etc.". Perhaps some of the smaller novelties in the book are stretching the definition rather a long way. If I have missed out anybody's favourite, or simply forgotten to do it then, perhaps, you could write and let me know for the next edition. Anyway, there are an awful lot of rivers in this book - enough for a lifetime or, at least, 17 years of Welsh paddling. "So, what now?" I have been asked. Well, I haven't paddled the Ogwen for a little while, so maybe I'll head back in that direction the next time it rains.

It is over eight years since *White Water Runs and Touring Rivers of South Wales* was published. This has long since sold out and was followed by a comparable guide to South West Wales. The books, paddling and adventure have kept me relatively sane whilst training and then working in earnest as a doctor. The first two books were received in good spirit, at least by most. The support I have had for this new, and far larger, project has been tremendous.

From the proofreaders, to people sending in photos and anecdotes, to the generous paddlers who bought a copy prior to publication, and for the general good wishes, a big thanks - it has all kept me going.

Of course, with writing any sort of guidebook promoting the use of the country-side there is the impact on the environment to consider. Not everyone approves the *raison d'être* of 'the guidebook'.

I have heard the argument of 'keeping local rivers for local paddlers'. I find it hard to agree with this way of thinking. Firstly, people will come and paddle without a guidebook regardless, if they so wish - after all, that's what I have done. The enjoyment of Welsh rivers should be open for everyone, not just a few. Not everyone will choose to buy a guidebook - it's a free world, and paddlers are not forced to use them. To take the parochial argument a step further would suggest, firstly, that objectors to 'outsiders' would never become outsiders themselves, and thus never venture to paddle on someone else's patch - and certainly would not, themselves, risk being caught using a guidebook!

Furthermore, I would hazard a guess that having the option to paddle one of 200 rivers may well take the pressure off some of the classics! In addition, there is no doubt that many canoeists appreciate some gentle direction and advice from a written source. Work is hard, weekends scarce (especially with good paddling conditions), and being able to use extra information to plan the best use of hard-earned time off is a good thing for many.

For each difficult encounter on a river, I guess I experience 20 or so friendly and positive ones. Most people I meet enjoy watching others doing their thing, especially so when they are polite, change discreetly, don't trample over gardens, and shut gates. Small groups on rivers greatly helps and considerate parking also plays its part. The countryside is there for everyone to respect and enjoy! I have tried to encourage this.

So, as I have put the finishing touches to the book, I couldn't help but to cast my mind back over the years. There was, I recall, the occasion of sitting my first finals examination in Bangor, when I saw this red-haired pate bobbing about outside the window. Smiling to myself, I managed to concentrate and finish the paper. I had guessed right: when I got outside, the boats were already loaded, my gear in the car, and I was cajoled into running the Ogwen which had come up on a summer storm. That first wave, relaxing me from the examination nerves, will stick in mind for years to come - a brilliant run.

Another memorable event was when I had my boat pinched by a difficult water bailiff (known to have refused help to a school hill walking party with a hypothermic child), only to be taken in, fed and looked-after by a gentle Welsh hill-farmer, who proceeded to retrieve my boat for me.

Whilst sitting on the banks of the Haffes after a long walk around the Horns of Mynydd Ddu with the water a mere trickle, just enough to soak my aching feet in, I pondered about life and then paddling. In 100 years' time, I wondered whether folk, after a long week's work, would still look to the skies over Wales for inspiration. And, if the skies opened, and the water came forth, would the paddlers appear from out of the woodwork of the drought? Would they strap the boats on the roofs of whatever vehicles are around then and head for the hills? The Haffes would have been "done", along with all the rest, a long time before but the computer or personal robot would, perhaps, still say it is a wonderful blast. But a guide - even in 100 years' time, can't paddle the Haffes for you. That's where all the excitement is - in the doing - I mean. That, surely, must still be there. I simply smiled. So, as I get old, just one run down the mighty Ogwen or Tawe and I'd die a happy man. Even then, if I were too stiff just one more chance to watch the Glaslyn in full flood and I'd be content, carried away once again by my love of the Welsh rivers.

So typically Welsh.

RIVER RUNNING AND USING THIS GUIDE

Canoeing and kayaking are more popular now than ever before. Paddlers are constantly looking for new rivers to run or for information on long-established classics.

Over the years, I found that I had paddled the vast majority of Welsh rivers and whilst paddling the rest, the concept of a complete guidebook to Welsh rivers grew. Unless otherwise stated, the information contained within this book is based entirely upon personal experience.

DISCLAIMER

These descriptions are based upon the situation found at time of paddling. I make no claim whatsoever that the rivers are safe in all conditions and for every canoeist. The decision to paddle must be yours alone - if you are not sure, don't paddle! I disclaim all responsibility for any injury or harassment caused to persons or property in this potentially dangerous sport.

CHANGING RIVERS

The rivers included in this guide (like any other rivers) change, sometimes dramatically, with time. Man, ever responsible, causes many of these changes in the form of weirs, canalization, pipes, bridges and neck-high barbed wire fences. Where new roads or bridges are built, there is always the possibility of debris being dumped in the river.

Nature, too, plays an important part in the shape of fallen trees and floods which change the river bed. The guide is written in good faith. However, with the best will in the world, one cannot always account for the human factor. It is also possible that misunderstandings between myself and the reader may arise. The message is clear: use the guide, but to avoid misinterpretation with un-pleasant consequences, *ALWAYS INSPECT BEFORE PADDLING*.

WATER LEVELS

Water levels are of fundamental importance to the decision of whether to paddle or not. The decision not to paddle may be due to the river being either too low or too high.

Common sense must prevail here. Too low, and the canoeing may be 'scraping the barrel' (or at least the bottom) making for tired arms and thin boats as you push yourselves into deeper water. Furthermore, a low level descent of the river may, firstly, be cheating the river and, secondly, cheating the paddler. I have seen paddlers getting off the Ogwen and Glaslyn at low, low levels and claiming that, firstly, the river is 'not up to much' and, secondly, probably kidding themselves that they are grade IV or V paddlers. This is not intended as a lesson from the 'prima donna' (any of my pals would soon dispel that) but the attempt to pass on some sensible advice from experience.

Usually, as above, the rivers tend to be a less serious proposition when low. However, this is not always the case: for example, the Fairy Glen and Wnion have unfortunately proved lethal when at low levels, because of the increased pinning possibilities. Sometimes low levels give a false sense of security.

In addition there is the environmental issue to consider. Plastic scraping along river beds may well impart some disturbance to them, and this should be carefully considered before launching.

Conversely, when the river is too high, the grade, and thus the seriousness, may change out of all proportion to that described here. This does not apply only to the high grade rivers. For example, the Gwendraeth Fawr is, as graded, I to II and is an excellent learning trip. However, in major flood, the river changes course through trees and around bridges, and becomes almost unrunnable. The gentle and bubbling class II Clywedog Brook was the scene of my fracturing and dislocating my ribs when in major flood - certainly more than its normal grade.

Most of these rivers require a steady rainfall to bring them up to a typical winter level on which most of these gradings are based. A few runs - for example, the Haffes, and Nant Peris - require exceptionally heavy rain to bring them into condition. Fortunately, Wales has more than its fair share of rain. However, it is perhaps sensible to say that with many Welsh rivers (especially the white water ones) - no rain - no paddling.

It is difficult to give clear advice on water levels in every case. Gauges do exist (a friend of mine even has one on his outside wall) but, more often than not, they are halfway down the run and difficult to inspect. Makeshift gauges are open to misunderstandings and I have made a point of not using these. I try to hint at good levels but, if you are paddling a flooded river, you should have the experience to judge for yourselves!

Grades often increase with rising water levels and I have used a dual grading system to try and cover this. Some rapids are decidedly hard at a particular grade, yet not quite hard enough to be a grade higher. I have tried to emphasise this, firstly, in the text and, secondly, by occasionally using a + or - to make the point. For example, the Pontardawe Clydach is grade III to IV in medium to "high-ish" water, yet becomes a continual IV+ rapid in very high flows. It is graded (III+ to IV) to IV+.

The message is clear - inspect everything before paddling, and make your own judgments.

ACCESS

Disclaimer

It must be stated from the outset that the words 'access' and 'egress' used in the narrative and maps of this book are no evidence whatsoever of any right to get on and off, or navigate, a river. The descriptions tell of what is physically, or was historically, possible to canoe or navigate! What is written here should not be taken as advice to trespass. If *you* decide to paddle on rivers without an access agreement, then you must use public rights of way, or ask the permission of the landowner.

Under the laws governing England and Wales many non-tidal waters are privately owned. These owners may or may not give permission to canoe along the waterways passing through their land. The canoeist does not have a legal right to paddle where he or she desires, unless there is a public right of navigation or an access agreement.

A book like this is a record of what it is possible to paddle in Wales, and may hopefully stimulate even further exploration. It is not however, and makes no attempt to be, a book of access agreements. I suspect, and hope, that this book will stay on the shelves for the next 20 years or more (albeit in future editions). The access situation is a dynamic affair. Agreements come and go, sometimes for the better and sometimes not. It is impossible for a text such as this to include meaningful agreements. This is not its purpose.

Certain rivers have excellent agreements - such as the Aberglaslyn gorge, where, now, a plaque cemented in the wall of the gorge gives details. Other well-known rivers such as the Conwy also have good river management agreements. Where these are working well, I have made a point of stressing the importance of sticking to these! These agreements have often been worked out amidst a great deal of blood, sweat and tears, trying to suit paddlers, fishermen and other countryside users alike. Recreation is important for all, and no paddler should try and spoil someone else's hard-earned time off.

There are many other, informal agreements, where fishermen and landowners have no objection to people paddling *out of season and given decent water levels.* Details change but up-to-date information can be had from local access officers or the Welsh Canoeing Association (WCA).

The WCA is the governing body for the sport in Wales. It is a democratic organisation and, therefore, almost by definition, I do not always agree with decisions arrived at. However, there are a few points that should be mentioned.

Most people involved with the WCA are real paddlers and, many, true pioneers of Welsh rivers or heavily involved with coaching or introducing people to our sport. Furthermore, they are extremely positive in involving the new generation of youngsters in paddling - and, after all, this is what it is all about.

The WCA and access officers have an often thankless task and difficult job to do. If you do not agree with them, or don't get the go-ahead you would like, do not be too hard on them (alternatively, get involved and make the necessary changes). A great deal of voluntary time and energy, not to mention a few grey hairs, have gone into some of the good working agreements so, in addition to this, where there are good working agreements, then *please adhere to them*.

If you think about it, mutual agreements between all users of a resource is the only way ahead. Canoeing and kayaking have grown tremendously over the past 15 years and there are literally tens of thousands of people wishing to try their hand on our waterways. The problem is that we have a finite volume of water, with various people wishing to use it. Morally, of course, we have a right to enjoy the heritage of the British countryside, but only with due consideration to, and not at the expense of other users.

Sometimes it is difficult to be positive when being bombarded by bricks, trying to disentangle oneself from anti-canoeing fences, or having a shotgun "let off" over one's head! However, the winds of change are, I am sure, in the air. The 'right to roam' policy being gently introduced through Parliament should affect our case. European laws and rights, too, may have a positive impact.

Furthermore, so may the National Lottery. There are various angling associations who are seeking grants to aid with various river-based projects. They should only be eligible for assistance if the funds allow more open usage of resources by all. Given such developments, I am cautiously optimistic that sensible agreements will eventually be worked out.

THIS FRAGILE ENVIRONMENT

One of the worst demonstrations involving a lack of sensitivity and common sense by canoeists that I have ever had unfortunate cause to witness was a university club roaring up to the Fairy Glen with two minibus-loads of paddlers. These rivers were never meant to support such numbers. Some of the Welsh streams are big enough *to take three or four paddlers, but no more*, in a team. Some time ago, on a Sunday morning, I saw three canoeists clambering over fences and trespassing over fields next to a South Wales river. I saw this because I was at a friend's farm at the time observing this with him, with some bemusement. One of the canoeists (and they had to be students) was wearing an all-in-one leopard suit, complete with tail! Luckily for him it wasn't lambing season! Anyway, common sense will prevail - I hope!

DESCRIPTIONS, CHARACTERISTICS AND GRADINGS

The guide is split into three sections: North, Mid and South Wales. This is actually quite a difficult thing to do as where, for example, does Mid Wales end and North Wales begin? It is a grey area, at least from the point of view of writing a river guide. In addition to this, many rivers start in one area and finish off in another. For example, the Tywi starts in the mountains of Mid Wales, but runs into the sea at Carmarthen which is in the South.

I have, therefore, divided the country by three somewhat arbitrary, but hopefully user-friendly lines. North and Mid Wales are split by a line that runs from Barmouth, via Dolgellau, through the Berwyn Mountains to Oswestry. Rivers north of this and the ones draining into them are included in the North Wales section.

Mid and South Wales are split by a line from Aberarth to Llandovery and via Hay-on-Wye to Hereford. The Mid Wales rivers are north of this and include rivers that flow into them.

The rivers are described in a clockwise direction, starting from west to east, (left to right) before completing a roughly circular path. They are also described as groups of rivers. This has been done by either choosing a main river, its tributaries and / or neighbours, or by selecting all the rivers close to a convenient centre. This has been done to aim for as user-friendly a format as I can make it. So far as possible, this is also convenient when referring to a particular Ordnance Survey (OS) map sheet.

Each river is shown on an approximately-scaled map to help with the description. The maps are drawn by a practising doctor and may, at times, sadly resemble my hand-writing skills. They are intended to supplement both the river and area descriptions, and should be seen as such. Figures and references from the appropriate OS maps are used for access and egress points and other major landmarks.

Each river description starts off with six lines of succinct information plus a short introduction. These are to enable the reader to make a very quick judgment as to the suitability of the river for their purposes. Firstly, the OS sheets within which the river will be found are noted. With 200 rivers, it is important to know in which part of the country the river is located. The grade is self-explanatory. The length is the overall length of the river and may be split into shorter and more manageable stretches within the text. The fourth line uses the heading of "Access". This is not referring, in any way, to the right of access but is to give a quick reference point as to how to get to the river. Generally, I include a road number and towns or villages between which a river runs. For example, access for the mighty Haffes is described as "A4067 Abercraf to

Sennybridge road". This means that the way to get to the Haffes will be some-where between these two towns along this A road. Using the text, finding the river should be reasonably straightforward. There are one or two rivers, high in the mountains, that really do require a large-scale map to find. I will usually state this in the notes. The fifth heading is "Notes", which is intended to briefly describe specific hazards which are important to paddling. For example, low trees, wires or fences and weirs may be mentioned. Lastly is a "star quality" rating graded from zero to five and described further on in the text.

The descriptions are not meant as an eddy by eddy, rock to rock analysis. They are meant to show suitable access and egress, notable falls, potential hazards, portages and an overall indication of what the river is like. I only hint at the best way to run a rapid, and that must be subjective to some degree. The real fun is left for you to discover. If at times I appear enthusiastic in the text, it is probably due to recollection of some fond memory.

There are various characteristics of the rivers in this guide that are of funda-mental importance to the paddler. The first is predominantly concerned with rivers high up in the mountains. This is the occurrence of flash floods which may alter the grade of a river out of all proportion. I have personally seen the Clydach Brook, a hard and gnarly run at the best of times, become a desperate prospect after heavy rain, on top of already high water conditions. *It is the paddler's personal responsibility to assess the water levels and, if neces-sary, portage, or choose another* river (see separate section on water levels).

The second characteristic is the presence of waterfalls on many of the moun-tains streams. It could be disastrous to run one of these by mistake.

Very importantly, many of these rivers pass through heavily-wooded areas where a tree or branch may block the canoeist's path. Due to the nature of some of these rivers it can be quite impossible to stop on some rapids if, for example, a tree blocks the way. The seriousness of the rapid may be increased out of all proportion to the grade. This should be borne particularly in mind after heavy storms and in closed-in gorges.

A fourth hazard is the presence of weirs or sluices on many Welsh rivers. Es-pecially in high water, these may produce very dangerous stoppers and towbacks. See the section on weirs. *Always, but always, be aware of the possibility of the "powers-that-be" deciding to build a new weir.*

A fifth danger on some of these rivers is the presence of low pipes that cross the river, and tunnels down which the river disappears. Tunnels are very excit-ing but there is no real way of knowing if they are clear of, for example, a tree, at time of paddling - unless you paddle them!

In addition to these, Welsh farmers hang many barbed wire fences across the rivers. These may change year by year as they rotate their stock around their fields.

A very important point regarding stock fences is that they often come in pairs (both ends of a field). Animals, too, can be a hazard. Six Charolais bulls with their bits and bobs swinging as they trundle down the middle of a river after you is enough to make even the weariest of paddlers liven up! Even rams can be a nuisance - see the section on the Afon Colwyn.

STAR RATING

Each river is given a star rating. There are six ratings ranging from the lowly 'no stars' up to the high-flying five stars *****. These are, without doubt, subjective and I make no apology for provoking a few raised eyebrows. Furthermore, they are not solely based on the white water quality, as this book is far more than a white water book, and covers all types of canoeing. A grade one river can achieve a five star rating. With the huge diversity of rivers found in Wales, five stars were needed to cover the enormous range of water available.

The star quality is given for the overall impression of the river and the type of paddling that it offers. For example, a grade I to II river through beautiful countryside, with abundant wildlife and crystal-clear waters, is the ideal touring section and will get a **** or ***** rating. Likewise, a hair-raising experience of continuous big, bouncy rapids, which tend to (though not always) occur through rugged scenery will also score high. I have attempted to be honest with the allocation of the stars but I, like most paddlers, sometimes just have a damn good day on the river - hence the inclusion of a few unlikely candidates.

GRID REFERENCES

Since certain places are difficult to describe, six-figure grid references are given for access, egress, and certain other points of importance. They indicate an area of land 100 metres square within which the location will be found. The Ordnance Survey (OS) Landranger map required for each section is indicated in the introduction.

GRADING THE RIVERS AND RAPIDS

The grading of rivers is a very difficult task. There are various problems with grading and the systems used. For years, paddlers have argued about, chewed over and spat out the systems that are available. There is still no universal grading system that every paddler accepts and, even if there were, people would still grade rivers differently. Paddlers are subjective, myself included, no matter how hard one tries to remain objective. It is tempting to grade a river as hard if one follows a poor line and takes a thrashing on a usually easy line: "it's a hard IV" - "No, it's an easy V"-type arguments are familiar to most.

The downgrading of rapids has also been a tendency over the past few years, especially by some experts or paragons of the sport. This would be fine if they followed a clear system for grading. For example, if having to make a series of complicated moves with the risk of a few back loops in a big hole, was graded III, then that would be fine so long as the system for grading described grade IIIs like this was consistent. None that I have seen do, and so problems inevitably arise.

Grades III, IV and V are usually where the discrepancies exist (and also *most* serious consequences) but this is not absolute. With harder and more dangerous rapids being tackled, there are more class VI rapids appearing. Of course, if one philosophizes, no grading system can be absolute. Where does class VI end and a new class VII start? Or, is it possible to extend grade VI as VI+, or 'super sixes' in order to cover all eventualities? Fortunately, in this book at the present time, I am not really forced to make that decision. It would be a lot harder to play on the world's stage where pushing of the grades is taking off each and every day. Today's standards are tomorrow's norms!

Terry Storry, somewhat bravely and admirably, brought in his dual grading system, which comprises a number grade for the technical difficulties, and a letter grade for the seriousness. Personally, I have found this system not an easy one to use when grading rapids. For example, the presence of a weir in a flat water river may make that section particularly dangerous but not affect the rest of the river. I would prefer to grade the river as one but point out clearly in the text that the weir is highly dangerous. An example might be the Mid Wales Clywedog Brook - a grade II stream best paddled in the week or so after heavy rain. In these conditions, it might be graded IIb. In flood, it becomes highly dangerous, flowing through trees and the odd fence. In fact, on this river, I had one of my worst accidents in flood conditions, fracturing one rib and dislocating two others under a barbed wire loop that I had not seen. It is still grade II paddling but I wouldn't know where to start if I were to give it a specific letter grade for danger. Should it be a D, E, F, or even C for careless? I guess it would need a different one for every water level. Better (in my mind at least), I feel, to grade it II in normal water conditions and stress the point that, probably, for most paddlers wanting to tackle this type of river, that it is best avoided when in major spate. Furthermore, it seems a little out of context to give a class V or VI rapid an extra dangerous grade. Class V and VI rapids are dangerous by definition.

Likewise, the presence of tunnels, sluices, and low bridges may increase the seriousness of particular rivers in particular places, and I have chosen to comment on this in the introduction and text sections of each description. Protection can, at times, make rapids and falls safer, as can prior knowledge of previous accident black spots, and I have tried to comment on this in the text.

If a river is continuous at a particular grade, it will usually make it more serious but not necessarily more technical. The moves may be the same, but, instead of having to perform them over 100 metres, it may be necessary to do so over a few kilometres! Many paddlers survive class IV rapids *but not* class IV rivers.

It is always harder to maintain skills over a sustained period of time. This, probably, along with the much bigger volume, are two reasons why many UK boaters get a shock to the system when launching on, for example, a comparably-graded US or even French river.

Lastly, grading rapids is not as specific as, perhaps, we would like. There are a range of "grades within a grade". By this I mean that there are "soft touch" grade IV rapids, and "top end" class IV with a whole host in between. The words "grade" and "class" are used interchangeably very much according to my whim - they mean the same thing. Occasionally, to emphasise the point, I use a + or - to clarify the grade as much as possible. I also comment strongly in the text. For example, if you have struggled down the isolated class IV Town Falls or Bala Mill Falls, don't expect an easy ride on the hard, continuous class IV rapids of the Pontardawe Clydach.

Perhaps the most important factor in grading is for the reader to know what I mean by a particular grade. Therefore, for class III and above, I have given a few examples of different sections of rivers that fit the grade - which can be used as an *aide-mémoire.*

DEFINITIONS

Grade I   Easy: moving water with the odd disturbances in the shape of small, regular waves and slight meanders.

Grade II   Moderate: the water is faster and rapids are more frequent; rocks, waves and small stoppers are found but always with an obvious channel.

Grade III   Harder: the pace quickens with fairly big waves, and stoppers which are quite capable of holding a boat firmly. Rapids are much more continuous and, although the route is fairly obvious, it is necessary to be able to manoeuvre the kayak well.

    Examples:

    i)   River Tryweryn, graveyard and slalom section, North Wales
    ii)   Upper River Leven (high water), Lake District
    iii)   Holme Pierrepoint (high release), Nottingham

Grade IV   Difficult: long stretches of heavy rapids and falls with irregular waves and often powerful holding stoppers. The route is not obvious from the water, and bank inspection is usually necessary. A mistake or swim could be serious.

Examples:

i)   Town Falls, River Dee, Wales
ii)   The middle Ogwen (usual high water conditions), North Wales
iii)   Cobden's Falls, River Llugwy, North Wales

Grade V   Extremely difficult: longer rapids, large drops with very big waves, dangerous stoppers and rocks to negotiate. This is a challenge to any canoeist. Although never absent in the lower grades, in grade V, substantial danger is always a possibility. Continual inspection and/or protection is often necessary.

Examples:

i)   The Aberglaslyn Gorge (just off flood), North Wales
ii)   The Fairy Glen, River Conwy, North Wales
iii)   The Middle Ogwen (in full flood), North Wales
iv)   The Wallowbarrow Gorge, River Duddon, Lake District

Grade VI   Limit of navigation: a line down exists - just. Luck may often play a part. There is always a real risk to life. Very favourable water conditions and protection may make rapids of this grade feasible. Very skillful paddling and the ability to pick the ideal days are also involved. Most of the time, however, they are too dangerous to canoe.

Examples:

i)   Upper two rapids of the Haffes, South Wales
ii)   Ceirw Falls (high water)
iii)   Pontardawe Clydach Falls, South Wales

Waterfalls *versus* class VI

It is only fair to say that the new generation of boaters are running harder and harder falls, and at higher and higher water levels. Therefore, there is a grey area where class VI runs into the, "waterfall usually portaged", description. If I offend anyone's efforts in running drops / class VI, then please forgive me - it is not intentional.

Many waterfalls are runnable only when the rest of the river is too low to contemplate. Perhaps, under these conditions, many could be described as bottleneck and back-testers! Often it is not feasible to run falls such as these when the rest of a river is worth doing. It is for this reason I tend to sometimes describe them as waterfalls, best portaged, rather than grade VI rapids, and not to challenge someone to prove me wrong.

Portages

"Uncanoeable sections", for whatever reasons, are marked as portages / 'X'.

Weirs

Dangerous weirs are marked as definite portages, whilst comments are made on those requiring inspection. Unusual spate water can make normally safe weirs dangerous. For example, in medium conditions, the horseshoe weir on the Afan can be run on the left. In flood it becomes a real killer with a towback of around 25 feet. Complacency towards weirs is always risky. I almost paid more than I bargained for whilst soloing a South Wales river because of this.

There are various pointers to the presence of a weir. Firstly, you may expect one because the guide say so. However, it is important to remember that weirs may change. New weirs may be built - eg. on the lower Tawe. "Bad weirs", may be made much "badder"! For example, the weir above Pontypridd on the Taff is now a definite portage.

There may be an unnatural slowing to the river - weirs are often used to control the flow. There may be a distinct horizon line. There may be a roar or rumble on a flat section - ask yourselves why, but remember that very quiet weirs can be extremely dangerous - eg. the ones below the egress on the Tryweryn! There may be an old mill on the banks - eg. Overton weir on the Dee. There may be new weir buildings or huts, or canalization as with the middle Ceiriog weir.

The message is clear - keep your eyes open, scout well ahead, and if in any doubt, portage. Remember, there are three categories of weirs:

i) Safe

ii) Dangerous

iii) Grey area - in which case they are dangerous! By grey I mean anything that the particular paddler isn't 100 percent sure about should be treated as dangerous.

The message is clear - if in doubt *PORTAGE*.

MAPS AND KEY TO SYMBOLS

Hand-drawn maps are included for all rivers, apart from the very lower sections of the Wye and Severn Bore. They are not drawn to exact scale and, in places, I have taken some liberties by bending and pushing the countryside to suit my purposes. They are intended to give quick visual information to the paddler: firstly, to help locate the river and, secondly, when used in conjunction with the text, to give a simplified overview which includes access, egress and some major landmarks.

Where possible, I have marked major weirs and waterfalls. However, some rivers have so many weirs and waterfalls, it is just not practicable to try and show all of them. Therefore, it should be noted that the maps do **not** show **every** landmark, fall or rapid. After a while, adding detail to sketch maps becomes meaningless.

Furthermore, whereas I have mentioned (where possible) permanent features such as low pipes that need to be portaged, I have made a particular point of not often marking all fences or fallen trees - though I certainly comment on these in the text. This is mainly due to, on the one hand, the dynamic nature of these obstacles and, on the other, managing the logistics of cartography.

Obviously, a large-scale map, preferably a 1:50 000 Ordnance Survey (OS) sheet would be advantageous to the visiting canoeist not familiar with the area. The names of relevant OS maps have been given in the descriptions. The maps are listed in each river description, and are also listed in the contents. Logistics have necessitated a little overlap on a few maps and, I hope, this won't limit their usage too much. Cartography, for me, is rather like facing an angry swan on the river: more time-consuming and difficult than the actual paddling.

Illustrations

There are three sections of full colour photographs in the book. Although these may be found within the North, Mid and South Wales sections the photographs do not correlate exactly with these areas. In other words, don't be too surprised to find a picture of the Llugwy in the South Wales section.

Key to Symbols Used

River	
Direction of flow	
Portage	Portage
Weir / Sluice	
Access	Start
Egress	Start / End
Gorge	
Bridge	
Main road	
B road / track	
Castle	
Old site of fort / castle	
Trees	
Church	
Sand / mud	
Reservoirs	

THE WELSH LANGUAGE

To the English ear, the Welsh language is, at most, an unmanageable jumble of sounds. Much of this is based on the idea that the Welsh alphabet is the same as the English one. This is not the case. In fact, the traditional Welsh alphabet consists of 28 letters. Certain sounds and words are notoriously mispronounced by the average English kayaker. Certain letters are actually double letters.

In my own, very much novice, way, I have tried to explain how a few of these should sound when pronounced correctly:

ch : as in the composer 'Bach'
dd : as in the name 'Pontypridd' rhymes with 'breathe'
f : like an English 'v'
ff : like an English 'f' - as in 'film'
ll : make the tongue say an 'l' and hiss. *Not*, as is often heard, pronouncing 'l' as in 'cl'an as in 'Clanberis'
w : as in b<u>oo</u>k
u : as in *hint*, therefore the North Wales River Llugwy is not pronounced 'Clugwi' but '<u>Ll</u>igowi', with a very short 'o' - if you see what I mean.

I have included a list of Welsh words and place names with their, or close to their, English meanings:

Aber	-	confluence or river mouth
Aberaeron	-	mouth of river Aeron
Afon	-	river
Allt	-	hill (usually wooded)
Bach	-	little
Baglan	-	saint's name
Bedd	-	grave
Bettws	-	chapel
Blaen	-	} head of a
Blaen-cwm	-	} valley
Blaendulais	-	source of the Dulais
Bont	-	bridge
Bryn cethin	-	hill of Cethin
Bryn coch	-	red hill
Cadair	-	chair
Caer	-	fort
Caerau	-	forts
Caerphilly	-	fort of ffili
Capel	-	chapel
Carnedd	-	stone / rock
Castell Carreg Cennen	-	Castle of the rock of the river Cennen

Cefn	-	ridge
Clogwyn	-	cliff
Clydach	-	rocky bed
Coch	-	red
Coed-cae	-	wooded field
Craig	-	crag
Creigiau	-	rocks or cliffs
Crib	-	narrow ridge
Cwm	-	hollow like mountain valley
Cymer	-	river confluence
Cyncoed	-	chief wood
Dinas	-	city or fort
Dinas Powys	-	fort of a tribal land
Du	-	black
Dyffryn	-	valley
Eglwys	-	church
Eira	-	snow
Ffordd	-	road
Gelli	-	small wood
Glas	-	blue
Gorseinon	-	the marsh of the Einon
Gwyn	-	white
Gwynt	-	wind
Gwyrfai	-	winding stream or river
Hafod	-	summer dwelling
Hendre	-	winter dwelling
Hen	-	old
Hirwaun	-	long meadow
Loughor	-	wet place
Llandaff	-	church on the river Taff
Llandeilo	-	church of St Eilo
Llyn	-	lake
Mawr	-	big
Merthyr Tydfil	-	grave of Tudful the martyr
Moel	-	bare round domed hill
Mynydd	-	mountain
Nant-Ffrancon	-	valley of the soldier
Newydd	-	new
Ogof	-	cave
Pen	-	chief, top or head
Pistyll	-	waterfall / spring
Pontardawe	-	bridge over the Tawe
Pontnewydd	-	new bridge
Pwll	-	pool
Raglan	-	the name of a person
Resolven	-	crop stubble
Roath	-	land near a fortress
Rhaeadr		waterfall

Rhigos	-	place of leather
Tondu	-	black lay land
Tref	-	town
Twll	-	hole
Ty newydd	-	new house
Tyn y pwll	-	house of the pool
Waun Felin	-	meadow of the mill
Yr Wyddfa	-	Snowdon
Ysbyty Ifan	-	Hospice / Hospital of Ifan

Richard Burton's birthplace at Pontrhydyfen.

NORTH WALES

Mick began to suspect that he had underestimated the size of the drop.

Afon Colwyn

Map:	Snowdon and surrounding area, no. 115
Grade:	IV - couple of sections of V
Length:	4 km
Access:	off A4058 Beddgelert to Caernarfon road
Notes:	some hard falls in a great spate river
Quality:	*****

The Colwyn draws from the Western flanks of Snowdon and via Llyn y Gader, the Nantlle Ridge. It can rise incredibly quickly and, at certain water levels, becomes an incredibly dangerous class V run. However, at normal high levels when linked with the Glaslyn's thundering gorge below, it makes for one of the best runs in the guide.

Hafod Ruffydd Isaf to Beddgelert: 4 km class IV with some V drops *****

It is possible to launch on the Colwyn at the A4085 Pont Cae'r-gors bridge but this section has a couple of fences and branches that needed portaging. It is better to take the small metalled road about a kilometre north of the forest picnic site to the bridge at the confluence of the two streams at Hafod Ruffydd Isaf GR575499. The locals here are really friendly so please don't drop the trousers in front of them! The river is fast and furious from the word 'go' with the first hard IV at the Forestry Commission bridge. Winding first right and then left the first steep drops occur a few 100 metres further on.

Freddie and the ram:

On a trip down here a ram took a fancy to a very good friend of mine whilst we were inspecting the steep drops. Unable to shake it off on land, Fred launched into the class IV to V drops. Amazingly the ram followed, only to disappear and then reappear, feet first. We hauled it out where it stood dripping wet with a bit of blood around the muzzle. It blinked a few times before deciding to take its chance with the next paddler in line - we all beat a hasty retreat.

There is a nasty little drop which is easier in medium to high flows, as a left hand route at these levels avoids a hidden boulder. This is immediately followed by a double drop. This is class IV to V depending on level.

Further down there is a steepening of the walls, with a sharp drop into a diagonal stopper. This has unseated some very good boaters who have spent time in the green room below. As the outskirts of Beddgelert are reached there is a significant class V drop below a stone bridge. This is easily inspected on the drive up. In big water there is a large stopper to be negotiated just below the bridge arch. A few good rapids follow until things ease off at the confluence, where it is easy to get off on the right bank GR591480. Just above the last grade V is a gauge which should be above 4 at a minimum level for the trip.

Afon Glaslyn

Map: Snowdon and surrounding area, no. 115
Grade: II and IV to V
Length: 16km
Access: A489
Notes: a beautiful gentle upper paddle with a thundering gorge below. Finishing off is a gentle meander to the sea.
Quality: ★★★★ and ★★★★★

The Glaslyn could be described as one of the true rivers of Snowdon as it drains many of the southern flanks of the mountain. The river becomes paddleable after moderate rainfall. The upper section is a wonderful beginners' river at medium levels. Due to the local copper deposits, it often runs for a few days after flood with an attractive blue hue. The gorge below is an entirely different prospect and, in full flood, is a fearsome sight. If the power station is running or the river is in spate, the section into Llyn Gwynant is nice at around II to III, though I haven't done it. Walk in from the power station and get on below the obvious big fall that is Cwm Dyli Gorge. The section from Gwynant to Dinas is also very pleasant.

The Glaslyn is, to my mind, one of the successes of a sensible access situation. There is now a plaque in the wall by the access for the gorge that says: *an agreement has been reached for paddling between 18 October and 1 April.* **This is brilliant, far better than some other ridiculous access agreements offering but a few weekends a year. We should stick to this - please, please adhere strictly to it!**

Upper Glaslyn - Llyn Dinas to A498 roadside: 4.5 km grade II★★★★

A layby, stile and footpath give excellent access onto the Glaslyn at Llyn Dinas GR612494. The first little rapid out of the lake gives a taste of the river's character. The only dangers are the occasional overhanging tree or rhododendron, which are fairly ubiquitous hereabouts. A long class II rapid is a bit of a surprise as the river enters Beddgelert. The Colwyn enters from river right, swelling the Glaslyn which turns southwards towards the forthcoming gorge. It is best to get out on river right, a little way below an old girder bridge. Walking down the bank, the happy paddler reaches a convenient layby GR592473.

The Aberglaslyn Gorge: 1.5 km class IV to V, depending on level*****

The Aberglaslyn Gorge is the stuff of myths and legends. Despite its shortness it is a test piece of Wales' water, and rightly so. The grade of the river depends so much on the water level. It is often paddled on a medium flood the day after a big spate. In full flood it is spectacular indeed, and only a very few paddlers have tackled it at these levels, when it is an extremely serious class V proposition.

A friend of mine, a quietly-spoken chap from Manchester, is quite a hair-boater. Rumour had it that he'd run the gorge with water lapping over the wooden bridge found on the left of the river by the main fall. On quizzing him about this, he replied quite characteristically, "no, it wasn't that high, it was at least a foot below the hand rail". Think of this the next time you are there.

A warm-up can be had in the first few 100 metres before the true gorge begins. From here on it's under the cosh all the way through waves, stoppers and falls galore. The largest drop has a bad reputation but appears to go through in most places, though far right or left normally work well. Below the large drop the river is still hard down to the bridge where, suddenly, it all stops and the river flattens out on a gentler course to the sea. Access river right 100 metres above bridge or left below bridge.

The Lower Glaslyn - Pont Aberglaslyn to Porthmadog: 11 km grade I*****

The start for families is a little problematical but, basically, access to the river is anywhere below the Aberglaslyn bridge. There are a few small laybys about one kilometre or so below the bridge where easy access can be made. It can be paddled at normal low levels and, as such, is an excellent touring river.

One way of avoiding fishermen is to try a full moon excursion - excellent fun in a well-organised, small group. Depending on the state of the tide, you may find shallows before and after Pont Croesor (B4410). To the right loom the most majestic of cliffs where brightly clad 'rock jocks' strut their stuff. This is Tremadog. This is a tidal area, where the sun's last rays strike golds and bronzes, and silhouetted seabirds take off and land. It is a wonderful place. Look over your shoulder and glimpse Cnicht, the Moelwyns or the Nantlle - the best of Welsh hills.

Egress on the *left* bank close to the Rebecca Toll booth GR583379. A convenient ramp is present.

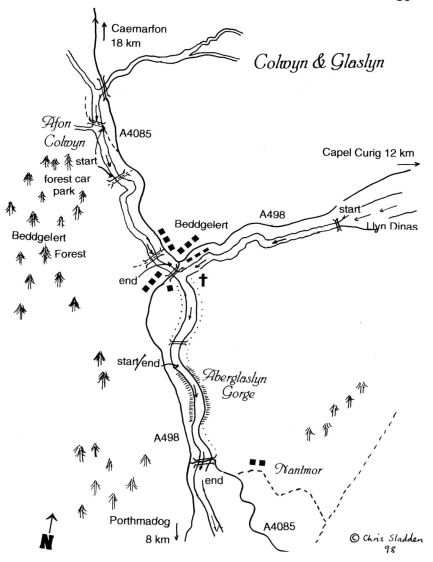

Caernarfon
18 km

Colwyn & Glaslyn

*Afon
Colwyn*

A4085

start

forest car
park

Beddgelert
Forest

Capel Curig 12 km

A498

start

Llyn Dinas

Beddgelert

end

start/end

*Aberglaslyn
Gorge*

A498

end

Porthmadog
8 km

Nantmor

A4085

© Chris Sladden
98

N

The Afon Nantmor

Map:	Snowdon and surrounding area, no. 115
Grade:	IV
Length:	4 km
Access:	A498 Beddgelert to Capel road
Notes:	wires need portaging
Quality:	***

"Haven't you done the Nantmor?" said a friend of ours who lives near the get-in point, "I saw some paddlers on it the other day and it looked really exciting - you must do it". So I did, and it was.

The time to run the Nantmor is when the other rivers look too big, as good spate conditions are needed.

Gelli-lago bridge to Bwlchgwernog bridge: 4 km grade IV***

There is a beautiful little back road that runs between the A4085 and the A489. This crosses the Glaslyn by turning off left between Llyn Gwynant and Llyn Dinas before eventually following a little stream - which is the Nantmor. Access can be made opposite an old quarry workings (parking), and below the small bridge GR632483.

The river is pretty full-on from the word 'go', as it piles down towards and under the following road bridge. A couple of wires stretched across the torrent below the bridge, and these needed portaging at time of paddling. However, I have it on good authority that in early '98, there was one wire and one rope course, both of which could be sneaked with care. The message is clear: fences change so, if unsure, always inspect. A gorge is entered through which you pass at top knots. Easier water for a bit until a second gorge is entered which is even faster and steeper than the first one. The line is far left and the stopper has been known to thrash even South America-hardened paddlers. Continual inspection is necessary. Trees are always a potential problem, but with some fierce bobbing and weaving and with the easing off of the current, egress can be made two bridges down at Bwlchgwernog GR611453. Just prior to this is the earlier-mentioned rope course.

If you have enough adrenaline left, quickly nip back upstream for another run.

Afon Croesor

Map:	Dolgellau and surrounding area, no. 124
Grade:	V to VI
Length:	2 km
Access:	turn off A4085
Notes:	possible portages
Quality:	***

The Croesor is a somewhat unlikely paddle, but certainly entertaining in its own way. From the gentle put-on in the village of Croesor, it reaches a point where it suddenly heads downhill at an alarming rate.

Croesor to A4085 bridge: 2 km class V to VI, with possible portages***

From the A4085 Beddgelert - Penrhyndeudraeth road, turn off in the village of Garreg Llanfrothen and drive up to the put-in by the river in the car park at Croesor.

During, or just after, heavy rain normally gives a suitable level for this exciting class V waterfall run. The river is a rocky grade II and III for the first 500 metres or so, before entering a series of drops with deep plunge pools. Though all of these drops have been run, the last - a double high squeeze onto guarding rocks and undercuts - is best portaged. This can be inspected by walking up the footpath river right from the egress point, below the cliffs of Carreg Hyll Drem GR615431.

Before paddling have a look at the knife-edged gorge of the Afon Maesgwm - again paddled, but not by me.

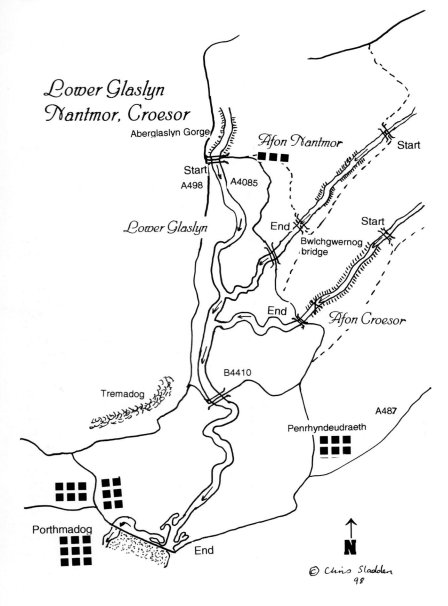

Lower Glaslyn Nantmor, Croesor

Aberglaslyn Gorge

Afon Nantmor

Start

Start
A498   A4085

Lower Glaslyn

Start

End

Bwlchgwernog
bridge

End

Afon Croesor

B4410

Tremadog

A487

Penrhyndeudraeth

Porthmadog

End

N

© Chris Sladden
98

Afon Dwyfor

Map:	Snowdon, Dolgellau and Lleyn sheets, nos. 115,124 and 123
Grade:	III to IV
Length:	12 km
Access:	A487 Porthmadog to Caernarfon road
Notes:	one weir - portage in high flows; trees ++
Quality:	**** *lower gorge only*

The lower section in big water is an excellent blast, a bit like a bigger and better Tryweryn.

Llanfihangel y Pennant to Llanystumdwy: 12 km class III to IV; portages****

Cwm Pennant can be reached either by working your way upstream, with the use of an OS sheet, from Llanystumdwy, or from where the A487 crosses the river higher up.

Draining Moel Hebog and the southern aspect of the Nantlle Ridge, in times of heavy rain the Dwyfor can get into a huge flood. Though paddleable from the end of the road in Cwm Pennant during high water conditions, this is a real pain because of the number of trees. Even further down, in high water the trees are immensely dangerous and the upper sections cannot really be recommended. A day or so after rain they are much more manageable. The bottom gorge, however, is a superb run in big water conditions.

Access can be made below the bridge in Llanfihangel y Pennant GR526450. The drop immediately at the bridge is a difficult one for starters because of the number of trees blocking the line. The river is only grade II until the main A487 trunk road bridge, but there was one set of wires under the Brynkir road bridge which required portaging.

A little way beyond the main road bridge is a weir that should be fairly obvious from the river. Two large central stanchions and weir buildings on the right, plus a definite horizon line, should alert the warning bells. This can be shot with speed when low-ish, **but looks lethal when in flood and is a definite portage.** Below this weir, rapids begin to build up and become grade III and IV in high water. These are absolutely superb rapids but they are a total nightmare because of the numerous trees ruining the lines.

Things improve remarkably once you have passed the bridge at Pont Rhyd y Benllyg, and indeed this is where I now get on. From here down, superb grade III to IV rapids lead all the way into Llanystumdwy. In good water, this is like a bigger volume, more continuous Tryweryn, and there are excellent stoppers and waves to shred. The big weir below the bridge in town can be shot left or right, but it is easier to egress up the small steps near the cemetery on the right.

Afon Dwyfach

Map:	Lleyn Peninsula
Grade:	II+ (one rapid III)
Length:	7 km
Access:	A489 Criccieth to Pwllheli road
Notes:	hazards - two definite wires needed portaging, plus trees
Quality:	**

This river turned out to be a good little run, albeit with a few portages around trees and fences. With competent leaders, good intermediate paddlers can have an excellent day out. If this river is up, it is safe to say, so is the Dwyfor, the bottom gorge of which is an excellent run at grade III to IV.

Fron oleu bridge to Bont Fechan: 7 km grade II+; a few portages**

Turn off the A487 Porthmadog to Caernarfon road along the B4411 where, about 2 kilometres down here, it is possible to turn off rightwards and cross the river at a small bridge by Fron oleu Farm GR474417.

The river is pretty well a continuous class II+ from the word 'go' and needs to be in spate at the put-in. However, it is important that the water is still well within the banks as, any higher, it becomes very dangerous at the grade. Some way down the river, a footbridge is passed and, just below this, was the first fence that needed portaging. A road bridge comes next, which is followed by some good rapids. Some way after, on the right hand bank, is an obvious country park-type area. Just below this, on a left-hand bend, is a small weir which can be easily run on the left. A little way below this, at time of last paddling (December '97) were a couple of trees that needed portaging. A Portmeirion-type house is passed on the right hand bank and, indeed, this was designed by Clough Williams-Ellis. Rapids continue down to the next road bridge, after which the river begins to ease off and one further fence required portaging. Pass under the main A497 road bridge and finish off at the next small bridge, which is Bont Fechan. Egress upstream right - there is a fence below GR463380.

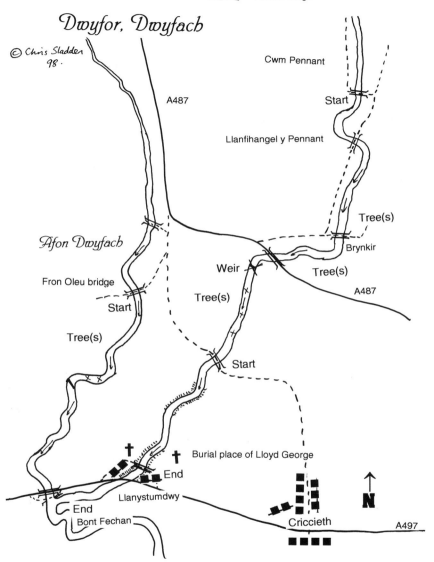

△△ Nantlle Ridge

Dwyfor, Dwyfach

© Chris Sladden
98.

Cwm Pennant

A487

Start

Llanfihangel y Pennant

Tree(s)

Afon Dwyfach

Brynkir

Weir

Tree(s)

Fron Oleu bridge

Tree(s)

A487

Start

Tree(s)

Tree(s)

Start

Burial place of Lloyd George

†

† End

End

Llanystumdwy

N

End

Bont Fechan

Criccieth

A497

Afon Llyfni

Map:	Snowdon and surrounding area, no. 115
Grade:	II to III
Length:	12 km
Access:	B4418 Rhyd Ddu to Penygroes road
Notes:	two weirs - sticky in flood and one low wire
Quality:	*****

An outstanding river at its grade. The bottom section is continuous rapids whereas the top section is quite unique and provides amusement for the needy. It is the next river down from the popular Seiont and Gwyrfai sections but, strangely enough, I could find no information on it until I paddled it. Go and see yourselves - it's great! It also runs for a good few days after heavy rain.

Llyn Nantlle to Pontllyfni: 12 km class II to III*****

Following the B4418 Nantlle to Penygroes road it is possible to put on the river just downstream of Llyn Nantlle GR508530. It is well worth it, just for the sheer entertainment value, to start on this upper section (unless the river is in big flood). After 100 m the flat stream enters 'the Everglades' and for 15 minutes or so you may paddle around looking for the exit. Be careful of floating logs for they may be **alligators!** There is one fence in here which can be passed either far left or right - if you can work out where far right or left is.

Once again in the open the river is flat and fast as it cruises under a railway bridge, and drifts through built-up banks towards the first road bridge. Two small footbridges are next before small steps and class II waves begin. As you enter Penygroes the rapids pick up and great surfing at the grade can be had. Soon the water becomes continual II as it shoots under the austere-looking railway bridge. Care is needed below as a few odd stakes are evident.

Soon the rapids are continuous class II+. As you pass a big house (an old mill) a gorge is entered. Following Corner Falls the rapids reach class III in good water and continue down to the beautiful little Pont y Eim. Just below are two weirs that, although easy in medium flows, become sticky in big water and some may wish to portage in these conditions.

The run finishes off down to the main A499 road bridge in Pontllyfni where egress can be made downstream right GR434526.

Afon Gwyrfai

Map:	Snowdon and surrounding area, no. 115
Grade:	III
Length:	5 km
Access:	A4085 Caernarfon to Beddgelert road
Notes:	upper section class IV and falls IV to V; few portages
Quality:	***

Storry and Hargreaves came out with the classic line of the Gwyrfai being enjoyed by aquatic dinosaurs (long necks and no brains). By today's standards, the Gwyrfai is not as fearful as its reputation suggests, but I just can't better this description. The trees and low bridges, not to mention wasps' nests, still demand respect.

The very upper section from the source at Llyn y Gader has been run at class IV GR568523. The pleasing falls at Betws Garmon go at IV to V depending on flow levels and the section down to Waunfawr bridge from here is only class II.

Waunfawr bridge to Bontnewydd: 5 km class III; possible portages***

From the get-in at the A4085 bridge GR526590 the river is a windy and technical class III. Trees may need portaging, depending on the height of the water. A small bridge about two kilometres down needs portaging in high flows, but can be rolled or sneaked when lower. The rapids continue at a good III with some interesting drops on the way down to Bontnewydd. There is an anti-scour weir in the village that becomes nasty at high flows and at such levels is best portaged. Egress can be made at either bridges in town GR486597. In '86 when we did a source-to-sea trip, we carried on to the river's mouth with no difficulties - apart from braving the sewage works at Pont Faen.

Afon Seiont / Rhythallt

Map:	Snowdon and surrounding area, no. 115
Grade:	III; one fall IV
Length:	13 km
Access:	A4086 Caernarfon to Llanberis road
Notes:	no portages, but one fall IV, plus weirs, plus possible anti-canoeing fences!
Quality:	****

The Seiont is a great paddling river but has seen its fair share of epics; most of them involving aggressive fishermen rather than rapids. Even in the very early '80s, the river was fraught with hassle. Often as the paddler was left on their own whilst the car shuttle occurred, they would be surrounded by three or four threatening figures objecting to their enjoying a hard-earned day out.

Stonings were more commonplace than in the Bible, and it seemed to matter little who the kayakers were. School children were equally fair game for some individuals. In 1987, the proverbial hit the fan when Ben Wright, a local paddler, was stoned and suffered serious facial injuries whilst assisting another paddler in distress. A mass rally / trespass was organised on the Seiont, by the Campaign for River Access for Canoes and Kayaks (CRACK). An enormous amount of publicity was raised, much in sympathy with the cause of paddlers. It is debatable as to the outcome regarding access to the Seiont but in the long tern, surely, it must have raised awareness of problems facing people wishing to enjoy the country's heritage. Personally, I am convinced that the day will come when the European Court of Human Rights will step out decisively on 'rivers for all'. In any case, the Seiont is still a great river. In '97 there were still fences slung across the river, many from local authority-owned bridges! I would suggest taking along a pair of wire cutters. *These are not stock fences but are deliberately placed to snaggle canoeists. I am not suggesting cutting fences but the wire cutters could* **save someone's life**. *This might be a fisherman or even a child who accidentally falls into the river: there has not been a lot of thought behind placing these fences.*

Pont Rhythallt pylons to Caernarfon: 11 km grade III; one fall (IV); few weirs ****

The river bed should be well covered at the get-in for the run to be worth doing. Historically, the *old* stone bridge at the mouth of Llyn Padarn (GR559624) was a possible get on point **but under no account should this be used!** There has been a successful prosecution of a canoeist for disturbing salmon-spawning beds here and it is not sensible to repeat this, especially as there is a far better access point below the spawning area. About two kilometres below the lake is a turning into Pont Rhythallt, where there is a bridge across the river. Crossing from north to south there is a small road on the right immediately after the bridge which leads to some electricity pylons where access can be made GR550636. Soon Pont Rhythallt is reached and passed and, a little way on, the largest drop is reached (IV). Inspection allows the easiest line to be judged and for many this may be their first class IV. It sticks in my mind - as the first time I successfully rolled in anger. Easier water leads to the next bridge, after which there are a series of excellent steps with the odd small weir to negotiate. The occasional branch can cause problems so it pays to be vigilant.

Before the main road bridge the river picks up, featuring some continual class III rapids interspersed with weirs - a super section this. The water eases off with the odd rapid and a few weirs on the way into Caernarfon. Some of these weirs can become a bit sticky in high flows. Under the A487, round a corner, and suddenly the paddler finds him-/herself in Caernarfon harbour. A great river: from below the slopes of Snowdon, to the ramparts of one of the great castles of Wales - and all this in one day.

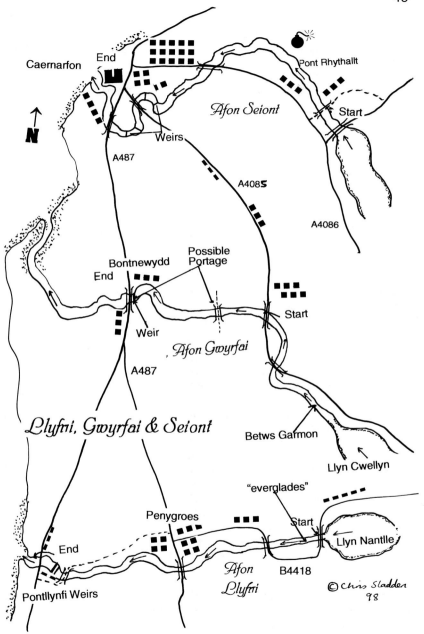

Caernarfon

End

N

Weirs

A487

Afon Seiont

Pont Rhythallt

Start

A408S

A4086

Bontnewydd

End

Possible Portage

Weir

Start

Afon Gwyrfai

A487

Llyfni, Gwyrfai & Seiont

Betws Garmon

Llyn Cwellyn

"everglades"

Penygroes

Start

Llyn Nantlle

End

B4418

Afon Llyfni

Pontllynfi Weirs

© Chris Sladden
98

Afon Arddu

Map:	Snowdon and surrounding area, no. 115
Grade:	IV to V
Length:	3 km
Access:	from A4086 Llanberis Road
Notes:	some portages though all but one of the drops have been shot
Quality:	*****

The Arddu is a wonderful expedition. From the shadows of the great cliffs of Clogwyn a wild ride can be had down into the town of Llanberis. What better use of one of those unique Summer storms than to trek into and ride out of the heart of Snowdonia.

Halfway House to Llanberis: 3 km of IV to V; some portages*****

Turn off near the Llanberis railway station and head up the steep road that parallels the Snowdon mountain railway. Reaching as far as is possible by car, one then has to carry the boats in for another one to two kilometres. Access can be made above a series of super drops GR592570. After the initial flurry, the river drops down to about a class II as it rushes downhill.

An old iron girder gives warning of a series of five drops; *class V* with some rock bouncing. The final drop is sheer magic - a Corsica-like fall between smooth boulders, into a seemingly bottomless pool.

Some 500 m of class III or so lead to the railway bridge. Here are the **Llanberis Falls**. The first drop is yet to be done to my knowledge - an extremely nasty fall. The main falls have seen a few audacious descents but the middle drop is one of the country's most perfect waterfalls and was run years before the main drop was first done. Incidentally, the other river dropping in from the left before the falls has some interesting if radical drops which have been run. Realistically it may be best to portage this whole class VI area. The section below the falls is perfect for photographs but beware the two main falls which have railway metalwork in them - both shootable.

Afon Nant Peris

Map:	Snowdon and surrounding area, no. 115
Grade:	V
Length:	2 km
Access:	A4086 Llanberis Pass
Notes:	one possible portage top end V
Quality:	****

Falling incredibly steeply over and around huge chockstones, the Nant Peris parallels the Llanberis Pass from Pen Y Pass to just before that most famous of climbing centres, where it pours its wrath into Llyn Peris. It can only be considered in very big water when the whole of Snowdonia is awash. In these conditions it is an excellent though somewhat frightening run. The river has actually been run from just below Pen Y Pass youth hostel in very big flows. If you do this section there is one footbridge that needs portaging.

Pont y Gromlech to Gwastadnant bridge: 2 km IV to V; one possible portage****

If you want a warm-up then do the Nantygwyryd falling down into Llynnau Mymbyr, before driving down the pass to where access can be made at Pont Y Gromlech GR630565. In good water it is very difficult to get under the bridge so get on below. The calm before the storm is only about 150 metres or so of paddling before the immensely steep layby rapids are reached. The water rages through huge chockstones in a tight right-sided line. Bearing in mind its relatively few descents over the years, the rapid has seen a relatively large number of epics! The grade is top end of V but, since the line is next to the bank, rescue is made that bit easier. Many portage this drop. A small road bridge is passed under.

Below this the water eases off only to wind up a notch or two above and below the next bridge down. Good water leads down to a huge fallen tree a little way above the following farm road bridge GR613576. This is a possible place to get out but it is better to continue to the next bridge and car park in Nant Peris.

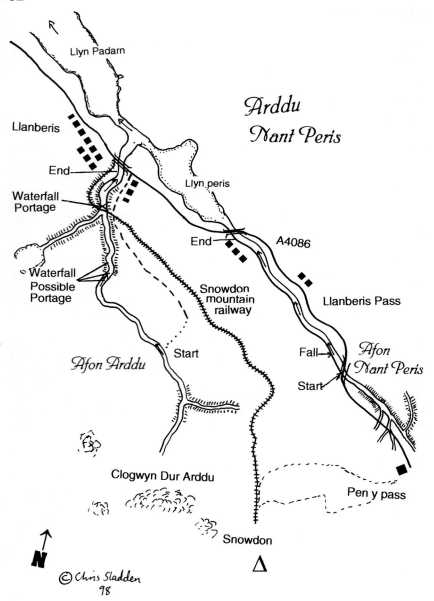

Llyn Padarn

Arddu
Nant Peris

Llanberis

End

Llyn peris

Waterfall
Portage

End

A4086

Waterfall
Possible
Portage

Snowdon
mountain
railway

Llanberis Pass

Afon Arddu

Start

Fall

Afon
Nant Peris

Start

Clogwyn Dur Arddu

Pen y pass

N

© Chris Sladden
98

Snowdon

Δ

Afon Ogwen

Map:	Snowdon and surrounding area, no. 115
Grade:	sections of III to IV, and IV to V
Length:	10 kilometres
Access:	A5
Notes:	no portages
Quality:	***and ****and *****

The Ogwen is a stunning river by any standards. Without any doubt, it is in the top ten great British white water rivers. The river is only worth doing after moderate to heavy rain, though some claim to have had a 'boring' run down the classic sections in lower water.

Draining seven of the Welsh 3000s peaks, the river begins its tumble over the mighty Rhaeadr Ogwen at the head of the Nant Ffrancon valley. Rumour has it that even these mighty falls have been run?

Some time ago I paddled, for completion, the section below the falls to Tyn Y Maes gorge, a four-kilometre, windy, flat section with a few barbed wires to dodge around. It detracts so much from the other sections that it cannot be recommended.

When all the side streams running into the Nant Ffrancon are white, you can be assured of some good sport on the sections below. It is convenient to split the Ogwen into three sections with one little novelty above in the shape of Tyn Y Maes. Levels can be inspected at various points, which is sensible so as to avoid the shock of the Llafar, Caseg and Marchlyn Mawr rivers doubling the troubles ahead! Ogwen Bank, the B4409, scout hut and A5 bridges are sensible viewing points.

Tyn y Maes bridge to Ogwen Bank: 1.5 km of grade I, and V to V+***

The small bridge crossing the river just north of the A5 Motel GR633643 allows a starting point if you want to try your luck at the drops below. The gorge is only sensible when the rest of the river is low but has been run at class V+ in higher water by a few paddlers. At these levels most will wish to start at Ogwen Bank.

Ogwen Bank to scout hut bridge: 4 km class IV - one fall class V****

Just south of Bethesda is the Ogwen Bank caravan park GR627653. It is worth looking at the first three little gems that the river has to offer before you launch, so as to pick the right place (depending on how you are feeling). The weir falling out of the pool is far easier than it looks and, at time of writing, had no nasty spikes to contend with. Immediately below the little bridge is the infamous 'scrap metal' or Ogwen Bank Falls. At medium levels this class V fall is actually a lot easier than its reputation suggests. It can be run into a pool on the right and then sneaked out to the left, thus avoiding all the nasties. Just below is the aptly-named Gun Barrel which was originally graded III! It is usually a good class IV but at certain levels reaches V - to my mind, at any rate. Some notable paddlers have spent definite down-time in some of the big, high water stoppers found towards the bottom of the barrel. This rifling of the water eases off but care needs to be taken at the next road bridge B4409 as in high water this is impassable!

Bethesda is not a pretty place but does sport the exciting class IV Bethesda Falls. Found on a tight, right hand bend some good manoeuvring, followed by drop and stopper, leads to easier water. The next two kilometres is only class II to III, topped up by the thundering Marchlyn Mawr entering river left. About 200 metres above the next road bridge is a steep class IV drop which runs immediately into the hard section. This is worth inspecting.

Scout hut bridge to A5 road bridge: 2 km IV to V; no portages*****

North of Bethesda is a crossroads leading off right to Rachub and left to Talgarth. The Talgarth road crosses the mighty Ogwen at the scout hut bridge. The river below here can be inspected from the right hand bank - sensible for those new to the run because of its continuous nature. If all the boulders are covered then you are in for a continual class V paddle. In massive spate this section may reach top-end, continuous class V, and even Dave Manby was heard to mutter that it was one of the few runs that had fettled him. There is a large eddy below the bridge that is a good access/egress point. The rapids below are simply marvellous. There are two islands that can actually be taken anywhere, and the best route should be left to the individual. Prior to the second island is a gnarly drop and stopper right up against the left wall. This is quite stern and is best shot middle to right and into the eddy. The river simply continues, brilliantly, all the way to the A5 halfway bridge. Egress can be made here river left, onto the small road GR607689 but is better to continue down the lower Ogwen.

Lower Ogwen - Halfway Bridge to old A55 road bridge: 3.5 km class IV****

For some, as an introduction to the harder, middle stretch this is a good place to launch your Ogwen career! In high water this is still a continuous and serious proposition. The island after the bridge is sporting a few potentially dangerous trees and should be approached with caution. There are a few broken weirs above the new bridge that require caution. The one under the green footbridge has to be portaged in very high water as there simply isn't the room to get under.

Egress by the council works car park just upstream of the *old* A55 road bridge GR602708. It is possible to continue the next 2 kilometres through broken weirs to the Ogwen's end at a small bridge just before the sea.

Afon Caseg

Map:	Snowdon and surrounding area, no. 115
Grade:	IV (V)
Length:	3 km
Access:	Via footpath from Gerlan Bethesda
Notes:	One fall class V+ certain falls / fences requiring portages
Quality:	***

A good river for those who enjoy the excitement of walking in with their boats. **During one of Phil Blain's excursions, so the story goes, he managed to persuade Loel Collins to walk in by suggesting that Rob Hind had started the run from much higher up. Competition being as it was, and Phil got his paddling partner. Of course, Rob hadn't been so daft as to walk too far up the river for that extra kilometre or so of easy water**. It needs to be raining to make the trip worthwhile: according to Phil this makes the walk just that little bit more special.

Afon Wen confluence to upper Gerlan bridge: 3 km class IV to V; portages***

Using an OS map, find the small bridge above Gerlan at GR636662 and leave a car for the get-out. By back-tracking downhill and taking the first right a small road can be followed to the start of the walk-in. By following the footpath that roughly parallels the river it is possible get on after some two to three kilometres of walking. The water runs at about grade III as the spate hurries to reach the Ogwen. After one and a half to two kilometres. trees begin to close in and you will want to be very careful of any low branches or fallers which lurk menacingly in the river. The grade is now a continuous IV with wooded danger. A few portages may be necessary. Just before the bridge is a class V drop into a big stopper. Get out river right. Below the bridge the confluence of the Llafar adds new power to the steepening river on its way down to the Ogwen. This has been run by a few hair boaters at around class V (continuous with significant danger). Phil suggests portaging the first gorge below where I finished and continuing on to the Ogwen: "excellent with some big stoppers" is how he describes it.

Afon Llafar

Map:	Snowdon and surrounding area, no. 115
Grade:	IV to V
Length:	3 km
Access:	from footpath from Gerlan (Bethesda)
Notes:	portages in the kilometre above the get-out
Quality:	***

The Llafar was one of the first 'expedition streams' to be run in Wales in the exciting period during the early '80s. Now, thanks to the pioneers of the time, many more of us seek the thrill of the wave off the mountain. The Llafar, like its parallel stream the Caseg, requires a fair effort to walk in.

Dafydd Falls to Gerlan: 3 km IV to V, with portages***

From the bridge described for the Caseg at GR636662, continue a little further until a second bridge is reached. From here it is possible to walk in to below the flanks of Carnedd Dafydd by following the *true* left bank of the river. Get on above or below a large fall (V) which can be run down the guts in suitable spate conditions. From here down the water is relatively easy until a weir is reached. A strange thing to find under the Carneddau's cliffs, but stranger things lie below. There is a good rapid running out from the weir which leads to a brick-work dam blocking the river. In high flood it is possible to run left or right over the little overflow but, otherwise, a portage is necessary before being sumped underneath. Rapids continue as the trees close in. The grade becomes increasingly difficult (V to VI through trees) and much of the last kilometre unfortunately requires portaging. A good expedition nevertheless.

Afon Marchlyn Mawr

Map:	Snowdon and surrounding area, no. 115
Grade:	IV to IV+
Length:	2 km
Access:	off the A5 in Bethesda
Notes:	few portages; steep stream paddling - low bushes cause some annoyance
Quality:	***

Mynydd Llandegai to spilling weir: 2 km IV to IV+ ***

If the Ogwen is too big for your liking an excellent spate alternative is the Marchlyn Mawr (MM). One of the roads in Mynydd Llandegai was commonly known as 'Instructor's Row' because of the number of centre people living there. It is not surprising then that MM was such a popular after-hours run.

Take the steep B4409 road up to Mynydd Llandegai where it crosses the MM at GR606655. Access onto the river at the bridge and immediately you are off downhill at a rate of knots. The paddling is relentless with steep rapids and some jungle bashing. Just before entering a small lake is an old wire fence that required portaging at time of paddling. See if you can recognise the overflow of this dammed area as you run it - it has appeared in the best instructional book on kayaking white water yet to be produced. Egress here onto the road and quickly nip back upstream for another run down. A tunnel downstream makes the trip to the Ogwen not really worthwhile.

58

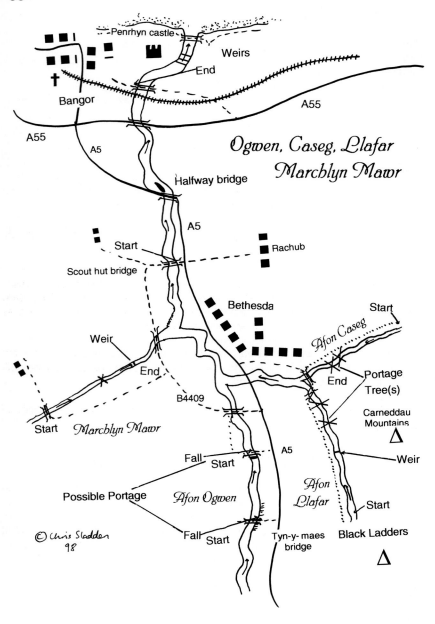

Penrhyn castle

Weirs

End

Bangor

A55

A55

A5

Ogwen, Caseg, Llafar
Marchlyn Mawr

Halfway bridge

A5

Start

Rachub

Scout hut bridge

Bethesda

Start

Afon Caseg

Weir

End

End

Portage
Tree(s)

Start

Marchlyn Mawr

B4409

Carneddau
Mountains

Δ

Fall Start

A5

Weir

Possible Portage

Afon Ogwen

Afon
Llafar

Start

© Chris Sladden
98

Fall Start

Tyn-y- maes
bridge

Black Ladders

Δ

Afon Rhaeadr Fawr

Map: Snowdon and surrounding area, no. 115
Grade: V to VI; IV to V; III to IV
Length: three 2 km-long sections
Access: access off A55 Bangor to Conwy road
Notes: various portages
Quality: ** and ***

There are three, distinctly separate, sections on the 'Aber' river that the adventurous may wish to run. Living in Abergwyngregyn back in 1980, we used to see the little river get into some angry spates and eventually we became brave enough to launch onto the lower section. Little then did I realise that the two upper sections and the Afon Anafon would ever be paddled.

Afon Goch section to Aber Falls: 2 km V to VI; three drops most will portage ***

This is an extreme expedition that only hardened (and slightly mad) paddlers will attempt. There is a long walk, climbing past the awesome Aber Falls (dare I say, totally uncanoeable) and further trudging up the stream and, as the river needs to be in spate, the weather is usually dreadful.

Start where you will. The paddling is hard and exciting. There are three big, big drops that fall steeply over large slabs and through narrow twists that most will want to portage - but they have all been paddled!

It is imperative not to go one drop too far and do ***a first and last descent of Aber Falls!!***

Aber Falls to Bont Newydd: 2 km grade IV to V; portages

I have not done this particular section though I have walked the area many times. I have it on good authority that, after walking in the two-plus kilometres to Aber Falls, it is possible to run most of the spate at hard class IV to V, with several portages - many tree-bound. However, there is a note on the National Nature Reserve that bans canoeing and so the section ***cannot*** be recommended, and I would urge paddlers to stick to this.

Bont Newydd to Laran Sands: 2.5 km III to IV; two bridges need portaging ***

Turn off the A55 in Abergwyngregyn and drive up to the car park at Bont Newydd GR662720. The river is best run in a medium flood (it has a big catchment area and can occasionally be too big for comfort) and at such levels will give an exciting and continuous class III to IV paddle. Trees may require portaging but all falls go. Where the river flows through the university farm, great care is required near the two bridges. Eddies are scarce and you may want a "catcher" to prevent being ensnared badly under the road and railway bridges. You may want to finish here, but it is a beautiful little trek finishing down to the Aber mud flats, reached by a small road just before the pub GR649735.

Afon Anafon

Map:	Snowdon and surrounding area, no. 115
Grade:	IV+ to V
Length:	2.5 km
Access:	walk in above the village of Abergwyngregyn, off the A55
Notes:	one portage - bushes
Quality:	****

The Anafon is one of the outstanding runs of its type, cascading steeply from the northern end of the Carneddau. The walk-in, though strenuous, is along a beautiful, rugged valley.

Llyn Anafon to forest area: 2.5 km class IV+ to V; one likely portage****

Turn off the A55 in the village of Abergwyngregyn and follow the signs for Aber falls. At the obvious car park head left up the steep road until a small parking area is reached GR676716. If you are very lucky as we were, and the gate is unlocked, then it is possible (with permission) to take a four-wheel drive right up to the get-in. With a good downpour the river is in fine fettle and this is clearly obvious on the drive up. About two and a half kilometres up the road access can be made onto the river about 300 metres below the actual lake. This is just after some very steep and narrow drops. The river is immediately fast and continuous IV+ or V as it rushes with awesome speed towards its destiny in the Menai Straits. Not long after the start are some obvious cliffs on the left below which, due to trees in the river, a portage is necessary. Tearing along below these with the odd moment of respite, a superb run is had. A good egress point is before the river plunges into the forest. There were, I figured, enough trees in the rest of the guide without me risking any more with this section!

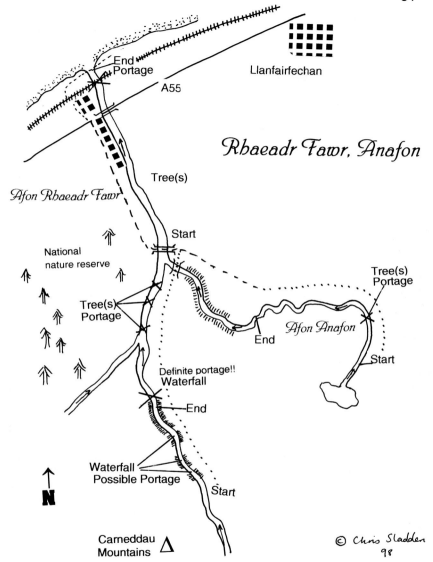

Llanfairfechan

End
Portage

A55

Rhaeadr Fawr, Anafon

Tree(s)

Afon Rhaeadr Fawr

Start

National
nature reserve

Tree(s)
Portage

Tree(s)
Portage

Afon Anafon

End

Start

Definite portage!!
Waterfall

End

Waterfall
Possible Portage

Start

N

Carneddau
Mountains △

© Chris Sladden
98

Afon Llugwy

Map:	Snowdon and surrounding area, no. 115
Grade:	sections of II to III, IV, V to VI
Length:	various sections, 14 km
Access:	A5
Notes:	few portages for most
Quality:	***and****

The Llugwy is a super run, with sections to suit all paddlers. It is one of the most popular rivers in this guide book and, furthermore, was the first ever river I paddled. Fond memories, then, from above and below as, in those days, swimming was an important part of my paddling, but I enjoyed it no less! The various sections go at different water levels. It was, and probably still is, one of the last major Welsh challenges: to paddle the Llugwy from source to sea, without portages, in one fell swoop. All the rapids have been run but no one, so far as I know, has dared to pit him- (or her-)self against the Llugwy's named drops when the upper Llugwy is paddleable. Therefore, portages are required.

Upper Llugwy - Helyg to Brown's Falls: 4 km class IV (IV+) with one class V****

This is a superb, but somewhat serious, spate run which goes after heavy rain. Occasionally, in midsummer after a thunderstorm, this can be run in the blazing sunshine. Put on the river somewhere near Helyg GR690601 and, for the first couple of kilometres, there is just fast, easy grade II before its true descent is felt.

The river quickly creeps up to an exciting and continuous class IV run with one fall, in particular, reaching class IV+ with distinct pinning possibilities. Good water levels will iron out some of the pinning potential. Between the houses, the river takes a right hand turn and plunges over the class V Brown's Falls. In normal levels this is easier than it looks with a left-to-right approach, duck the branch, and come hurling out skywards through the bottom stopper. In very high spate this reaches V+. Finish here into the car park right GR720582.

Brown's Falls to Pont Cyfyng: 2 km grade II to III; one IV to V; one usual portage***

Either continue down from Brown's Falls, or put on at the little class II rapid below the Plas y Brenin footbridge. This is actually on the Nantygwyryd and is reached via a footpath just past the centre GR716577. Near the A5 garage a small, grade II rapid flows under Jim's Bridge - a statement to one of the most entertaining of paddlers. Below, as the walls close in, the class IV Cobden's Falls is reached. The car park is owned by the hotel and, at present, there are signs requesting that paddlers do not access, egress or change here. The bridge, however, leads to a footpath from where the falls can be surveyed. In high flows, Cobden's reaches class V with some very meaty stoppers to avoid. In normal flows it is still a classic drop and is preceded by a tricky little slot just above. Some very well-known paddlers have been unseated hereabouts!

Easier rapids lead to the falls at Pont Cyfyng which start just above the bridge. These are best portaged on river right, though all the falls including the last twisting drop have been run by a few colourful characters. This is normally at a lowish level when the rest of the river is boney!

Pont Cyfyng to Forestry Falls: 3 km grade II to III; likely portages****

The following run is the classic easy section of the Llugwy. From the right bank, a muddy path steeply winds to below Pont Cyfyng where access can be made. In high water there are one or two stoppers in the first rapid that beginners will remember. The rest of the river is full of excellent, easy rapids down to the Forestry Falls. Normally taken left then back to the middle and over the final drop, this is the first class III many paddlers will do. Egress river right below the falls GR753575. There is a pull-in on the little back road that parallels the river, and notices showing the egress point.

Forestry Falls to Betws y Coed: 5 km class V to VI; likely portages****

If you continue down from Forestry Falls the water is class II until the mighty Swallow is reached.

The first descent of these huge falls in '86, by Shaun Baker and Fred Wondre represented, to my mind, one of the major landmarks in pushing the grades! Waterfall-jumping had arrived. These three large falls have since seen numerous descents but nearly always in low water. Inspiration to writers such as Watts-Dunkin and Borrow, the 'Swallow Falls' is probably a misnomer. The gentle 'swallow falls' is translated as 'Rhaeadr y Wennol', whereas the more fitting Rhaeadr Gwynol, which means 'foaming falls', was probably the original name.

Below the Swallow in high water is an exciting one and a half to two kilometres of class III to IV culminating in a drop that often loops the surprised paddler. Extreme care is required here, as at this level the following 500 metres of foaming fury to the Miners' Bridge is class VI at the very least - and has *probably* not been paddled in these conditions. Even when lower, the run down to Miners Bridge is a serious undertaking at class V+ to VI - but all of these drops have been done at such levels though the area is notorious for trees! Below the Miners' Bridge itself is a class IV+ to V- rapid, (level-dependent) which is an excellent shoot.

Easier water runs down towards the tourist hot spot of Betws y Coed. Here, one of the least paddled drops in North Wales, Pont y Pair, throws down a (seldom picked-up) gauntlet. In high flows there is a superb line right over the now-covered central boulder and through an angry stopper below. It has been run in low water down the formidable slot on the left - a necky line if ever there was one.

Egress above into the car park GR792567. Below lies one kilometre of class I to II before the Conwy confluence.

Nantygwyryd

Map:	Snowdon and surrounding area, no. 115
Grade:	IV; one fall V+ usual portage
Length:	5 km
Access:	off A4086 Capel to Beddgelert road
Notes:	one fall requires caution and most will portage
Quality:	****

If the upper Llugwy is up then it is usual for the Nantygwyryd, known locally as the Gwyryd, to be at a good level - so, too, may be the harder Nant Peris. Fed by the Western flanks of the Moel Siabod massif and the Northern Glyders, the river rises and falls very quickly.

A4086 to Garth farm bridge: 5 km class IV; one fall V+****

Just below the Pen y Gwyryd hotel (steeped in climbing history) access can be made onto the stream. Look upstream and maybe, as I did one day, see Phil Blain hurtling down the impressive slides above - but for most of us the access is below the bridge. Flat at first, the stream soon picks up and hurtles downhill at a tremendous rate. About a kilometre down here, a little way after the Nant Llys enters, is a fallen concrete and old iron girder spanning the river. Immediately below is a nasty fall plunging into a rock wall. To my knowledge, this has been run by only a few paddlers at a hard V+ grade. Most will portage right. The last time I was on the Gwyryd there was no sign of this iron bridge and I can only assume, for the water was in a huge spate, that it was covered! This is the only time I've seen a sensible line down the drop - but it was not for me that day!

Below this drop the water eases but beware a fallen telegraph pole bridge which can snaggle the unwary at certain water levels. The difficulties ease off until Garth Farm Falls. At normal levels this is easily shot far right to left but, in high flows, the trees become very problematic. Egress here or continue through the lake to the Brenin.

65

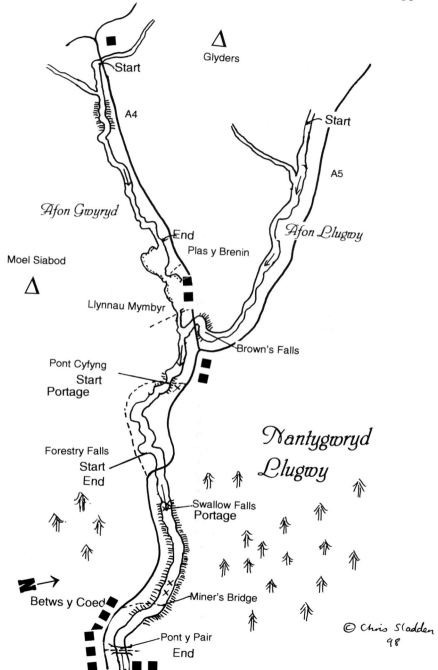

Glyders

Start

A4

Afon Gwyryd

Start

A5

Afon Llugwy

End

Plas y Brenin

Moel Siabod

Llynnau Mymbyr

Brown's Falls

Pont Cyfyng
Start
Portage

Nantygwryd
Llugwy

Forestry Falls
Start
End

Swallow Falls
Portage

Betws y Coed

Miner's Bridge

Pont y Pair
End

© Chris Sladden
98

Afon Lledr

Map:	Snowdon and surrounding area, no. 115
Grade:	various sections of class II, IV, V and VI!
Length:	15 km
Access:	A470
Notes:	several prudent portages; beware debris in river at Pont y Coblyn
Quality:	***

Although brilliant in places the Lledr is not as popular a river as might be expected. This is probably due to the erratic nature of its grade, which varies between II and VI. Saying that, there are some mighty drops to run which are of superb quality. It is probably sensible to break the run down into two sections. Due to the hydrology of the river, the water can rise at an alarming rate during the paddle - a frightening experience.

Blaenau Dolwyddelan to Pont y Pant: 9 km of IV to V interspersed with flat***

By turning off the small road just west of the A470(T) bridge and travelling for about two kilometres past another bridge, access can be made near Blaenau Dolwyddelan GR699516. The beauty of this section is its two classic class V drops before easing off on the run down to the Roman bridge of Pont y Coblyn. Here is another classic and hard grade IV (or V in very high water) fall. However, at the time this book was going to print, the road was being totally changed with evidence of considerable debris going into the river ... *beware*.

Class III rapids follow in an exciting little gorge but, after a short while the river opens out and meanders, via a couple of broken weirs, down through Dolwyddelan (a good bunkhouse here) to Pont y Pant.

Pont y Pant to Beaver Pool: 6 km of class III to IV, with sections of V to VI***

Most people will scrabble down the steep bank to put on above, or below, the last drop of the Pont y Pant Falls. Some will run the drops in low water, but the whole section at *class V+ to VI* has been run in enormous water by that man from the Towers - and the photos are an impressive sight!

The water eases off considerably until a double drop - visible on the drive up - is reached. This is an exciting class IV to IV+ run, the bottom stopper of which has thrashed a few good paddlers.

This heralds the approach of the class V Rhiw Goch gorge. At a low level - just enough to run the river - the first drop has a runnable tongue by the right wall. Any higher and an exceptionally dangerous stopper forms - **I know of no one who has tried their luck with the 15 foot towback that occurs**. However, in higher water still, a line over the rock shelf on the left allows clearance of the towback. The consequences of a 'cock-up' are immense and I only know a couple of paddlers who have suffered these.

This first drop (or the whole gorge) can be portaged scarily along the (Jacob's) fisherman's ladder or, more soundly, along the right hand bank. Below this first drop, the gorge is a fantastic class V with big stoppers to negotiate.

The river eases off before a small bridge and then class III to IV rapids lead towards the railway viaduct falls. Paddled at a hard grade when the river is very low, this is a definite portage at decent levels (right or left). The final two kilometres of water is excellent value with many great play waves, but there is a sting in the tail. It is well worth scouting the double drop below the little stone bridge, found just above the Conwy confluence. At big levels the first narrow squeeze is a definite and dangerous class V, though this drops a grade when the river is lower. There have been some frightening swims in here, and it is quite common for multiple back loops to occur. As you finish into the Conwy, your helmet twisted by the power of the last stopper, you might just have the energy left for a run down to Beaver Pool.

Afon Machno

Map:	Snowdon and surrounding area, no. 115
Grade:	I
Length:	4 km
Access:	B4406 A5 to Penmachno road
Notes:	large drops just below egress
Quality:	****

The Machno is best paddled during the few days after heavy rain, when the water will be a blue colour, within its banks and, hopefully, with the sun shining. In these conditions it is a super meandering paddle, suitable for beginners, down to the egress at Penmachno Mill.

Penmachno to Penmachno Mill: 4 km class I****

Turn off the A5 at the Conwy Falls cafe and head up the B4406 until you reach Penmachno Woollen Mill. Here, it is a very good idea to checkout the falls that are just above the bridge which will reinforce the correct egress above! Even larger falls, which drop steeply over and under huge chock stones, lie about 500 metres downstream - these are very impressive to look at. Drive upstream, through Penmachno to where access can be made via one or two convenient footpaths which meet the river about a kilometre above the village.

There are a few low bushes which require some steering-around but, at the suggested water levels, these are not dangerous as the water bubbles along. Pass through the village until a second bridge is reached, below which is a tiny weir that first-timers will enjoy surfing on. A little further down is a slightly harder, perhaps grade I+ rapid which weaves around a few boulders. Egress on the right above the Mill by the National Trust car park: ***this is before any rapids start*** GR807528.

Just below are some pothole-ridden and dangerous class V drops.

A5

Fairy Glen

Penmachno Falls
B4406

Portage

Beaver Pool

Woollen Mill
End

End

Penmachno

Afon Machno

Viaduct Gorge
Portage

Start

Rhiw Goch
Possible
Portage

Pont y Pant
Portage

Dolwyddelan

Lledr, Machno

Start

Afon Lledr

Pont y Coblyn

A470

© Chris Sladden

Start

Afon Conwy

Map:	Snowdon and surrounding area, no. 115
	Denbigh and Colwyn Bay area, no. 116
Grade:	sections of I to II; II; III to IV; IV and V
Length:	various sections totalling 44 km
Access:	A5 & A470T
Notes:	few portages
Quality:	quality sections of*** and**** and*****

By any standards the Conwy is a truly majestic river. Rising as it does from Llyn Conwy at a height of some 1488 feet, it winds and roars and glides its way downstream until it enters the sea in Conwy. Here, still standing in extremely good nick, is one of the most powerful of the English castles built in Wales.

By canoe the Conwy is navigable from some 23+ miles upstream but, long prior to the visiting paddler, the river was used as a navigation system. Back in the reign of Elizabeth I, the Conwy was used to float oak timber down to the coast. So it comes as no surprise that much of the upper Conwy still supports fine native oaks along its banks.

The Conwy has the reputation for being canoeable after other rivers have run dry. To some extent this is true, fed as it is from the Migneint ('the place of swamps'), one of the largest, wild, moorland places in Wales. The harder sections, being more gorged, are paddleable after the main sections drop - the 'Glen', for example, is often do-able a few days after rain. Though many paddlers happily bounce down the Conwy at all levels, the river should be clearly 'up' for its true mettle to be felt. There are various viewing points - Waterloo Bridge in Betws, and the riverside road bend a little way below Bryn Bras Falls, both places of which should have the shelves and rocks covered for good levels. The Glen itself is normally done in the first few days following high water as, in flood, it is one mean piece of water.

At the time of writing, there is a reasonable access situation on the Conwy, agreed by the WCA to which would seem prudent to adhere. This obviously changes from year to year and up-to-date information should be available from the WCA, or Cotswold Camping in Betws. A great deal of hard work has gone into this agreement and I would urge paddlers to stick to it.

Upper Conwy - Ysbyty Ifan to A5 bridge: 7 km class III to IV; one portage***

Put on the river in Ysbyty Ifan where access is clearly marked. After good rain it was possible and traditional (historically) to launch onto the river at Pennant bridge and footpath GR824469 (south of Ysbyty Ifan on the B4407). *However, I should point out that the access agreement does not include this section of river and these notes are just for interest.*

Getting on above Ysbyty Ifan will put the access agreement in jeopardy so, please, don't do it. The river is fairly easy until a class VI fall near Pandy Uchaf is reached. This has been run by a few people but is normally a portage. In any case the last time I was there a tree was blocking the line. A little way below is a steep weir before the falls at Ysbyty Ifan. This weir itself is straightforward unless in very high flood, where it suddenly hits a level at which it becomes much, much nastier! Beware. The class IV falls are excellent value and worth inspecting for the right line. It is as well to remember that an unfortunate fatality occurred on this stretch some years ago.

Ysbyty Ifan itself has an interesting history, taking its name from a hospice founded in the twelfth century by the Knights of St John to give lodging and shelter to those in need when crossing the Migneint (see earlier). Later on the hospice was granted the right of sanctuary and became a safe place to those wanted by the law - sanctuary for canoeists from persecution? Access can be made here GR842488 but not on Sundays. The rapids down to the A5 bridge are fairly straightforward, apart from perhaps the attractively-named 'Hargreaves' Folly. Egress can be made river right of the A5 road bridge.

A5 to Rhydlanfair Bridge: 4 km grade III to IV; no portages****

From the A5 layby at GR857512, access can be made along the little footpath through the trees and thus onto the river. This totally avoids playing Russian Roulette along the A5. Back in the days of my youth, this section was considered a true gem and a local challenge. It still is worth every little bit of its four star status.

With the addition of the Caletwr and Merddur, the river picks up new power as it carves its way through the Foelas Estate (the Merddur itself has some good rapids but is crossed by numerous fences and isn't worth the bother). First runs can be intimidating to the newcomer as the river surges and boils its way around moss-covered boulders and through high vertical walls. First a footbridge, and then the road bridge, are passed as the river becomes more continuous through the Padog Farm narrows. Down under the A5 bridge, the river starts to wind itself up for a rush down Bryn Bras Falls (class III when low, or IV when up). 16 years on, I vividly remember my first run through the stopper at the bottom - great!

The river relaxes as it becomes visible to the A5 and, before long, reaches the get-out at Rhydlanfair bridge GR828524.

Rhydlanfair Bridge to Penmachno Bridge: 2.5 km grade IV, with two big class V drops plus exciting egress prospects****

A medium spate is probably the best level to run this rather serious section of the Conwy. The river soon picks up to class III and IV for the first kilometre or so in its run up to the first of two hard class V rapids. This is run down a series of drops on the left and through a stopper at the bottom. It is potentially serious if cocked-up. The right side has been blocked with trees in living history (portage left). The second fall, a few 100 metres below, is also pretty gnarly. It can be run left to right, or straight down the right - both lines ending over a large drop into a big stopper. The portage is quite tricky even with the wooden ladder put in for just that purpose. To avoid going through an SSSI, a big seal launch into the pool below is required. However, at time of last paddling a large tree blocked the river just below. Some thought is needed to negotiate this!

Below this drop are some excellent and hard class IV rapids leading down to the get off above Penmachno bridge. The first of these has a large undercut rock in the middle which to my knowledge has been swum under at least once. This section is now notorious and has featured in various TV rescues and news programmes! Much to my amusement, on the left bank are now a series of markers counting down to the egress point **100 metres before** Penmachno Bridge. This is actually visible *across* the bend and though the trees to the keen eye. The problem was that certain parties missed the egress and found that paddling under Penmachno Bridge committed them to entering the "unrunnable" upper part of Conwy Falls. Looking from the bridge into the foaming chaos of water passing under and around huge rocks, one particularly large rock island is visible. From here various (including one well-known) paddlers have been hauled off under the watchful eyes of TV cameras! I call this section "unrunnable" but, in point of fact, I should give it a major class VI rating as it has been done in medium and high flows. However, the person I know who has paddled this rapid is an exceptional boater - don't be deceived!

The Fairy Glen - Penmachno Bridge to Beaver Pool: 2 km class V; one usual portage (V+ to VI fall)*****

'Opened up' in the early eighties, this section is one of the best hard runs at its grade in the country. It is a British test-piece and, as such, is immensely popular. It has seen its fair share of epics plus at least one fatality. Guarding the entrance to the run are the Conwy Falls. One of the big five waterfall tourist attractions in Wales even they, in their entirety, have been paddled. The lower falls, topped up by the raging Machno, have been run both left and right in very low water. They are extremely dangerous and, with the advent of the new salmon steps, are 'illegal' to attempt. Just as well - I have personal experience of a near-drowning in which the canoeist only escaped because both his legs broke and he was washed free of the boat - enough said.

Access can be made down the footpath on the river right from below Penmachno bridge car park. A low to medium spate is the best condition for running the Glen, as many of the dangerous siphons are covered, but the waves and stoppers still manageable. There are two main gorges split by a usually easier section plus a class V+ to VI fall. Most of the drops need inspection. The river opens with a bang as a large fall taken right to middle is shot, with the paddler disappearing totally below. Immediately below is a small drop up against the left wall, with a vicious stopper. Next is a boulder-choked run right up against the left cliff. The water needs to be a medium level to do this and is not possible when low.

A little way below used to be one of the most pleasing and aesthetic drops on the river: a steep drop into a big stopper guarded by siphons above and below. Over the past five years or so this has fallen in fully, firstly creating a monster, before settling down to a somewhat easier fall to shoot. It may well be worth noting that, unfortunately, this drop has been the scene of a fatality plus a few near misses. A few, steep drops follow before a fantastic long rapid is run between steep and sculptured walls.

The gorge opens out with a small road visible high up on the left bank, where the water gets easier and, theoretically, less dangerous. One small vertical drop should be viewed with caution: once, in very high water, a paddler with an incredible 47 previous Glen descents swam in it for a long time - much of it underwater. Not much farther on is a major class V+ to VI fall, which has been paddled a number of times - usually at low-ish levels. It is possible to portage left or right and then re-enter the second gorge. Beware of the drop just below as pinning is a serious possibility.

The tale of two guidebook writers:

One, not a million miles away, pinned and swam here, only to have the second guidebook writer turn up in the following group to rescue the boat. With a mischievous grin he told me [oops!] "you've got to watch the pins here". On the last-but-one drop the tables were turned - almost exactly - and his boat was rescued. Moral? What goes round comes round!

The next-but-one drop, known as the pipeline, is probably the most aesthetic on the river and is technical at all levels. Best run left to right, an escape route to the right exists. A large 'S' type rapid follows before a short flat section leads in above the last drop. It is best to inspect this drop before paddling as it is, frighteningly, almost impossible to do so from the river (at certain levels it is possible to get onto a ledge on the left bank). Best run just left of centre, there are undercut boulders on both sides.

Here, at normal levels for doing the Glen, the rapids ease off to class III+. However, they should not be underestimated in big flows when they contain some enormous gobbling stoppers. On the way down, past the Lledr confluence, is a bouncy, class III run into Beaver Pool. Egress river left below the bridge (A4707) GR798547.

Beaver Pool to Dolgarrog Bridge: 14 km class II to II+; no portages***

Access is a problem on this section of river. In big water, the rapids tumbling out of Beaver Pool and down to the Waterloo Bridge reach class II+. There are some superb surfing waves and stoppers but, at these conditions, it is a big river and can be a bit intimidating for absolute beginners as it thunders down left and right of washed-out islands. The rapids ease off to fast-flowing water and where the Llugwy joins it becomes very much a touring river down to the egress at Dolgarrog GR780668.

Dolgarrog Bridge to Conwy Quay: 14 km II (grade for tidal conditions and jet-skis)***

This section is excellent for touring parties with experienced leaders. It is suitable for both paddling down, and also up, on the tide. The ever-popular Conwy ascent is now a regular occurrence. I even did part of my SI here, but that was many years ago!

Which-ever way you are going to try this section of river, it is important to time your run with the tide. If you are doing the ascent it is best to utilise the flood tide rushing in by leaving Conwy within one hour, and certainly within two hours, of the low water tide. This gives a number of hours to utilise the flood before high tide - when it is best to return on the ebb. On big springs the tide can race in both directions at around six knots so an experienced leader is sensible. That being said, in good conditions it is a great touring run for *experienced* families.

From the main road a track can be walked along to the access at Dolgarrog bridge. The river meanders through areas of SSSI and is frequented by myriad wildlife. There is one area in which the ebb produces a small, class II, tidal rapids. This is just upstream of the Ferry Hotel and Tal y Cafn bridge. A few old stakes remain of the original bridge and these should be treated with caution.

Below here, a gentle paddle under the brooding shadow of Edward I's Conwy stronghold brings the paddler to the egress at Conwy Quay, just south of the bridge GR783776. At least, here, the stamp out at low water includes some sand underfoot.

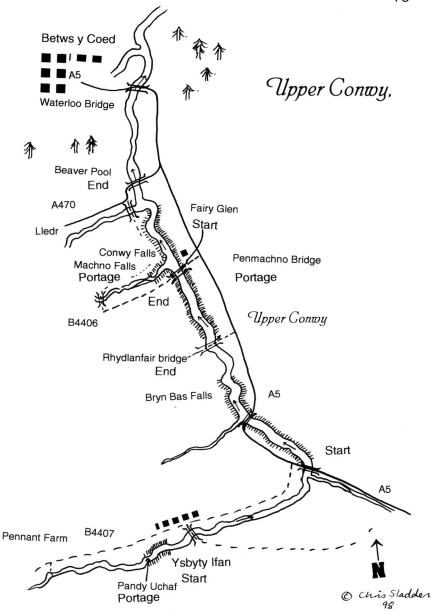

Betws y Coed

A5

Waterloo Bridge

Beaver Pool
End

A470

Lledr

Fairy Glen
Start

Conwy Falls
Machno Falls
Portage

End

Penmachno Bridge
Portage

B4406

Upper Conwy

Rhydlanfair bridge
End

Bryn Bas Falls

A5

Start

A5

Pennant Farm   B4407

Ysbyty Ifan
Start

Pandy Uchaf
Portage

Upper Conwy.

© Chris Sladder
98

N

Afon Crafnant

Map:	Snowdon and surrounding area, no. 115
Grade:	IV to V
Length:	2 km (but seems a little further)
Access:	Trefriw to Llyn Crafnant
Notes:	various portages particularly fences
Quality:	very little

There are several rivers that fall very steeply off the Eastern flanks of the Carneddau and into the lower Conwy. These rivers are in hanging valleys and fall incredibly steeply downhill - in places at over 600 feet in half of a kilometre! For a long time this gradient has been harnessed for the production of power, as it is still, for the Dolgarrog Aluminium Works. The waters of the Porth Llwyd are held at bay and used from a small lake with tipper gates on its dam. Essentially these are an all-or-nothing phenomenon! If the water exceeds demand and builds up in the lake, the gates suddenly open and pour the most incredible cataract downhill at an alarming rate. *Not even thinkable* in a canoe, this is an alarming but awe-inspiring sight if you happen to be in the area at the time. The Crafnant is the only one that could remotely be described as worth paddling and even this is not really worth the effort. However, it has had various descents over the years, so here it is.

Cae Crwn to Trefriw: 2.5 km class IV to V; various portages

From the village of Trefriw drive up the extremely steep road towards Llyn Crafnant (we stayed here at New Year a few years back, and got to know just how steep the road was at chucking-out time!). This steep road hides the Fairy Falls which is a total misnomer and has not, to my knowledge, been paddled. It is worth checking Bro Geirionnydd weir, situated by the large greenhouses, as egress has to be made above this beast!

If you are still keen, then continue up the road for about two and a half kilometres where access can be made by a small stone hut next to the Crafnant, although you can get on at the lake. The river rushes off downhill at an alarming rate through a few wooded gorges. There are quite a few tree portages en-route but all drops have been paddled or, more accurately, bashed. Several portages are sensible depending on how brave or silly you feel. There are a few places where easy escape can be had if you're fed up. Egress above the weir on the right bank GR778630.

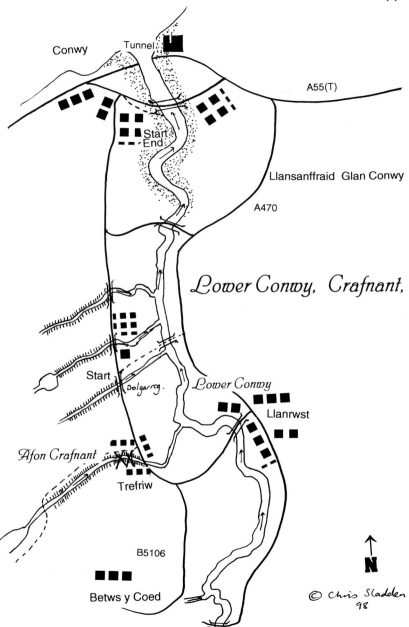

Conwy

Tunnel

A55(T)

Start
End

Llansanffraid Glan Conwy

A470

Lower Conwy, Crafnant,

Start

Dolgarrog.

Lower Conwy

Llanrwst

Afon Crafnant

Trefriw

B5106

N

Betws y Coed

© Chris Sladden
98

Afon Cledwen

Map:	Denbigh & Colwyn Bay area, no. 116
Grade:	II to III
Length:	17 km
Access:	A548 Llanrwst to Abergele road
Notes:	various fences and tree portages
Quality:	**

A beautiful little mountain river passing through several small but sculptured gorges. The various fence portages ensure it only gets two stars but well worth the visit if you are in the area. Paddleable for a day or so after rain; in big flood it would be quite dangerous!

Gwytherin to Llanfair: 17 km grade II to III; various portages**

About 10 kilometres east of Llanrwst is the village of Gwytherin. Here, access can be made to the river GR878616. The river is immediately grade II+ (in good flows), but the first kilometre is a bit of a pain, with much fence portaging.

Before and after the bridge at Ty'r Felin Isaf are two harder sections reaching grade III. The second gorge, in particular, is extremely attractive and in big water a few of the stoppers are meaner than they look. The river continues at a good class II, with the odd fence/tree portage down to Llangernyw where the trip can be shortened if required. From here down to the finishing point the river is wider and deeper with the odd ripply rapid to float. There was just one fence along here that sticks in mind - an all-wooded, staked affair that could be sneaked on the left through a hole (but remember this is repairable!). Egress at Llanfair Talhaiarn onto the A548 GR927703.

Afon / River Elwy

Map: Denbigh & Colwyn Bay area, no. 116
Grade: 14 km
Length: III
Access: A548 Llanfair Talhaiarn
Notes: one weir portage
Quality: ****

Somewhere above Llanfair Talhaiarn, the Cledwen becomes the Elwy. It is a surprisingly good river which runs from a few days to about a week after heavy, prolonged rain.

Llanfair Talhaiarn to Bont Newydd: 14 km grade III; one portage****

Access in Llanfair at the above egress point. A little way below the main road bridge is a large but easily shootable weir, which can be run left or right, so missing the salmon steps in the centre. **Best left for the salmon these**, as they are never pleasant to try and descend!

A couple of further weirs follow that are safe enough to shoot, both of which have brilliant surfing waves below. It is very easy to spend a couple of hours at these two play-spots! Further down, bouncy but easy rapids are found. The Aled roars in from the right doubling the volume, and the new power is easily felt as you cruise on by.

From here down to the get-out, the Elwy digs deeply through some beautiful gorge sections, with good grade III rapids to run and play. The gorge itself is really quite unique to the Elwy and the section is excellent at the grade. Two places particularly spring to mind though, **where caution is required**: the first is at Pont y Ddol (the third 'proper' road bridge after the Aled). Immediately under the bridge is a steep weir step with a powerful stopper. It is wise to inspect this and, although it can be punched at normal flows, if in any doubt make a *portage*. The second is an altogether more vicious, triple-stepped weir found between here and the egress. To the trained eye it is obvious from the river, and looks particularly unpleasant. **I recommend a portage on the left.** Egress at Bont-newydd by the footpath upstream right of the bridge GR013708.

Alternatively, continue to St Asaph but I haven't managed to get around to this yet!

Afon Aled

Map: Denbigh & Colwyn Bay area, no. 116
Grade: II+ to III
Length: 8 km
Access: A548 and A544 Abergele to Llansannan road
Notes: weirs; low trees
Quality: ***

The Aled is a pleasant enough little river running, as it does, northwards to join the Elwy downstream of Llanfair Talhaiarn. It runs out of Aled Isaf Reservoir and really needs to be spilling over the dam to be worth doing. It has an upper eight kilometres above the section described, that begins with a tumble over the mighty Rhaeadr y Bedd. Below this, it runs through an impressive gorge which, I think, contains class IV and V drops at the very least, but I know little more about this section.

Llansannan to Elwy confluence: 8 km class II+ to III; few weirs ***

Llansannan is situated about 15 kilometres inland from Abergele, and can be reached via the A548 and A544 roads. The latter crosses the river in town, where access can be made from the public footpath GR936658.

The river needs to be clearly up to be worth paddling and, for the first two kilometres or so, runs at a gentle grade II+. There is then a series of half a dozen or so three-foot weir steps, which have clearly been placed to create fishing pools. These are really good fun to bounce through. The first village, Bryn Rhyd-yr-Arian, is passed and then, about a kilometre later, is a more formal weir. This should be obvious from the river because of concreted sides, weir buildings and a gauge on the left bank (reads 8 to 9 on bottom scale at good levels). At time of paddling, early '98, there was a tree in the central salmon ladder, but an easy line on the left.

Just above the next bridge is the hardest fall on the river - a good class III that may need a quick look before descent. The rest of the river to the egress is pleasant but easy, with no trees requiring portaging at time of paddling. It is possible to pull out below the little wave under the next bridge, where there is a stile and a public footpath GR953717. Alternatively, for a longer trip, continue down the excellent Elwy.

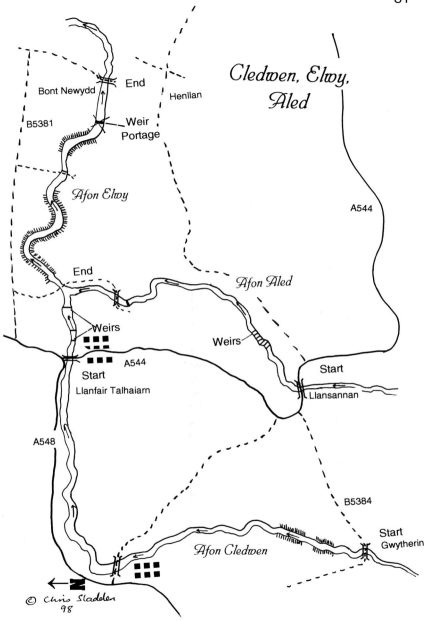

Cledwen, Elwy, Aled

Bont Newydd

End

Henllan

B5381

Weir
Portage

Afon Elwy

A544

End

Afon Aled

Weirs

Weirs

A544

Start

Start
Llanfair Talhaiarn

Llansannan

A548

B5384

Start
Gwytherin

Afon Cledwen

© Chris Sladden
98

N

Afon Clwyd

Map: Denbigh & Colwyn Bay area, no. 116
Grade: I
Length: 15 km
Access: A525 Denbigh to St Asaph road
Notes: few overgrowing trees/bushes
Quality: ***

The Clwyd is a fine salmon river and, as such, it would seem entirely reasonable to keep off it during the season! All the locals I have met are very friendly, and I would hate to give reason for this to alter. The river runs for a good week after heavy rain during the winter season. In fact, it is best when a couple of feet below its normal banks at the suggested access point. In flood, it sets up between fences and trees and becomes an extremely dangerous flat river!

Pont Glan y Wern to St Asaph: 15 km grade I; no portages***

The little road from Denbigh to Waen crosses the river at GR091659. Downstream on the true left bank are some useful steps onto the public footpath which follows the river. Here access can be made.

The first five or so kilometres weaves around tight bends and, occasionally, through branches and fallen trees to the main A541 road bridge. The large farm with its beautiful ivy-covered, stone bridge that is passed en-route, is Lleweni Hall. From the A541 down, the river is less fraught with trees and becomes pleasant touring water.

There are footpaths at most of the following bridges, which allow a shorter trip should this be desired. Otherwise, pass the grand-looking Llannerch Hall and finish off at the old A525 road bridge which offers perfect egress. This can be reached by carrying straight on instead of turning sharp right to Denbigh in St Asaph GR044748.

Afon Clywedog

Map:	Denbigh & Colwyn Bay area, no. 116
Grade:	II+ to III
Length:	8 km
Access:	A525 Ruthin to Denbigh road
Notes:	weirs - two portages, and a couple of wires and trees
Quality:	*** (none for the bottom 8 km)

I quite enjoyed this river with its unexpected limestone gorges. In flood, the grade may be a little harder and the trees could be a bit of a nuisance.

Cyffylliog to Rhewl: 8 km class II+ to III; various portages***

From the sewage works downstream of Cyffylliog GR063578, the river is class II+ and III as it rushes over shale-type steps. The odd tree and fence may need to be portaged depending on storm damage and water height. Just before the second road bridge in Bontuchel is an enormous vertical weir. I have no idea how deep the plunge pool is. It is probably best to **portage** along the road and either down the steep bank below, or past the Bridge Hotel, where it is possible to follow the hedge-line back onto the river (polite to seek permission).

From here down is a grade III gorge. There is a wire stretching across the flow just after the first few grade III drops, which is a bit awkward.

Below here a path on the left hand bank follows the gorge as it rushes over class II+ and III steps. One fall, by a small white and red house on the right, is a bit harder than the others and has quite a sticky stopper in high flows.

A little below as the gorge closes in is a steep, three-stepped weir - **best portaged on the left**. Finish the run at the first bridge in Rhewl GR108603.

Rhewl to Pont Glan y Wen: 8km class I

It is possible to continue down the Clywedog until it joins the Clwyd. I did this but, be warned, as it is eight kilometres of pretty dreadful water. Not recommended unless you enjoy talon-like thorns, barricade-like trees, not to mention garrotte-like neck-attracting wires.

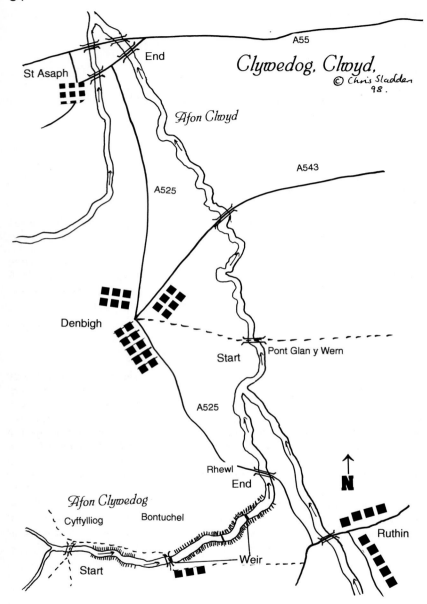

St Asaph

End

Clywedog, Clwyd,

© Chris Sladden
98.

A55

Afon Clwyd

A543

A525

Denbigh

Start

Pont Glan y Wern

A525

Rhewl

End

Afon Clywedog

Cyffylliog

Bontuchel

Start

Weir

N

Ruthin

Afon Dyfrdwy / River Dee

Map:	Bala & Lake Vyrnwy & surrounding area, no. 125
	Chester & Wrexham, no. 117
Grade:	sections of I and II, and III to IV
Length:	various sections; total more than 140 km
Access:	various, including off the A5 and A483
Notes:	few weirs - prudent portages at high flows.
Quality:	sections of ***and ****and *****

The Afon Dyfrdwy or "The Dee", as it is better known to most, is one of the all-time classics of Welsh paddling. The Dee rises from below some impressive crags in the hills south west of Bala, after which it flows for about ten kilometres before entering Bala Lake (Llyn Tegid). The canoeing sections start from below the lake and continue on a winding course through Wales before entering England a little way above Chester - a distance of some 140 kilometres.

The Dee is always paddleable - that is, it always has enough water in to paddle - if only the access situation were similar! It is a fine salmon river and is jealously (or should it be 'zealously') guarded, with access to the well-known sections only being allowed two or three weekends a year.

A tale by Stuart Fisher:

As Scottish students, we were blissfully ignorant of the access situation further south and decided to paddle some of the less extreme rapids of the Dee somewhere between Corwen and Llangollen. We parked by a bridge over the river and struggled into our wetsuits, watched closely by a man in another car. We untied the boats and the paddles, donned our spraydecks, life jackets (yes, it was a long time ago) and helmets, tidied away unwanted items, locked the car and were ready to launch. At this point, our observer emerged from his own car and informed us that he was the bailiff and that, if we put our boats on the water, he would call the police. Adopting what appeared to be a more conciliatory tone, he then explained where his stretch ended, below which point he would not be concerned about us, and invited us to follow him there. He drove off, leaving us to load up again. Eventually, we arrived at the described spot to find him with another man, the bailiff from the next section.

For many years, when the Mike Jones Rally was held here, thousands of canoeists would descend on the sleepy town of Llangollen in order to try their luck with the waves and stoppers of the famous Serpent's Tail, Tombstones and Town Falls, to name a few. Now the Jones has temporarily retired the WCA weekend is, perhaps, the next most popular.

Most canoeists have stuck to these open weekends - myself included. It seemed tradition that the Dee was open but a few days a year. Morally, of course, this is a wholly different matter. The lower sections seem far less problematic and I have met only with friendliness when steering my Canadian along these more placid stretches.

Hilnant to Llandderfel bridge: 5 km grade I to II****

It is possible (good access) to put on at the bridge where the Dee flows out of Llyn Tegid, but I have *not* done these first few kilometres and it is just the type of section where an unpleasant weir could lurk - **beware**. Where the B4402 crosses the little Hilnant river it is possible to park, and then walk downstream past the class V falls that are about 200 metres below the bridge. There are just a few, easily shot, small weirs between here and the Dee confluence. It takes about 5 minutes to walk down the pleasant footpath (right hand bank) - *the most important thing, of course, is to make 100% sure you get on below the class V*.

Once on the Dee, the river carves a fast, but flat, path through beautiful rustic countryside. There is one class II step found by a big house about halfway down to the next bridge. Egress is onto the left hand bank (public footpath) just below Llandderfel bridge   GR982366.

Llandderfel to Corwen: 20 km class I to II****

Access as above at Llandderfel bridge. This is reached by turning off the A494 Corwen to Bala road in the hamlet of Bethel and following the B4402 to the bridge. If the river is over its banks and hence flowing through the trees lining the side, then it is not really suitable for beginners or families, but at normal levels or even summer lows it is a beautiful touring stretch.

Just before the Ceidiog enters from the river right is a house at Cilan. This is "Goose city", - due to the number of birds that live there. The dismantled railway bridge in the middle of the river has a few old stanchions remaining that deserve respect in low conditions.

Otherwise, enjoy the river and egress at the bridge below the A5 bridge in Corwen   GR082439.

Corwen to Horseshoe Falls: 19 km grade II; portage at Horseshoe Falls*****

Access can be had at the small bridge in Corwen GR082439 for four kilometres of fast but flat water down to the Carrog bridge. The latter is a more usual starting point, especially during the Open Days. To reach this, turn off the A5 in the small village of Llidiart y Parc.

This is a lovely touring section of river through a rich and shaded valley. When the leaves are turning myriad shades of golden brown, then this must be one of the most idyllic places to float along. In high water, the river booms along, washing out many of the shingle-type rapids which are found on this stretch. Some way down here is a small diagonal weir step, which is ideal for playing in, and is best at low to medium flows. Further down, at high spate in particular, the rapids approaching Berwen are bouncy at the grade.

At the bottom of the trip, around a lazy sweeping right hand bend, are the **Horseshoe Falls**. The water is suddenly slowed from its natural flow, warning as to what is causing the rumble that can increasingly be heard. Egress *well above* **this weir**, on the left GR196433.

Horseshoe Falls to Llangollen: 3 km class III-IV*****

This is the 'classic' section of wild water Dee. Steeped in tradition, linked with Dr Mike Jones and other famous paddlers, this is the provider of many people's canoeing adventures. It is here that many paddlers have had their first taste of paddling and, indeed, swimming grade III (and above) rapids.

Park in the Chainbridge car park - well signposted on 'match days'. From here it is easy to walk by, or float along, the feeder canal to the Horseshoe Falls. In anything higher than low water this weir is **exceptionally dangerous** through the main drop. It can, however, be easily shot far left, thus avoiding the vicious weir towback. Under a bridge and the water begins to pick up through waves and holes. Warm, dry spectators in the Chainbridge Hotel smile at the sport below.

Next comes the famous Serpent's Tail rapid, graded III to IV. In low water, spectators crowd the left bank and cheer those with, and without, boats as they descend the tail. In high water, this is covered with good stoppers and the main route is big and bouncy until through the final stopper. In years gone by a few brave hearts would test the stopper at the bottom of the Tail. It is a mark of a new generation of boaters that all kinds of acrobatics are now performed with regularity.

The Tail carries on downriver in a flat and meandering fashion where boats and bodies are usually reunited. Next comes a broken weir followed by a railway bridge. Another weir which is easily shot follows next.

Next, comes the Nomads' slalom site which runs along by Mile End Mill. Here, there is access to this short play section throughout the year. Bunkhouse accommodation is also available which is warm, economical and convenient. Report in to the canoe shop complex at Mile End Mill for access. The entrance rapid to the Nomads' site is the Tombstones. This is a lot safer than it used to be as most of the old 'tombstone stanchions' have been removed (using funds raised from the rally). Unfortunately, in days gone by, a fatality occurred here before the stanchions were blown out. There is still some debris left in mid-channel and, as for any broken weir, this should be borne in mind.

Below is a brilliant play stopper which just gets better and better as the water rises. The hardest move is getting into it alongside all the other boats! A sharp drop on the left with an excellent play wave is the last drop before the long run in to Town Falls.

In high flood this is quite an intimidating rapid, as you weave your way through a couple of weirs before the falls proper. The main shoot is on the right - the line is left for you to decide but always with that nagging thought of the **un-pleasant weir** below in mind. In big water an exciting line through boat-sticking stoppers can be taken under the left arches.

Below the bridge, and visible from it with a sharp horizon line, is the infamous Town Weir. In high water, its middle and right hand side form a **vicious swim-mer-holding stopper**, and this part is best avoided at all costs. Divers on the right hand bank perform an excellent job during *most open days* pulling the swamped refugees to shore. However, it's best not to rely on this.

The weir is safely shot far left through an obvious shoot. The only trick is to reach it. Egress into the obvious car park left GR212422.

Llangollen to Trevor: 6 km grade II to III***

Many will end the run in Llangollen and head straight for the local pub but, below, is a pleasant section ending in the historic Trevor Rocks rapids. The water is fast but relatively flat until a few 100 metres above Trevor bridge. In big water, this produces a few good waves and stoppers but will seem tame after the rigours above. Egress by the footpath river left below the bridge GR268421. Before driving off, take time to look back upstream at the site of the first British Slalom competition.

Trevor to Erbistock / Overton Bridge: 16 km grade I to II; two weirs often portaged*****

A superb section, best done in normal water conditions (well below the flood), when it is great for Canadian canoes and suitably-led families.

Put on below the bridge at Trevor, in view of the impressive Froncysyllte aqueduct passing high overhead. During good weather, weekends and holidays, barges can be seen passing overhead at dizzy heights above. There are lots of grade I to II easy rapids along this beautiful section of water. Further on, an equally-impressive viaduct dwarfs the passing boater. Newbridge bridge is next, followed by the modern A483 road bridge (both very difficult and arduous access). The rapids continue, interspersed by beautiful flat sections. At a large bend in the river the Afon Ceiriog enters from the right but, at usual touring levels, this will look a rather sad affair. In high flows this is a good river in its own right. There are some very impressive houses in the valley along with the fishing rights. However, nearly all the fishermen and locals were extremely pleasant.

Towards the end of the trip, about 500 metres before Erbistock, is a small weir. This should be obvious from the river as it has a central block of concrete sticking out. If water is flowing only down the right hand shoot, then it is safe enough to shoot with speed. Any higher though, although small, it is worth being cautious and portaging left/right.

Moor alongside *The Boat* inn in Erbistock where one or two old rowing boats are usually found and wander up into this superb watering hole for a drink or so. In fact, you may wish to egress here where an excellent meal can be had (footpath just downstream of pub).

Continue on for one and a half kilometres to where the water slows through black meandering pools. This heralds the approach of a ***large, angled weir***. There is a large old mill house on the left which gives warning. It is easy enough to shoot on the right down the angled rocky shoot but most will **probably wish to portage**. Again, in flood this is an extremely different proposal. 500 metres further on is the *Cross Foxes* pub and egress can be made from the footpath river left, downstream of the bridge GR354427.

Overton Bridge to Bangor-is-y-Coed: 9 km grade I***

From below Overton Bridge the river winds its way down through rich pasture land on its way seawards. This is a lovely touring section with just a few ripples to keep the paddler awake. Bangor racecourse is passed some way down. Egress below the old stone bridge onto the footpath river right in Bangor-is-y-Coed GR388455.

Bangor-is-y-Coed to Farndon: 15 km grade I***

It is possible - after seeking permission - to park in the car park of the *Royal Oak*, found by the old stone bridge in Bangor-is-y-Coed. From here access can be made on to the pleasant touring section between here and Farndon. A little way down from here the Clywedog enters from the left (an "interesting" little adventure in its own right), after which the river goes into a huge series of winding turns. Where the Worthhenbury Brook enters from the right, the river becomes the border between England and Wales. Egress can be made above the ancient stone bridge in the village of Farndon GR410534.

Farndon to Chester: 20 km grade I****

Farndon is found along the A534 Wrexham to Nantwich road. There is excellent access / egress at the Cheshire County Council picnic area by the ancient Roman bridge. There is ample car parking before the excellent *Boat House* restaurant. History is told here; etched in the sandstone rocks of the ancient Dee cliffs is evidence of ancient Dee floods.

The river is flat all the way and perfect for touring and families. It is paddleable all year round - with the proviso that it isn't in big flood when newcomers could get caught out. The river is a 'no-man's land,' forming a border for much of the way, and is fairly straight until a large bend when the Alun River enters from the left. Along here are numerous weekend shacks of all sizes and descriptions but - what the heck - not a bad place to spend your Saturday and Sunday.

The Pulford Brook enters sharply from the left and, a kilometre or so on, the Dee passes into England. But continue nevertheless as the river is still excellent.

Passing on some way, an early 19th century iron bridge is passed: a good place this, for photos. This is all part of the Eaton Hall estate and grounds. If you find it hard work here then it may be because on a big tide, the effects of the sea are felt, even this far up. Indeed, the Dee is one of the few rivers that experiences a bore but, don't worry, no wave of water will come flying around the corner up here. Egress is possible at the small road on the left by the Eccleston village GR415622. The noise of the A55(T) is soon heard before the main road bridge is snuck under. About three kilometres further on egress is made into the car park river right along Sandy Lane, Chester. This is immediately downstream of the Chester Sailing and Canoe Club GR420656.

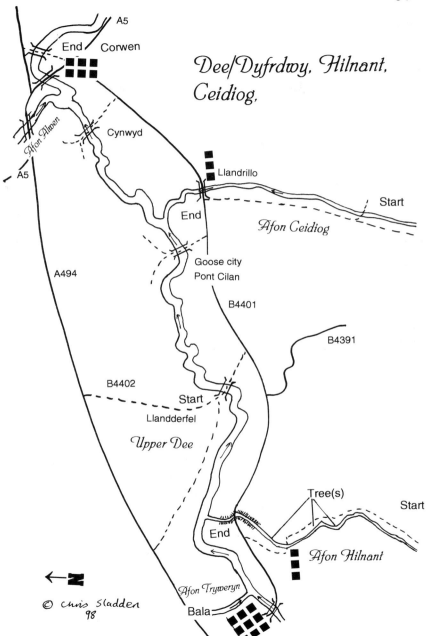

A5

End Corwen

Dee/Dyfrdwy, Hilnant,
Ceidiog,

Afon Alwen

Cynwyd

A5

Llandrillo

Start

End

Afon Ceidiog

A494

Goose city
Pont Cilan

B4401

B4391

B4402

Start

Llandderfel

Upper Dee

Tree(s)

Start

End

Afon Hilnant

N

© chris sladden
98

Afon Tryweryn

Bala

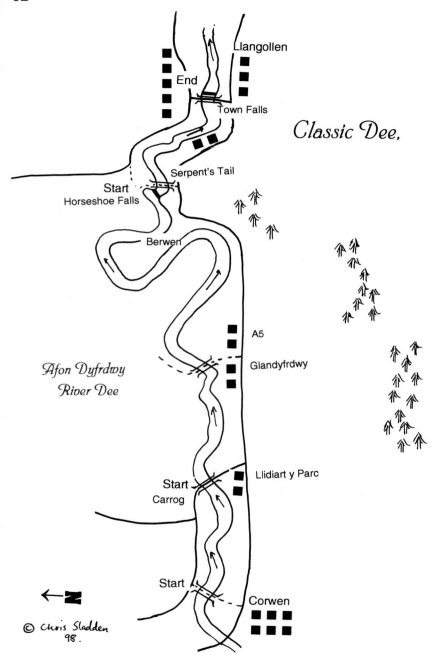

Llangollen

End

Town Falls

Classic Dee,

Serpent's Tail

Start
Horseshoe Falls

Berwen

A5

Afon Dyfrdwy
River Dee

Glandyfrdwy

Llidiart y Parc

Start
Carrog

Start

Corwen

N

© Chris Sladden
98.

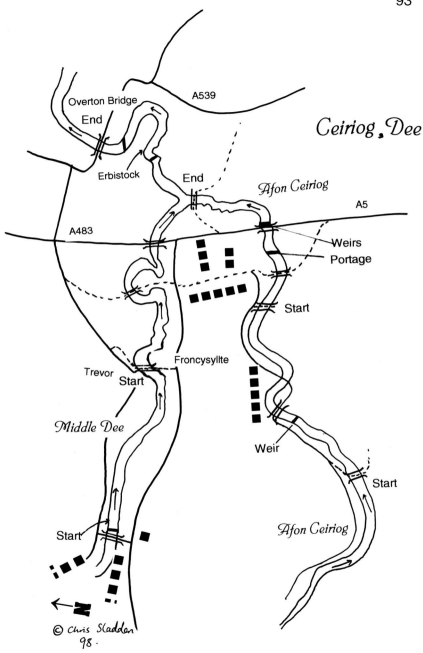

Ceiriog, Dee

Overton Bridge

End

Erbistock

A539

A483

End

Afon Ceiriog

A5

Weirs

Portage

Start

Trevor

Start

Froncysyllte

Middle Dee

Weir

Start

Afon Ceiriog

Start

N

© Chris Sladden
98.

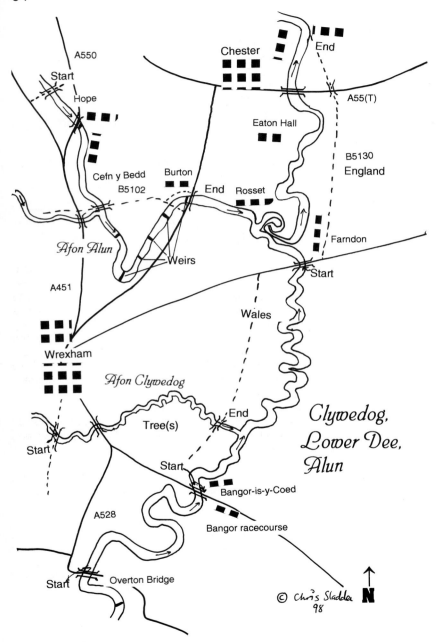

Chester

End

A55(T)

Start

Hope

A550

Eaton Hall

B5130
England

Cefn y Bedd

B5102

Burton

End

Rosset

Afon Alun

Weirs

Farndon

Start

A451

Wales

Wrexham

Afon Clywedog

Tree(s)

End

Clywedog,
Lower Dee,
Alun

Start

Start

Bangor-is-y-Coed

A528

Bangor racecourse

Start

Overton Bridge

© Chris Sladden
98

N

Afon Ceirw:

Map:	Denbigh & Colwyn Bay area, no. 116
	Bala & Lake Vyrnwy & surrounding area, no. 125
Grade:	II to III; one long section VI
Length:	8 km
Access:	off A5 north of Corwen
Notes:	the VI is portaged by most
Quality:	***

The Ceirw is a surprisingly good, intermediate river so long as care is taken with the portage. Reminiscent of the easy middle Llugwy, the bottom section is excellent value. The hard V+ to VI gorge has had a few runs but not by me. In full spate it is an awesome spectacle.

Ystrad Bach Bridge to Maerdy: 8 km class II to III; one portage ***

Start the run at Ystrad Bach bridge GR975455. This is two bridges down from the B4501 Bala road. From here down the water is flat but fast, with very well defined eddies, which are perfect for practising break-outs etc. The first stone bridge had a strand of barbed wire strung from it but this was easily sneaked. It is wise to inspect the class VI before paddling - from the road to Gaer-gerrig and the old A5. Walking down this new footpath, it is hard to imagine that the A5 main road actually ran along here. The best way to portage is to egress the river 200 metres **before the cataract** and climb up onto the old road. This allows a ten-minute, easy wander along here and down a well-marked footpath to the river well below the falls.

Take time to look at the considerable class V+ to VI drops which have now seen a few descents. Along the old road note the plaque to George Borrow who thought this "***the wildest place in Wales***" - not far from the truth!

Back on the river, it is possible to paddle the final ***stiff* class IV** or get onto class II to III water. The rapids from here down are superb, with some brilliant small stoppers and surf waves - excellent at the grade. A couple of broken weirs are found just before good egress river left at a small stone bridge, which is found down the little lane opposite the sign to Betws Garmon GR016446. 100 metres below is a weir that can be run at medium to high levels, which allows continuation down and onto the Alwen. I don't think any more nasties occur on the section below the weir, but I have not paddled the final 800 metres to the confluence.

Afon Alwen

Map:	Denbigh & Colwyn Bay area, no. 116
	Bala & Lake Vyrnwy & surrounding area, no. 125
Grade:	III
Length:	14 km
Access:	B5015 Cerrigydrudion to Ruthin road
Notes:	wires and weirs - one of which is very dangerous
Quality:	**

The Alwen is not a marvellous river by any stretch of the imagination, but it certainly has a few good rapids along its length. There were various fences en-route, all of which could be sneaked when paddled in '97. The big weir below the Ceirw confluence is *potentially lethal!*

Llanfihangel Glyn Myfyr to A5 road bridge: 14 km class III; one prudent portage**

Turn off the A5 in Cerrigydrudion and head eastwards on the B5105 towards Llanfihangel Glyn Myfyr. Access can be made on to the river from the little road upstream of the bridge,GR992493. The river flows out of Llyn Brenig and the flow is often restricted. When the other rivers are in spate there tends to be a limited release which is topped up by various side streams entering the river. Shoot the first weir, **(which, in big spate, might be quite nasty)** and navigate your way around the following Island. Apart from a few fences that were easily passable, the river is easy until a little way above the first proper road bridge (Hendre). Just above here is a splendid mini gorge, graded III

Between here and the next road bridge at Bettws Gwerfil Goch is a steep weir, which was runnable middle to right over its large constructing blocks. A little way below the bridge itself was a *difficult-to-sneak* **fence**. From here on down, the rapids get a bit better, just about touching Grade III.

The Ceirw enters from the right, significantly increasing the volume downstream. In flood it is like a steam train, leading the paddler through some bouncy grade III rapids and a broken weir. The water eases off, down to where a footbridge crosses the river at Pen-y-Bont. *With any kind of water level above low, the weir that is immediately below becomes exceptionally dangerous*. Don't be deceived by the first bouncy ramp that puts paddlers into a stilling pool. This sanctuary could better be described as a prison as, once captured, the canoe-ist is forced to run the following step. This carries an exceptionally dangerous stopper which looks like a **"drowner"**.

I paddled this river with a couple of young hotshots, who ran the weir without inspection! They signalled me down their line - a hard boof on the left. I got a tremendous shock when, out of the corner of my eye, I saw the horrendous

Phil Blain takes the drop splitting the two gorges of the Fairy Glen.
Photo: Phil Blain collection

Tranquillity on the Lower Dee. Barges cross the Froncysyllte
aqueduct high overhead. Photo Clare Jefferson

In the early '80s someone once said, "if you spill your drink someone will come and paddle it" - proving the point on Pont Cyfyng (Afon Llugwy). Photo: Chris Sladden collection

How do you grade this? 'Main-lining' on Swallow Falls.
Photo: Foxy

Ross Purdy up to his arms in a class V section of the Conwy.
Photo: Foxy

Phil Davidson, "a legend in his own lifetime" on the first of the two
big drops on the Conwy above Penmachno bridge. Photo and
comments by Ian Walsh

The last-but-one big hit on the Colwyn. Photo: Ian Walsh

Rhiw Goch gorge on the Lledr. Photo: Ian Walsh

Stream paddling par excellence:
above) Nantygwyryd. Photo: Loel Collins
below) Ysgethin. Photo Clare Jefferson

'Pipeline rapid' in the Fairy Glen. Photo: Foxy

Warm-up on the Afon Gain. Photo: Clare Jefferson

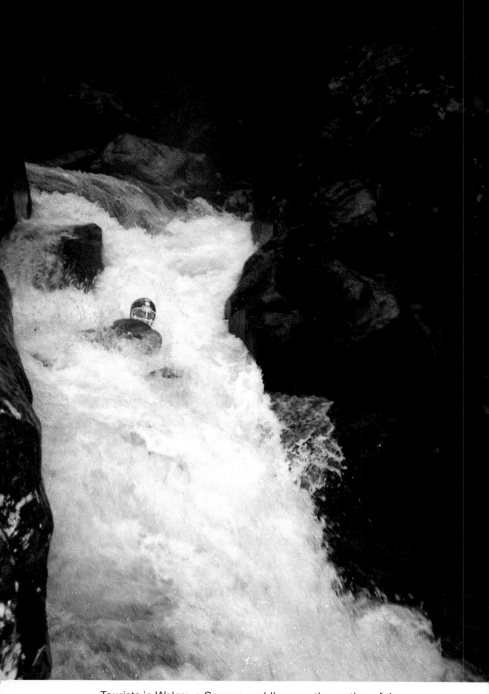

Tourists in Wales: a German paddler runs the section of the
Llugwy above the Miner's Bridge. Photo: Ian Walsh

stopper beckoning. The moral of this tale is: don't always trust hotshots - I would never contemplate doing this weir again.

I strongly recommend an easy **portage** along the road on the left. It is also easy to finish the trip here, GR043437. Otherwise, continue down to the main A5 road bridge, shoot the broken weir and pull out below on the right bank GR051435.

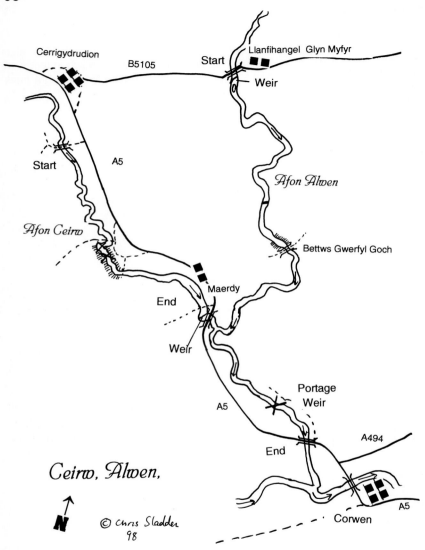

Cerrigydrudion

B5105

Start

Llanfihangel Glyn Myfyr

Weir

A5

Start

Afon Alwen

Afon Ceirw

Bettws Gwerfyl Goch

Maerdy

End

Weir

Portage
Weir

A5

End

A494

A5

Ceirw, Alwen.

N

© Chris Sladden
98

Corwen

Afon Hilnant

Map:	Bala & Lake Vyrnwy & surrounding area, no. 125
Grade:	IV; gorge IV to V
Length:	4 km
Access:	B4319 Bala to Corwen road
Notes:	trees, trees and more trees
Quality:	not recommended

The Hilnant is a vicious little stream running downhill to join the upper Dee. There are one or two drops that are worth doing but the river is fraught with tree dangers. However, the lower section does actually give very good alternative access to the upper Dee.

Tyn y Cwm to Garth Goch: 4 km IV; various portages, one V

The B4319 crosses the river at Pont Ceunant where, just west of this, it is possible to head upstream to a small place called Rhos y Gwaliau. If you cross the river here and carry on for a further two kilometres, a convenient access place is found at a small parking area GR956335. The water starts off at a good grade II to III but, almost immediately, there is a fence just below that requires portaging. However, there are some reasonable little drops towards the next village.

Below this the rapids steepen and become class IV, but are very dangerous because of the number of trees - two required portaging. The road bridge is reached but the narrow drop below had a tree firmly jammed in the shoot at time of writing. Just around the corner is a good **class V** drop that proves a challenging run. All that remains is a broken railway bridge and a few small weirs, before the Dee is reached. A little path allows access and egress from this point and, indeed, you may wish to start a run on the upper Dee from here.

Afon Ceidiog

Map:	Bala & Lake Vyrnwy & surrounding area, no. 125
Grade:	II
Length:	3 km
Access:	off the B4401 Llandrillo to Bala road
Notes:	one fence required portaging
Quality:	***

The Ceidiog is a pleasant little stream running out of Cwm Pennant towards the Dee. In fact, it can be used as an alternative starting point for the river Dee, if you so wish.

<u>Pennant to Llandrillo</u>: 3 km grade II; one portage - fence***

From the beautiful village of Llandrillo (on the B4401), turn off upstream just west of the river and continue for about three kilometres to where access can be made at the little Pennant bridge GR027342. This is by a public telephone.

The river needs to be in a reasonable spate to be worth doing. It pays to get on about ten metres downstream of the bridge, thus avoiding an annoying fence that is just out of sight around the corner. The river is a beautiful Grade II as it hurries down to reach the Dee. There were a few fences but only the one under the bridge at Cadwst needed portaging. There are also a few foot-bridges that are passed en-route, one of which is a contender for the most dilapidated in Wales.

Finish the run just below the little weirs at the bridge in town. These are good fun to play in at the right level GR035362. From here to the Dee, the river should be flat, but I haven't done this last section.

Afon Ceiriog:

Map:	Bala & Lake Vyrnwy & surrounding area, no. 125
	Shrewsbury & surrounding area, no. 126
Grade:	II to II+ and III
Length:	22 km
Access:	off the B4500 Chirk to Glynceiriog road
Notes:	weirs, two of which are best portaged, in flood it is an altogether more nasty river
Quality:	***upper section, **lower section has irritating portages

A reasonable river - consistent at the grade and best paddled in medium levels. A few fences and a fallen tree required portaging at time of paddling.

<u>Pont-y-Meibion to Pont Faen</u>: 16 km of class II to II+; two weirs***

During a thunderstorm, the drive up the B4500 towards and through Glyn Ceiriog is a sombre affair. One can almost picture ancient skirmishes between the Welsh and the English in the valleys below, and on the slopes above. The river is best done in a medium spate and, maybe, with luck the sun will be out, brightening up the valley. As the road passes through Pandy it rises away from the river to where, about a kilometre later, a small road goes off to the left and down to a bridge over the Ceiriog. There is a convenient yard for parking and access can be made down the short bank GR196352.

The rapids are pretty continuous class II to II+ and excellent value. Just before the village of Glyn Ceiriog is reached there is a **_weir_**. With care this can be shot through the salmon steps on the right in medium levels. This drop can easily be seen during the drive up the road. The rapids ease off as the river swaps sides now and again with the road alongside.

In between Castle Mill and Pont Eaen bridges is a boulder weir across the river. This is easily shot on the left by the 'Beware Guard Dogs' sign. Egress can be made river left downstream of Pont Eaen bridge onto the convenient footpath GR280371.

Pont Eaen to Ddôl bridge: 6 km III; two weirs best portaged; frustrating fences**

This part of the river is found on the OS sheet covering Shrewsbury and surrounding area, no. 126. In flood this hammers down under the huge viaduct and aqueduct, and the paddler is dwarfed as he passes underneath. The river here is 'no man's land', the right bank being Shropshire, the left Clwyd. The next bridge, the B5070, used to be the A5 until the new by-pass was built. A few 100 metres below this is an ***unpleasant double-stepped weir***. A horizon line and a weir hut on the right gives indication of its arrival. This is best **portaged on the right**. Just below is a fence, so make sure you put on below.

Below the huge following (A5) road bridge, on a left hand sweep, is a further weir where the river passes over a concrete ford. This is again unpleasant at high flows and, again, has a fence below. Portage left or right with a bit of effort. There is another fence at the end of the next field so care is needed - portage right. The beautiful little stone bridge leading to Brynkinalt is passed - a fine place this, for photos. Good rapids lead under Pont y Blew. Halfway between this and the next bridge is the best surfing wave on the river - marvellous fun. A couple more fences need to be negotiated before the get-out at Ddôl bridge on river right GR316392.

Afon Clywedog

Map:	Chester, Wrexham and surrounding area, no. 117
Grade:	II
Length:	9 km
Access:	off A525 Whitchurch to Wrexham road
Notes:	two little weirs; numerous tree chokes
Quality:	none for paddling; many for SAS training!

The Wrexham Clywedog has the dubious distinction of being about the filthiest river I have paddled in Wales. Oddly enough, it starts off in the Country Park running over lovely shingle and pebbly reefs, before being used as a municipal rubbish dump by some local people. Sad that the local children have to fish in such surroundings as, if cleaned, this would be a pretty little stream by which to grow up.

Country Park bridge to Pickhall Hall footpath bridge: 9 km grade II

Go there if you dare, but I can't recommend this to anyone other than salvage workers. The little Country Park found just south of Wrexham can be reached either off the A525 or B5426 at GR336484. Access can be made below an attractive little bridge, built in 1845. The river should be up enough for the boat to clear any obstructions in the first 100 metres or so but, under no account, should it be in flood!

The river starts off pleasantly enough before rapidly going downhill (not in gradient). A first bridge is passed on which the local youth have left record of who has 'scored' with whom over the years. A chap called 'Daz' appeared to be doing particularly well. Some huge pipes and an old bridge are passed. A sewage works appears on the right bank - there is no mistaking this! After this, the river meanders through the Wrexham Industrial Estate, during which a tiny weir is found. There are numerous tree chokes which increase in number en-route down. Many can be breached using siege tactics, but some are just plain awkward portages up the muddy banks. If you want an old fridge, lawn mower or motor cycle helmet, then you are likely to find it here!

Before the B5130 is another tiny weir, Egress here, or be a sucker like me and continue down to the next footbridge, where the footpath off right leads to a small back road   GR398476.

Afon Alun

Map:	Chester
Grade:	II to III
Length:	14 km
Access:	A483 Chester to Wrexham road
Notes:	weirs - a couple are prudent portages
Quality:	***

The Alun is not a bad river at the grade; it never really hits the mark but is well worth doing if you are in the area.

Hope to Rosset: 14 km II to III; various weirs; some prudent portages***

About two and a half kilometres north of Cefn y Bedd it is possible to turn off towards Hope crossing the river as you do. Using some stone steps by the bridge allows good access to the river GR302585. The river needs a good flow to make it worthwhile. In flood it moves quickly along. Easy meandering water with the occasional fence, brings the paddler down to a beautiful little bridge. About 500 metres past this, and just below the next bridge (built in1838), is a large, angled weir that can be easily shot. The people in the mill house on the left bank are particularly friendly.

About a kilometre below this is a short section with a natural weir drop that just, at a pinch, reaches class III in big water. A large double bridge is next, followed by the Cegidog spilling in its murky flow from the right. Further down on the right are two mounds of orange rock which presumably contain some kind of iron. Easy water under the next and then B5425 road bridge leads to a large bend south and then north through a large estate. A few houses on the left are followed by a small bridge with a "bouncy rapid-like thing" below. This is about a grade III - the wave below the bridge is superb for surfing or looping in. Just below is a barbed wire which can just about be sneaked. A few 100 metres further on is a boxed-in weir - shootable down the left channel in a low to medium spate, the right side in flood looks particularly unpleasant. If any doubt **portage**. Passing under the next bridge the river straightens up through a wooded area. Take care here, as a little way below is a small, odd weir which is very quiet but has a big towback in spate - **beware**. This towback is about 15 foot in high water and just quietly rushes back to the foot of the drop carrying all kinds of rubbish. Although it is probably "punch-able" at medium water, I recommend **a portage!** 50 metres below is another one, but this can be shot on the right down the tongue, where the banks have fallen in.

Below here the water rushes down through a few easy rapids and under the next bridge. There is one further weir which can be safely shot on the right before Burton weir is reached. This large weir is next to the main road at the suggested get-out point. It can be easily shot far left but in flood the central salmon steps look extremely nasty. Egress onto the small road below the weir GR360572.

Afon Tryweryn

Map:	Bala & Lake Vyrnwy & surrounding area, no. 125
Grade:	III (IV-) and II (IV)
Length:	8 km
Access:	off A4212 Bala to Trawsfynydd road
Notes:	no portages
Quality:	****

The Afon Tryweryn is the best of the small handful of rivers in Wales that are dam released. It releases water, on average, for over 200 days of the year in its capacity for keeping the Dee high. This is not necessarily when it is raining. Indeed, if the rain is heavy, then I would recommend checking out one of the 200 or so other rivers in this guide book. The high number of releases means that it is available for a large number of paddlers and adventurers from all over the country. It is the National White Water Centre and, as such, is a resource open to many water users. The centre has hosted the World slalom and River Racing Championships and plans are underfoot to upgrade the facilities even as this book goes to press.

There is a charge to get on the water but, remember: the water is pretty clean, the waves are reliable, and there are excellent plans to include impromptu coaching sessions. The river is also regularly used for rafting - but then, if you paddle abroad, you quickly get used to this.

It is always best to ring the centre for release and accessibility as, often, when releases are on, there may be a competition which restricts access. Midweek is usually available. The river is closed for environmental purposes from December to the beginning of February. During October and November the lower, easier section of the river is also open.

Information on releases - Tel: 01678 520826
To call the Centre -   Tel: 01678 521083

The class of water varies according to a release, but guidelines are as follows:-

Full release: 8-10 cumecs   Grade III(+)
Full and natural flow: 12 cumecs   Grade just reaches IV
Half release: 5 cumecs   Class III, just

To reach the centre turn off the A4212 in Ciltalgarth - the centre is well-signposted.

Llyn Celyn dam to Tyn y Cornel bridge: 2 km class III (IV)****

If you are going to start up at the dam it is best to check for availability with the Centre, as one is not always allowed onto here. A road to the top allows access and paths along the river bank allow easy inspection - great for newcomers.

The water from the dam flows out into a stilling basin and over a steep weir. This is good for airtime. Many rescue courses have people swim in the weir and experience the green room effect as they spend a lot of down time.

Below this, easy rapids lead to where the old the Irish Bridge was situated. This has now been removed because of danger from its potential strainers. Plans are underfoot to totally change this. Easier water leads down to the metal fish pass below which the usual access can be made.

A short, flat section, to warm up before the class III graveyard, is entered. This just about reaches IV in high flows (12+ cumecs). This is an excellent, long rapid, which has not earned its name for nothing. A short break before the so-called 'ski jump' is reached with its play hole at bottom. The infamous Fedwr Gog Falls follows a short, bouncy shoot and is directly below the stone bridge. Despite most thinking the easiest shoot is on the right, I disagree, and feel far left is simpler - right into the eddy. Have a look, watch some of the other boaters run it and decide yourselves. At one time, with changes in the river bed, the stopper below became quite dangerous but this has now been rectified. Loel (Centre Manager) assures me that it has lost its teeth ... well maybe, perhaps, blunted (Loel is a very good paddler indeed)?

The Dog Leg, with its small stopper and surf wave, is followed by another bouncy rapid, then the scaffold bridge with its popular haystack wave. That done, and easy water leads down to the last big drop, Chapel Falls. Finish off at Tyn y Cornel bridge, a couple of 100 metres downstream. Most paddlers will already be heading back up for another run!

Tyn y Cornel bridge to Bala car park: 6 km grade II to III; one fall IV****

On open days or during the months of October and November, it is possible to paddle the rest of the Tryweryn. This should not be missed as it is an excellent stretch of river, but at a lower grade. It is also more wild in that here, like on all other Welsh rivers, other things like the occasional tree need to be borne in mind.

Frequent grade II rapids lead down to just before Bala where the so-called Factory Pool is reached GR920368. If you don't like the thought of a class IV rapid, then it is possible to egress here by the path on the right. The river cranks up a grade in the next few 100 metres on the lead down to Bala Mill

Falls. This drop is one of the first class IV rapids that many paddlers attempt. **It can only just be described as a IV, but that said, a run down through the main channel on the right is an achievement nevertheless and not to be scoffed at** - a left-sided chicken shoot is a possible alternative.

A good friend of mine, Dr Dave Evans, ran Bala Mill - his first class IV. The cheeks were puffed, the eyes on stalks, as he took a superb line down the falls. In the pool below he broke out and visibly relaxed before capsizing - these tricky flat pools!

Below Bala Mill, continue down to below the main road bridge and egress out into the convenient car park GR929362. Below this are some small, innocuous **but very dangerous weirs** - don't be tempted!

The upper Tryweryn:

Running into Llyn Celyn is the upper Tryweryn. Once graded as class III it is, in fact, in its lower parts, a full-on, class V spate paddle with at least one or two portages.

Tryweryn

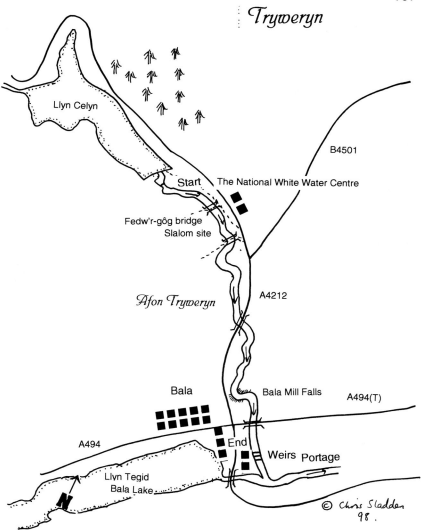

Llyn Celyn

B4501

Start   The National White Water Centre

Fedw'r-gôg bridge
Slalom site

Afon Tryweryn   A4212

Bala   Bala Mill Falls   A494(T)

A494

End   Weirs Portage

Llyn Tegid
Bala Lake

N

© Chris Sladden
98.

Afon Llafar

Map:	Bala & Lake Vyrnwy & surrounding area, no. 125
Grade:	II
Length:	2.5 km
Access:	off 4494(T) Bala to Dolgellau road
Notes:	two fences - one of which needs portaging
Quality:	***

An excellent little spate river, especially so for the grade. For those wanting to get into spate paddling this is a good river, with continuous but easy rapids, surf-able waves and a few playable stoppers.

Parc to Pont y Lafar: 2.5 km grade II - one fence portage***

Turn off to Parc near the south western end of Llyn Tegid (Bala Lake). Good access for *small* groups can be made by the small bridge in town (though I strongly suggest changing out of sight of the houses!) GR876339. The river needs to be clearly 'up' to be worth doing.

Exciting grade II, bouncy rapids start just around the corner and continue nearly all the way to the egress. There are loads of really good, beginners' surf waves, with good eddies to be carved. At time of paddling there were two fences on the first half of the river, one of which was easily sneaked, the other a definite portage. Egress at the main road bridge GR893324.

Afon Lliw

Map:	Bala & Lake Vyrnwy & surrounding area, no. 125
Grade:	IV to V
Length:	5 km
Access:	off A494 Dolgellau to Bala road
Notes:	various class V to VI drops which most will portage
Quality:	***

The Lliw is quite an exciting little expedition. It runs through a wild valley and over even wilder drops, many of which are prudently portaged; though all of them have apparently been run.

Lliw falls to Bryn Gwyn: 5 km grade IV to V; various portages***

The Lliw runs into Bala Lake from the opposite valley to the splendid Twrch. It can be done after a warm up on the Twrch if you fancy a more radical paddle. A medium spate is the ideal level for the Lliw as, in flood, it is extremely dangerous.

Turn off the A494 just before it crosses the river, and head up to and through the village of Dothendre. Continue up the steep road until the huge Lliw waterfalls are visible. Access can be made here by the farm buildings a few 100 metres **below** the cataract. Use the footpath to get down to the water, GR828325.

Class II and III lead down to a right hand bend. Immediately below is a class V fall - ***don't miss the break out***. The fall is dangerous because of the nature of the bedrock. A slight "gorging up", gives a hint of its presence. Below, some excellent class IVs lead somewhat surreptitiously into a long **300-metre cataract**. Some of these drops can be run in the right conditions but it is easy enough to portage river left via a small path by the fence line, to where the cataract clearly eases off. It is a mark of today's standards that all of these class V and VI drops have been done. Some class IV+ drops complete the gorge till it suddenly pops out above a caravan park. From here down to whatever egress point you choose is class II - the road is right next to the river at a little bridge at GR861308 - a good get-out.

Afon Twrch

Map:	Bala & Lake Vyrnwy & surrounding area, no. 125
Grade:	IV to V
Length:	4 km
Access:	turn off B4403 at Llanuwchllyn, SW end of Llyn Tegid
Notes:	one weir - possible portage
Quality:	*****

A storming run with increasing difficulties until a final flourish over two big drops. The grade changes quite considerably depending on water levels and, in big flood, it is nail biting stuff. It is a great river for the more experienced paddler, but it is a good idea to walk along the footpath upstream of the egress point to see what you are letting yourself in for.

Talardd Bridge to Llanuwchllyn: 4.5 km IV to V; one weir a possible portage*****

The Twrch is found at the southern end of Bala lake. Turn off the B4403 in Llanuwchllyn along the steep road just east of the river and continue upstream for about four kilometres. There is a small road that goes off left to several farms, with a telephone and letter box visible.

Start at the bridge, GR894270. Soon grade III rapids are reached that twist and turn excitingly down to below the footbridge at Cae Porth. Things pick up and grade III and IV rapids bring you around an island to a *five-foot horseshoe weir*. If you are struggling it may be advisable to consider backing off (path on left) as, after this, things hot up! The weir itself can be bounced far left, but the stopper looks particularly **dangerous** elsewhere and a portage is easy if you don't fancy the shoot!

Class IV leads you to a sharp mini break-out above a **class V drop**. There was a tree here that needed portaging around, before ferrying out midstream to run this hard drop through the guts. Below are some excellent and hard grade IV rapids leading to the top of a *second frightening class V drop*. This is about 60 metres above the egress bridge and, again, with enough water is run through the guts. It can be easily inspected before paddling, from the egress point. A partially natural weir lying under the bridge is easily taken, before egress is made below left into the convenient car park.

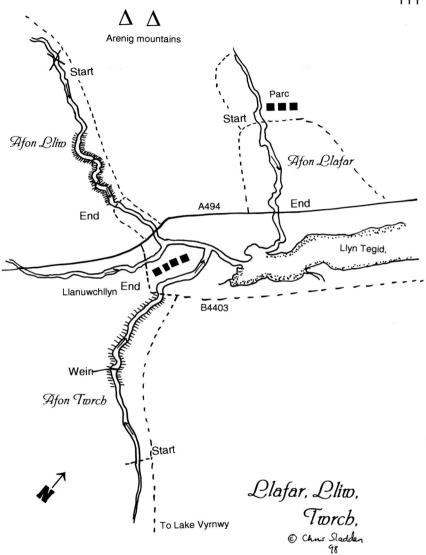

Arenig mountains

Start

Afon Lliw

Parc

Start

Afon Llafar

A494

End

End

Llyn Tegid,

End

Llanuwchllyn

B4403

Weir

Afon Twrch

Start

To Lake Vyrnwy

Llafar, Lliw,
Twrch,
© Chris Sladden
98

Ffestiniog rivers:

There are three rivers which run into the Vale of Ffestiniog to eventually form the Afon Dwyryd. The Dwyryd is a beautiful grade I paddle suitable for family and lovers alike. The feeding rivers are wholly the opposite - all steep, hard, frightening and dangerous.

Of the three, the Goedal is most regularly paddled and is, probably, the best quality; the Cynfal is an awesome river with good, short sections, and the Teigl - well, the Teigl is a nasty little number.

Afon Goedal

Map:	Dolgellau & surrounding area, no. 124
Grade:	grade V to VI
Length:	3 km
Access:	from A496 Porthmadog to Blaenau Ffestiniog road
Notes:	serious and steep creek paddling; one portage
Quality:	*****

The two most important points to note about the Goedal are, one, find the correct access point and, second, pick the water level. The access is in GR693440, below some pylons and by a wooden bridge, immediately above a large but shootable fall. Do not make the mistake of getting on above at the next bridge up which has a dangerous and radical drop below (though even this has now been run). The water is released from Tanygrisiau reservoir. It normally goes a few days after rain but the spills are unpredictable - I've been lucky in midsummer, so look if you are passing. The river is topped up by the Afon Cwmorthen and the Afon Barlwyd, both of which have been paddled. If the reservoir is releasing in addition to these two streams going, then the Goedal becomes pretty much unrunnable.

Wooden bridge to Tegel confluence: 3 km V to VI; portages *****

The Goedal is a very serious paddling trip fraught with potential danger from start to finish. It has seen more than its fair share of epics, with at least two near-drownings - to my knowledge. It is well worth checking it out before getting on to paddle, firstly, to check water level and, secondly, the type of drops involved. Although you can walk the whole river by the excellent path system, the access and egress points and at Rhaeadr Cwmerau, which is next to the layby, are good points to check. The river has two distinct gorge sections, the second one having a possibly un-run drop in it.

The river starts with a bang and needs to have enough water flowing over large slabs at the bridge to be runnable. In flood it is horrendous. The river is unrelenting. **Most of the drops are regularly paddled, but they are all water dependent!** Rhaeadr Cwmerau is a well-known and somewhat infamous drop - if a lot of water is flowing over it, it may be best taken on the unlikely looking left-side - the right shoot at high conditions is very dangerous. However, in this kind of water the situation is marginal, and the stopper becomes capable of holding swimmers and boats viciously underwater. It is often a prudent portage.

Below Rhaeadr Cwmerau is another equally testing gorge but this time containing a portage. Its third drop is yet to be run (to my knowledge) and is an extremely dangerous prospect.

Enough said - if you can paddle this river, you don't really need a guide.
Egress at the Teigl confluence, where there is a convenient footpath GR689423.

Afon Teigl

Map:	Dolgellau and surrounding area, no. 124
Grade:	V and VI
Length:	2 km
Access:	footpath below Pont y Pandy GR704429
Notes:	nasty; various portages - trees/drops
Quality:	**

The Teigl is a nasty, steep, somewhat tree-ridden little number. Phil Blain assures me that I am over-reacting, and that even the upper section from Cwm Teigl down is good sport.

Pont y Pandy to Goedal confluence: 2km V to VI; various portages**

Basically, the river starts with steep, narrow falls before dropping sharply through a boulder jungle. Following this is a second narrow gorge. In flood it is unpaddleable. Medium water allows certain lines to be taken. About three to four portages are probably (though apparently all drops have been done) necessary depending on tree damage. **A horrible river**, but there we are.

Afon Cynfal

Map:	Dolgellau and surrounding area, no. 124
Grade:	V to VI
Length:	7 km
Access:	junction B4407 / B4391, Bont Newydd
Notes:	some big falls and trees need careful inspection; various portages
Quality:	***adventure

I am very grateful to Phil Blain for putting together these notes. I did paddle part of the river, with Phil, about ten years ago but for the life of me couldn't remember details apart from how hard and dangerous it was. Thanks to Phil, I haven't had the worry of having to paddle it again:

The Cynfal is a hidden gem or your worst nightmare depending upon taste. This river is only for the adventure enthusiast and requires group tactics to inspect, portage and protect. Ropework and climbing skills are essential. It is best run in low to medium levels and after rain. When it is high or rising the narrow gorges become a more difficult proposition. The river can be run complete, or as two sections, -advisable.

Pont Yr Afon Gam to road bridge GR735414: 3 km class V to VI***

Pont Yr Afon Gam, GR747419, is east of Llan Ffestiniog and at one time was the site of the highest petrol station in Wales. If the river looks full or dark peaty brown the descent will be difficult and **the stop above Rhaeadr Y Cwm most interesting**.

Grade II water leads to a narrow gorge which can only really be run in high water when the rest of the river becomes a horror show. It has a choke on entry but finishes with a steep little fall on a bend. Most will want to portage - river left. Easy water then takes you to a steep sided gorge which towers above you. It hides the impressive Rhaeadr Y Cwm. Some interesting falls lead to the lip of this. To my knowledge **no one has yet run this fall**. Most will want to abseil from here. The river now descends into a steep sided gorge with a series of difficult drops that most will want to portage or be selective. The river now eases considerably - egress at a bridge GR735414. It is possible to continue but a difficult fall nestles directly under the road bridge at Bont Newydd heralding the change of difficulty.

Bont Newydd to Pont Tal Y Bont: 4 km V to VI; portages***

Follow a small road downstream from the bridge to a layby and footpath. Access the river wherever you feel confident to put on.

A good level is a couple of days after rain or low to medium depending upon your ability. It is worth having a walk to look for trees and inspect falls as some sections are difficult to portage. Prior to our first descent it took several weekends of hard work to clear the trees. A series of drops leads to Sweetness and Light, two contrasting falls - one boney - and the second an impressive waterfall which marks the end of this section. Some portages may be necessary, but all of this section has been run.

If you still want more then continue under the impressive viaduct and head for Rhaeadr Cynfal. The Pulpit, an impressive island in the middle of the gorge, signifies the beginning of the difficulties. You may want to portage before this. There is an impressive viewpoint above the fall, river right, which will rapidly decide your course of action. I believe it has been run, though personally I abseiled, swam it and then walked away.

The river continues over a series of falls and steep drops. Depending upon the water level and trees you will need to make important judgments. Portages usually go best on river left. One fall is particularly gnarly and needs a lot of water to do! The river eases slightly and the keyhole arrives on a bend in the river. Water level is significant here as is all too obvious, most will want to portage river right. Depending upon trees the rest of the river can be a delight as it narrows, twists and turns to bring you to the final difficulties, a series of falls below a distinct narrowing. Depending upon river levels, these are worth a walk upstream from Tal Y Bont just to do them. The A496 bridge indicates that your journey is over. Downstream of this, river right, is a small road. If you have come from the top you will have had an impressive day and I would recommend a pint or two to calm those shattered nerves.

Just writing this brought back exciting memories, I feel as drained as I did when I crawled out of the river.

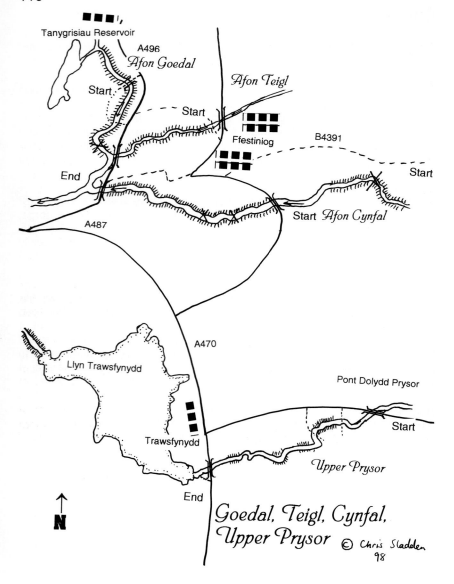

Tanygrisiau Reservoir

A496

Afon Goedal

Afon Teigl

Start

Start

Ffestiniog

B4391

End

Start

A487

Start *Afon Cynfal*

A470

Llyn Trawsfynydd

Pont Dolydd Prysor

Trawsfynydd

Start

End

Upper Prysor

N

Goedal, Teigl, Cynfal,
Upper Prysor © Chris Sladden
98

Afon Dwyryd

Map:	Dolgellau & surrounding area, no. 124
Grade:	I to II (for tidal conditions and jet skis!)
Length:	11 km
Access:	4487
Notes:	no portages
Quality:	****

Four of the hardest rivers in this area, the Goedal, Teigl, Cynfal and Lower Prysor empty into, and become, the placid and delightful Dwyryd. The bottom section is easier on an outgoing tide and, with properly qualified leadership, this is a great trip to do. The upper section from Dol y Moch bridge is a beautiful class II GR685417.

<u>Lower Prysor bridge to Borth y Gest harbour</u>: 11 km grade I to II****

Access can be made a little way below the little bridge over the Lower Prysor GR653397. Alternatively, there is a small layby right by the river and situated on the A487 between Maentwrog and Porthmadog GR648402. However, both starts *need fairly high tides to be useable*.

The river is flat and delightful as it winds its estuarine way past the fascinating village of Portmeirion. Many will want to visit this most well-known of Clough William-Ellis' designs.

Borth y Gest harbour (via Porthmadog) makes for a charming finish. Good parking, toilets, plus a café which serves steaming mugs of tea - what more could a paddler ask for? GR565375.

Afon Prysor

Map:	Dolgellau & surrounding area, no. 124
Grade:	II to III (IV)
Length:	6 km
Access:	off A4217 Trawsfynydd to Bala road
Notes:	two harder falls
Quality:	*****

A brilliant little river with four outstanding little gorges. Best done in medium spate.

Pont Dolydd Prysor to Trawsfynydd: 6 km grade II to III; two falls of IV*****

This super little run needs to be in a medium spate to be in prime condition. It is a great intermediate run for introducing this type of mountain stream. Put in at the first A4210 road bridge over the river GR747362, where the river should be obviously 'up', but not over its banks.

Gentle little rapids lead to the first of the small gorges, situated between two footbridges (III). Easier water again and then the walls obviously close in, and a super little class III rapid is entered. A little further on and there is a large drop which, in high water, is a class IV. This exciting drop is best run left of middle.

A little way before the main road bridge in Trawsfynydd is a series of natural steps that reach IV in big conditions. You need to be a little cautious about the stoppers on one or two of these if the water is very high. An excellent river - egress river left 50 metres below the main road bridge, up a small track GR710351.

Lower Prysor

Map:	Dolgellau & surrounding area, no. 124
Grade:	V to V+
Length:	2 km
Access:	turn up steep road just before A496 crosses the river near Maentwrog power station
Notes:	one possible portage
Quality:	*****

The Prysor fills Trawsfynydd lake and is an excellent class III run whilst it is drained by the Lower Prysor or, as it is occasionally known, the Rhaeadr Ddu. The misnomer arises from the spectacular runnable drop at the get-on to the section described. This river is often empty as water is diverted down pipes near the glow factory of Trawsfynydd Nuclear Power station. The water in the lake was used for cooling purposes whilst the piped water went to generate electricity downhill in Maentwrog. If the pipes were in need of repair there was guaranteed water. This is still very much the case even with the closure of the top power station, unless there is extremely heavy rain. If you arrive in summer weather then it is an excellent gorge walk.

Rhaeadr Ddu to A496 road bridge: 2 km class V to V+; possible portage*****

The upper gorge has been paddled at a hard grade VI with several portages. It hardly ever has water in it. The waterfall, Rhaeadr Ddu, has also seen its fair share of descents. The televised descent by Shaun Baker was particularly spectacular. This is reached by walking in with boats from the road up to Gellilydan (the steep road uphill by the power plant). Put on below the main drop GR666388. The water is exciting class V. Two drops, in particular, have mean and dangerous stoppers in high flows and should be viewed with caution.

Some way down there is a large drop into a 60 foot deep pool (dived by Paul Fessi) which immediately drops into a long slide and undercut. This may need to be portaged (grade VI) if the water is high, but is otherwise a fantastic and radical run. Further exciting paddling brings you down to the main road bridge where egress can be made. It's unlikely that you'll have the energy for another run down!

120

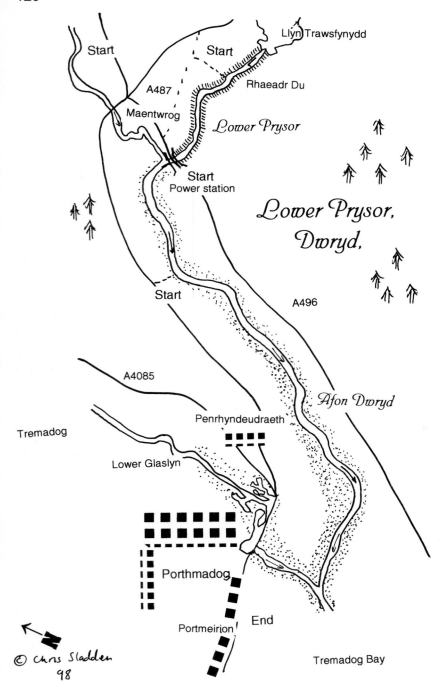

Llyn Trawsfynydd

Start

Start

A487

Rhaeadr Du

Maentwrog

Lower Prysor

Start
Power station

Lower Prysor,
Dwryd,

Start

A496

A4085

Afon Dwryd

Penrhyndeudraeth

Tremadog

Lower Glaslyn

Porthmadog

Portmeirion

End

© Chris Sladden
98

Tremadog Bay

The Afon Mawddach

Map:	Dolgellau & surrounding area, no. 124
Grade:	sections of II, IV and V
Length:	21 km
Access:	off A470(T)
Notes:	portages for most on upper section - one big weir needs caution in flood
Quality:	sections of ***and ****and *****

Rising, as it does, in the high marshland of Waun y Griafolen ('the moor of Rowan') the Mawddach is a true river of gold. Not only is it still producing small amounts of the precious metal but it is real gold in canoeing terms. Cascading over large drops, and surging through rapids and waves, it is paddleable from source to sea with just a few portages for most mortals. More important is that there are sections that can be enjoyed by all.

Upper Mawddach - Pont Abergeirw to Pont ar Eden: 9 km grade V; several portages*****

To reach the upper Mawddach an OS sheet is useful. Otherwise, head up the small roads through Coed y Brenin forest, paralleling the Wen, and carry on until you reach Pont Abergeirw crossing the river. The river *needs* to be in a reasonable spate to be worth doing. A few years back, a friend and I made the mistake of launching when the river was too low - it made for a long day. We were eventually 'rescued' by the Forestry Commission - but that is another tale.

The first couple of kilometres of river are straightforward but very pleasant, before the first of several steep falls is reached. This vicious class V drop has a nasty left hand slot that I have seen a couple of good paddlers have religious times in! Most portage. Increasingly interesting rapids, over the next one and a half kilometres or so, lead to the next big drop. This is about six metres in height, solid class V and with a big hole at the bottom, but goes hard through the guts over the centre slab. Many choose to portage.

A little way down from this, and with the appearance of workings and about 50 metres below a stone bridge, is the awesome Rhaeadr Mawddach. In days gone by the power of this waterfall was exploited in the turning of a huge water wheel. To do this the water was directed, in part, down a mine shaft! This large double drop has been run several times! The original pioneers netted the entrance to the shaft as a precaution! Most of us portage easily down the right hand bank. As you do, look up the Afon Gain (also a great river) at Pistyll y Cain - it says something about the determination of paddlers that this has now, reputedly, had one or two descents !

Below the confluence, class III water leads to the first of two class V gorges which contain some fabulous drops. Before this gorge is a weir-like structure next to some houses on the right hand bank. This has a big stopper in high water but can be run on the left. However, it is formed by a stone footbridge which is sumped in the middle. It would be **extremely dangerous** to swim above this! This first gorge is known locally as "the three nasties", which gives some indication of its enclosed, and difficult to inspect, rapids. The second gorge, possibly a little easier, ends with a bang just above the confluence with the Eden. Egress can be made onto the little road on the right (GR729248), or down below Public Toilet Falls.

Eden confluence to Precipice: 5 km class IV; one weir needs caution***

This section contains the famous Public Toilet Falls (PTF) or, as Terry Storry so succinctly stated, "the SHF". This is a good section in big flood, hard and testing, but nowhere (bar the wrong place in the big weir) desperate. When new to the grade, a run down PTF in big water will stick in mind for a long time.

Immediately below the Eden confluence is a large sloping weir that produces a nasty keeper in times of high flow. There is normally a good central shoot but, if unsure, then discretion is the better part of drowning … as they say. A little below is PTF, a good class IV that can be inspected by walking upstream from the public toilets car park in Ganllwyd. In good flood there is a big wave dead centre that provides an exciting shoot. When lower, a boulder is exposed with a left or right choice. Below this the mighty Gamlan rages in from the right, and a little while after is a short, bouncy rapid. Below is a bridge that provides egress, if required, into a suitable car park GR730234.

Author's tale:

when new to the sport some (quite a few) years back, I was taken to the Mawddach to try my luck at PTF etc. By mistake, I spent many a worried minute looking at how I was going to the tackle the "grade IV Gamlan" …

Below this, on a sharp bend is an excellent rapid extending over a few 100 metres or so. Scattered with boulders at the right levels, this is filled with excellent waves and holes. It is possible to egress close to the Wen confluence or, continue downstream for about two kilometres on fast flowing class II, to where an angled footpath allows a more sedate carry up to the small back road on the true left bank of the river. There are a couple of small pull-ins and the river is obviously close to the road GR729210.

Precipice Walk to (*The George*) Penmaenpool: 7 km I to II; boulder weirs****

To reach the put-in, turn off the A470 just south of the Mawddach bridge and head upstream past Cymmer Abbey. After about three kilometres you reach the get-in, as described above. You may wish to pick an outgoing tide for this journey but, even with the tide on the flood, it is a lovely journey. The river can, with the odd scrape, be descended even when low. There are a few rapids and a couple of gentle weirs, before a large bouldery weir stretching diagonally from left to right across the river is reached. This has a safe shoot on the *right*. Cruising under the beautiful Llanelltyd bridge, the grip of the sea is felt and the water becomes tidal. With the sun setting the colours are just so typically Welsh over the ramparts of the majestic Cader Idris. The paddler can egress just before, or just after, the toll bridge at Penmaenpool, river left GR695185. In either case, *The George* is less than a stone's throw away.

Afon Wen

Map:	Dolgellau and surrounding area, no. 124
Grade:	IV; two IV+ drops; one class V
Length:	4 km
Access:	A470 Dolgellau to Ffestiniog road
Notes:	numerous tree portages
Quality:	**

The Wen runs through a stunning gorge to join the Mawddach River a couple of kilometres below the well-known Public Toilet Falls.

It has some good rapids but is fraught with tree portages - seven at last count, but I think it was about eight in early '98! Perhaps the Forestry Commission might remove them to improve recreational facilities in Coed y Brenin?!?

Capel Hermon bridge to Copper Mine car park: 4 km grade IV; numerous portages; three harder falls**

The Wen is reached by crossing the Mawddach by a little road about one kilometre south of Ganllwyd (Public Toilet Falls), just before the Tyn y Groes pub, and then heading downstream until a little bridge which crosses the river, is reached. Alternatively, the road which runs parallel to the Mawddach on its east bank crosses the river at the same bridge GR737226. Just below the bridge and north of another little river, the Afon Las (Babi), is a car parking area which is a suitable egress point. The Afon Las itself is a steep knife-edged gorge through which water rages in flood - it has possibly been run but not by me.

Following the road on the east bank of the Wen, it is possible to get to the access point after about four kilometres GR751256. There is a telephone box by the road and a small weir below the bridge.

The river is basically class III and rapids with three harder sections but is graded IV because of the **considerable tree danger!**

The first and biggest drop occurs about 500 metres after the start, and ends in a big drop into a strong stopper just above a footbridge. Footbridge Falls is class V and needs some nifty ropework to lasoo a tree branch and pull it out of the line of attack. The pool is deepest on the left - it is beautiful for swimming in summer lows.

Below here, easy rapids littered with trees, continue to the next footbridge. There are two harder rapids between here and the following road bridge, but both needed to be portaged because of yet more trees. Finish the run about 100 metres after the road bridge and into the convenient car park on the left bank.

Afon Eden

Map:	Dolgellau and surrounding area, no. 124
Grade:	III to IV-
Length:	8 km
Access:	A470(T)
Notes:	small weirs, few fences on upper section
Quality:	****

The Eden is a superb run. The river needs to be in a medium or higher spate to be worth doing but, when like this, gives a great middle-grade run. It is in places very continuous and, therefore serious, if an unforeseen tree blocked the river. As the Eden runs deeply through Coed y Brenin this is worth bearing in mind. It can easily be combined with the lower Mawddach.

Pont y Grible to Pont ar Eden: 8 km III to IV-****

Driving north through Coed y Brenin a small left turn can be made off the main road a little way before the village of Bronaber. This leads to Pont y Grible where access can be made to the Eden GR708305. The river needs to be in a good spate to make it worthwhile.

Easy rapids, apart from a few low stock fences, carry the excited paddler past two small bridges. The Afon Crawcwellt enters from the right (this has a few interesting little numbers upstream, as it parallels the Gamlan!) swelling the flood. The river creeps up the grade, with some excellent class III and IV rapids to be tackled on the way down to the Coed y Brenin visitor centre. This is an excellent alternative access point; out of the sight of any disapproving eyes from the main road! Alternatively, if the river is low, get out the mountain bike and go and try the fabulous "Red Bull route" up in the forest. Above and below the main A470, excellent class III rapids continue on their helter-skelter towards the Mawddach.

The trees close in and the Eden starts to cut a deeper bed. Soon, the river narrows and the paddler finds himself in a small rocky gorge. This is absolutely lip-smacking for those new to this type of paddling. On a trip some years ago I remember three of us snatching eddies above a fallen tree - totally blocking the river: *something to be borne in mind,* depending upon the amount of damage done by winter storms!

The river is a good class IV- in **flood**, with a couple of steep rapids just before the get-out at Pont ar Eden GR726249. Alternatively boat the small weir on the Eden, join the Mawddach and get out to inspect the much *more fearsome weir downstream!*

Afon Gain

Map:	Dolgellau & surrounding area, no. 124
Grade:	IV+ to V
Length:	6 km
Access:	off A470(T)
Notes:	one definite portage - other portages at high levels V+ to VI falls
Quality:	*****

Rising as it does in the hills high above Coed y Brenin, the Gain twists and tumbles over numerous drops and rapids, on its way to fill the Afon Mawddach. It is a brilliant white water river with some significant drops to negotiate. According to Phil Blain the purist will want to go higher and navigate down the peat ditches. He claims an ethereal experience with the added bonus of frightening unsuspecting walkers when the mists are down.

Cattle grid to Pistyll y Cain: 6 km grade IV+ to V; one definite portage plus class V+ falls*****

Turning eastwards off the A470 in Bronaber, and heading past the dry ski slope road and the old firing ranges, it is possible to access the river at the bridge found at GR734312.

The river needs to be in a good medium spate but if over the banks at the get-in, it may best be left till another day. From here until just before the next bridge, Pont y Llyn Du, the river is flat which allows a warm up for the class III series of drops leading under the ancient bridge.

From here on down good rapids and falls lead on for a kilometre or so until an obvious steepening is reached. It is wise to inspect this first class V - a 50 metre run-in to a sharp fall between large boulders. From here on down the river rushes and tumbles through beautiful small gorges. There are various class IV+ and the odd class V drops that you may wish to have a good look at. One, where a hard push left misses a large boulder, particularly springs to mind. In 1998 (early) the old foot bridge shown on the map had been washed away. At the first bridge, a stone archway, great care is needed and it is imperative to inspect the falls under this **and especially the ones just out of sight around the corner**. In high water, these look a major class V+ to VI triple affair - but when lower are more manageable (V). At high water most, if not all, will portage. Below this is an enclosed gorge, with four or so major class V drops. This carries on for about 200 metres or so, **but**, and it is a very big **but**, continual inspection and cover is needed, as tagged on just below a particularly severe fall is Pistyll y Cain, an awesome fall. Rumours abound that even the mighty Cain has been paddled - but surely not when the rest of the river is going - **a definite portage**. The rumours don't clarify who the paddler was!

In big flood a good alternative is to portage the whole of this short bottom gorge along the forest track on the right bank. Below this, it is easy enough to launch on the lower two gorges of the upper Mawddach - a brilliant run in its own right.

Afon Gamlan

Map:	Dolgellau and surrounding area, no. 124
Grade:	V to VI
Length:	a <u>short</u> kilometre
Access:	A470(T)
Notes:	sustained difficulty, but no portages
Quality:	★★★★

The Gamlan is a ferocious little river draining from the southern end of the Rhinogs (Y Llethr). Much of the section above the one described has also been paddled, but not by me. Having mountain-biked around this upper piece, it looks exceptionally hard but I have it on good authority that all but, perhaps, two of the drops have been done. *Phil Blain laughed at my description of the Gamlan being a short kilometre and says, "I always find it a very long kilometre".*

Rhaeadr Ddu to Mawddach confluence: one short km V to VI; no portages★★★★

The grade of the Gamlan is very water-dependent. In big flood, it is an extremely serious run and is graded VI. It is most well-known from Shaun Baker's excellent video, which actually gives an almost-perfect water level where the grade is a hard, relentless V. The land around the river is National Trust-owned and there is little objection to sensible and considerate paddlers. The Gamlan joins the Mawddach in the village of Ganllwyd just downstream of the public toilets (of PTF fame). Access can be had via the little road up the left hand bank and the National Trust footpath leading to the Black Waterfalls (Rhaeadr Ddu). Good access can be made onto the plunge pool **below the main horrendous drop** but above the following perfect 25 footer GR722244. From here on down you are under the cosh all the way until just before the Mawddach where egress can be made on the left GR729243.

128

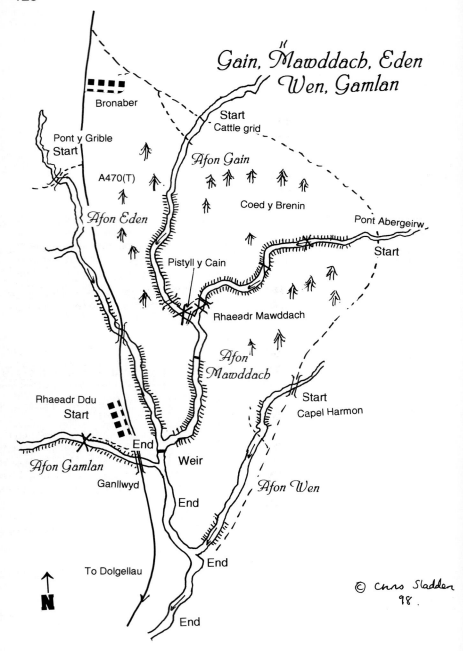

Gain, Mawddach, Eden Wen, Gamlan

Bronaber

Pont y Grible
Start

Start
Cattle grid

Afon Gain

A470(T)

Coed y Brenin

Afon Eden

Pont Abergeirw

Start

Pistyll y Cain

Rhaeadr Mawddach

Afon Mawddach

Rhaeadr Ddu
Start

Start
Capel Harmon

End

Weir

Afon Gamlan

Ganllwyd

Afon Wen

End

To Dolgellau

End

End

N

© Chris Sladden
98.

The Wnion

Map:	Dolgellau & surrounding area, no. 124
Grade:	sections of IV and II (III-IV)
Length:	16 km
Access:	A494 Dolgellau to Bala road
Notes:	narrow gorge; no portages
Quality:	**** and *****

Most paddlers run the upper Wnion but the lower section is a super run at medium levels for intermediate paddlers. There is just one harder fall during the first kilometre that is easily portaged if required.

Esgairgawr bridge to Bontnewydd: 6 km grade IV (V)*****

The river can be inspected (or photographed) from the dismantled railway line which criss-crosses its path or from the road on the drive up. It is sensible to have a quick scout of the lower gorge for the potential of fallen trees which could easily block the channels, for once in there you're in! There has been a tree partially blocking one of the upper shoots for some time now - inspected near a small building GR777203.

There are various access points to the river from footpaths or the old railway but it is quite pleasant to launch from the footpath at Esgairgawr bridge (signposted) GR817229. Apart from one or two low fences there is an excellent warm up down to the first "hit" at Pont Llanrhaiadr, a few bridges down. Check your line for, in high water, the stopper in places is very weir-like. Easier then for a bit until the walls obviously gorge in and steep rapids occur. This is full-on stuff in big water and reminds me very much of the Ogwen - it probably warrants *a class V- rating* in these conditions. The walls then close in further down as the water bends round and heads down a narrow sheer-sided gorge. In big water this is quite intimidating and the grade may rise a fraction. However, stoppers and waves, on the whole, appear to flush through.

I am convinced in some ways, rather like the Fairy Glen, that the water *may* become more dangerous when low because of pinning possibilities. Indeed, sadly, a fatality occurred in just such a manner a couple of years ago.

Egress can be made at Bontnewydd (B4416) about a kilometre after the end of the best the Wnion has to offer GR772203 .

If you fancy more and even better drive up and do the fabulous Twrch just up the road.

Lower Wnion - Bontnewydd to A493 bridge: 10 km class II; one fall III to IV****

Access at the Bontnewydd bridge GR772203. Grade II bouncy water for one kilometre then a large grade **III or IV ledge drop** across the river. This is easily portaged if you know of its presence. Dolserau bridge is reached with its little weir beneath. The Clywedog, or Torrent, enters from the left and by the time the main bridge is reached the rapids have eased off. Continue through and past Dolgellau till the get-out at Fairbourne road bridge. Egress into the Mawddach trail car park by the old railway bridge GR714183.

Afon Clywedog - *Torrent Walk*

Map:	Dolgellau and surrounding area, no. 124
Grade:	V to VI
Length:	1.5 km
Access:	B4416 Brithdir road
Notes:	various portages depending on water levels and storm damage
Quality:	*

Like the Teigl it is hard to recommend this short section of river, especially so as it drops through an SSSI. If you want this grade of paddling check out the Goedal, Gamlan, Mynach or Lower Prysor - they are far better quality and equally as testing.

Brithdir to Wnion: 1.5 km V to VI; various portages*

From Brithdir bridge GR762179 the river drops increasingly steeply down a myriad of twists and drops - many with shallow and pinning-type landings. Trees or common sense may suggest the odd portage. Egress at the small road bridge before the Wnion confluence GR753188. My memories of this river are a long, arduous and not very worthwhile day! Be warned.

Wnion,
Clywedog/Torrent,

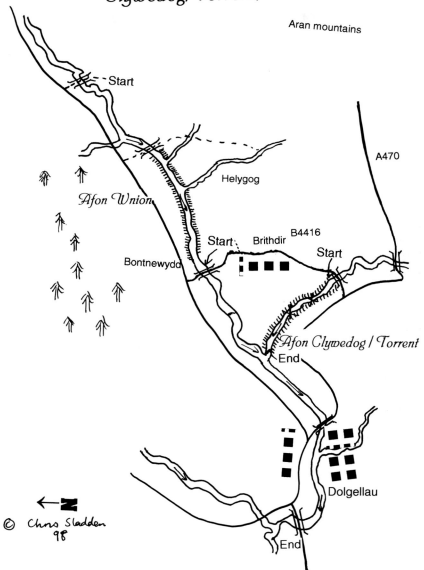

Aran mountains

A470

Helygog

Afon Wnion

Start   Brithdir   B4416

Start

Bontnewydd

Afon Clywedog / Torrent

End

Dolgellau

© Chris Sladden
98

End

Afon Cwm-Mynach

Map:	Dolgellau and surrounding area, no. 124
Grade:	V+
Length:	2.5 km
Access:	A496 Llanelltyd to Barmouth road
Notes:	two tree portages; one or two falls in lower gorge that most will wish to portage
Quality:	***

The Cwm-Mynach is an audacious little river rising from the eastern flanks of Diffwys. It is difficult to get the right water level for both stretches. The upper needs much water to blot out some sizeable boulders whilst the lower gorge becomes very frightening at these conditions - at least for me. Piers Nesbitt tells a horror story of being firmly held under water, by one of the more vicious stoppers in the lower gorge at high water.

Garth Gell bridge to Pen y Bryn: 2.5 km class V+; possible portages ***

Just before crossing the river on the A496 turn off upstream on a steep little road, and drive up for about two kilometres until it is possible to put on at a small bridge GR684205. The river is easy at first as it rushes down a beautiful gorge, with one or two trees that needed portaging. After about 600 metres things hot up, with some class V boulder rapids that are steep and hard.

Below here there is a short respite before the second and more gnarly gorge is entered. This is just below the old gold workings. Here the river cascades incredibly steeply through a series of increasingly large narrow drops. At high water some of the lines get tricky, whilst some of the stoppers become ex-tremely sticky. *Inspection and discretion* are the name of the game - or at least were when we paddled. One or two of these drops are prudently por-taged. Suddenly, as you pass a works yard on the left it is all over - until another day.

Afon Gwynant

Map:	Dolgellau and surrounding area, no. 124
Grade:	IV to V
Length:	4 km (bottom gorge 2 km)
Access:	A493 Dolgellau - Fairbourne road
Notes:	various tree portages plus one vicious weir
Quality:	***

The Gwynant is a hard and dangerous little stream which drains the northern flanks of Cader Idris. It can be paddled from the main Cader car park at Ty Nant if you fancy a real expedition, or from near the Kings Youth Hostel. Either way, you will need to keep your wits about you but, certainly, have an extremely exciting paddle. It is best paddled in a medium flood as, in full spate, it's a frightening sight - this should be fairly obvious as soon as you look at it!

Cader car park to Abergwynant main road bridge: 4 km class IV to V; one definite portage***

Take the main A493 out of Dolgellau until just before you cross the river at Abergwynant. Turn up the very steep little road which follows the river. This will enable you to decide where to get on, and whether like the look of things. The Kings Youth Hostel is about two kilometres up here but if you follow this road further, it is possible to reach the road below Cader Idris and to find the Ty Nant car park GR698153. From here down, the water is fast grade III with the ever-present tree ready to tip you in. A small bridge and tributary coming in from the left are passed and, about 200 metres after this, was a fence that required some careful negotiation at time of paddling. The rapids start picking up to excellent class III to IV but there was one tree that required portaging at times of paddling (late '97 - early '98).

Kings is reached, which is an alternative access point. Two bridges cross the river; the smaller one of which is difficult to get under if the water is high! **Below this is probably the hardest rapid on the river - a good class V**. The tree that used to make this a portage was washed further downstream in the floods of early '98 and it is now just the hardness of the rapid to worry about. Below this are nearly continuous class IV+ rapids all the way down to Abergwynant.

About 200 metres before the bridge is a particularly ***vicious three-stepped weir that is a sensible portage***. Egress just before the main road bridge on river left. About 13 years ago I paddled the section from here on down. Apart from trees galore it had little to offer.

134

Lower Mawddach, Cwm Mynach, Gwynant,

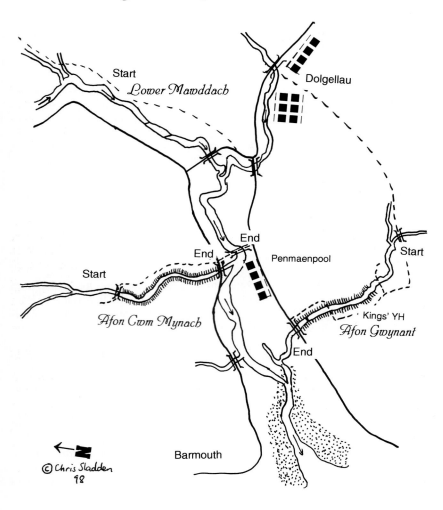

Start
Lower Mawddach

Dolgellau

End
Penmaenpool

End

Start

Start

End

Kings' YH
Afon Gwynant

Afon Cwm Mynach

© Chris Sladden
98

Barmouth

Afon Ysgethin

Map: Dolgellau and surrounding area, no. 124
Grade: IV medium water; V high water
Length: 4 km
Access: small road off A496
Notes: an outstanding expedition
Quality: ***

I had first noticed the Ysgethin many years before when doing MLC navigation exercises in the Rhinogs. Here was this beautiful lake, Llyn Bodlyn, feeding a steep river, the Ysgethin. However, the lake was dammed and the sluices locked! In these lean years, it takes a good flood for the river to come up. Even when we paddled it after two days of heavy rain, Llyn Bodlyn was ten foot lower than the overflow channel and we had to put on much lower down.

Craig y Dinas to Talybont: 4 km class IV to V; some tree portages***

Between Barmouth and Harlech is the village of Talybont. There is a cross-roads 500 metre north of the bridge in Talybont which leads up a road on a very stately home-looking drive. Drive up here as far as you can until a gate which says 'no cars allowed'. We asked the local farmer, a very nice chap, who allowed us to drive up. A sharp right hand then left hand bend in the track, and you reach a place on the road before a gate, where you can park the car GR617234. Here, a five-minute walk downhill, and then five minutes up the little river allows the launching above or below a class V drop.

The river starts reasonably enough but soon steepens to a continual gradient towards the sea. There are no big drops, but the river is steep. The grade is definitely IV or V (depending on the height of the flood) because of its continual nature, the need for exact boat control, and continual inspection. A long one and a half kilometres on, and the beautiful 18th century Pont Fadog is passed as the river heads into a forested area. Steep rapids, snatched eddies, and a few trees to portage bring the paddler towards Talybont. Two footbridges and it's nearly over. Egress in the public car park with roadside conveniences GR589217. So few descents but worth its stars for the uniqueness.

Afon Artro

Map:	Dolgellau and surrounding area, no. 124
Grade:	III
Length:	5 km
Access:	A496 Harlech to Barmouth road
Notes:	no portages - trees depending on winter damage
Quality:	****

An excellent spate run. It is possible to get on at Llyn Cwm Bychan for a source to sea trip but there are some tree problems up here.

Cwm Yr Afon to Llanbedr: 5 km class III; no portages****

The Artro is one of the first spate rivers I paddled and I still remember the buzz it gave me. It is a good warm up for paddling the dangerous, but exciting, Cwm Nantcol which joins lower down. Draining the north western end of the Rhinogs, it rises and falls quickly after rain and is only good during flood.

Drive upstream from Llanbedr, keeping to the true right bank of the river. Access can be had from the footpath at the small bridge leading to Cwm Yr Afon GR622298. The water is fast grade II to below Pen y Bont bridge when it increases in speed and steepness to class III. Around a left then right hand bend is a steeper drop, plus stopper, that is more memorable than the other rapids. Continue down past the Nantcol, entering from river left. Egress is possible at the first road bridge in Llanbedr.

Afon Cwm Nantcol

Map:	Dolgellau and surrounding area, no. 124
Grade:	V+
Length:	2 km - extended to 5 km
Access:	from Harlech A496
Notes:	a few portages
Quality:	***

A hard and dangerous run that will attract the brave of heart. It has, unfortunately been the scene of a fatality and is not to be undertaken lightly.

Pont Cerrig (GR634262) to Artro confluence: 5 km grade V+***

Purists can start the run at Pont Cerrig - if you wish to bash along a ditch (even
by my standards) over the moors. However, there is a short section of class III
and with one steep drop to contend with at the top (IV+) before the tufted grass
and tree bashing begins. One footbridge is too low to get under and has to be
portaged before the next stone bridge is reached. A little way below a class IV+
drop leads around an island best taken on the right. Easier water leads into the
first of the Nantcol gorges. This is a narrow and formidable class V+ run with
certain drops you may wish to portage (with difficulty). After this nasty and
frightening experience easier class II water leads past a picnic site and into a
small lake. The "outflow weir-type thing" needs **portaging**, below which starts
the second gorge. In good water (the only time to run this) this is a continuous
and hard class IV rapid running below a large water pipe and eventually under
two stone bridges to join the Artro. Egress here (or further down the Artro)
GR601272.

Artro, Nantcol, Ysgethin

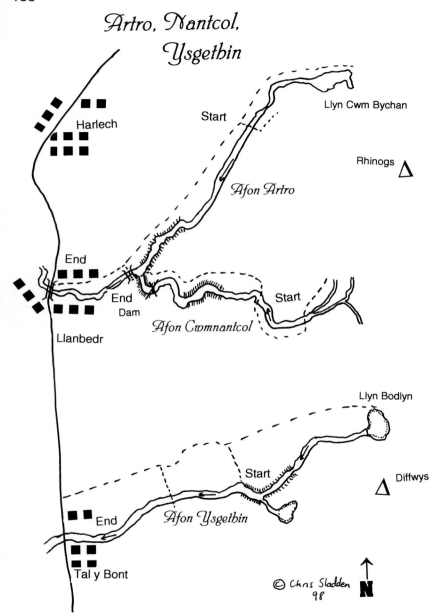

Llyn Cwm Bychan

Start

Harlech

Rhinogs △

Afon Artro

End

End
Dam

Start

Afon Cwmnantcol

Llanbedr

Llyn Bodlyn

Start

Diffwys △

End

Afon Ysgethin

Tal y Bont

© Chris Sladden
98

N

MID WALES

Boris always liked to be the first down the river.

Dysynni

Map:	Dolgellau & surrounding area, no. 124
Grade:	II
Length:	12 km
Access:	on B4405 above Abergynolwyn
Notes:	A beautiful touring run; no portages
Quality:	****

A beautiful touring river on crystal clear water below the heights of Cader.

Abergynolwyn to the old Bryncrug road bridge: 12 km grade II****

East of Abergynolwyn, parking can be made a **discreet** distance from the cemetery. A stile allows access on the river just above a tiny weir step. GR683074. Fast, clear, easy water leads down to below the village. Below this the happy canoeists enter the grade II Gamallt gorge. In *flood* it becomes more dangerous simply because of the water setting up in trees and bushes. Best at off-flood levels it is excellent for intermediates or, when lower, beginners. **This gorge actually gives open, and a lot easier, access and you may wish to start your trip here** GR674072.

There is a sharp south west turn towards the sea just after the confluence with the Afon Cadair. Below the following road bridge the river flattens out apart from three small weirs, all of which are easily shot, though in high water the third one forms a deceptively strong stopper. The water becomes tidal from here on to the sea. Overall the river is excellent for expeditions and touring.

Egress on the right at the old Bryncrug bridge GR599039. Alternatively, it is possible to continue downstream to a small tidal rapid below the Broadwater - incidentally the site of the only slalom I have ever attempted. As with any ebbing river don't stray too far or risk getting washed out to sea!

Afon Cadair

Map:	Dolgellau & surrounding area, no. 124
Grade:	III; one V above access
Length:	2.5 km
Access:	B4405 Tywyn to Dolgellau road
Notes:	fences
Quality:	**

The Cadair can be used as an alternative access to point to the Dysynni river trip but needs to be in a good spate to be worth doing.

Mary Jones cottage to Dysynni confluence: 2.5 km class III; low bridge and fences**

Just at the end of the Gamallt gorge on the Dysynni is a small turning that goes up to the village of Llanfihangel-y-pennant, passing en-route the monument of Castell y Bere. By continuing on the road and then a track it is possible to follow the river on its true right bank for some way. Here it is possible to launch onto an excellent series of class III rapids which lead down and under the road bridge. They need a fair amount of rain to make them worthwhile. After this the rapids ease off to the odd class II en-route to the Dysynni, though there is one weir to contend with as well. There were a couple of fences that required caution and one low bridge which you may have to duck. Finish at the following road bridge or further down the Dysynni. Above the access is a 15 foot fall that is quite fun to paddle, but has quite a stiff stopper to punch through.

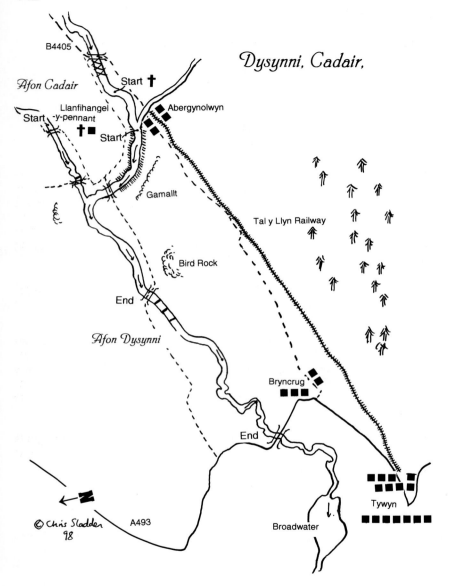

Dysynni, Cadair,

B4405

Afon Cadair

Start ✝

Llanfihangel
-y-pennant

Start

✝■ Start

Abergynolwyn

Gamallt

Tal y Llyn Railway

Bird Rock

End

Afon Dysynni

Bryncrug

End

Tywyn

© Chris Sladden
98

A493

Broadwater

Afon Dyfi (Dovey)

Map: Bala & Lake Vyrnwy & surrounding area, no. 125
              Dolgellau & surrounding area, no. 124
              Aberystwyth & surrounding area, no. 135
Grade: sections of I to II, and III+, with one short stretch IV to -V
Length: 37 km
Access: A470(T) Machynlleth to Dolgellau road
Notes: trees in upper gorge; one section of IV to V

Quality: sections of ***and ****

The Dyfi is a beautiful mountain river rising from Creiglyn Dyfi, which lies below the crags of the Aran mountains. It is a fine fishing river and is guarded in its lower reaches by banner proud fishermen. However, that said, all the farmers we have met on our various journeys down the river have been exceptionally kind. I very much believe in sport for all and so would ask paddlers to keep off the river during the fishing season - that would be seen to be reasonable on our front.

Llanymawddwy Bridge to Cywarch Bridge: 14km III (+) and one fall IV+ to V****

Turning off the A470 in Dinas Mawddwy it is possible to follow the river upstream until access is found at the small bridge in Llanymawddwy, GR908194. The river is beautiful as its winds its way down under several bridges in a very easy and relaxed fashion. After about five kilometres or so there are a few class III rapids as the walls begin to close in. One of these had a tree a jammed in it at time of paddling which required a portage.

Above the little bridge in Cywarch are a series of three drops which are grade IV+ to V, dependent upon water levels. The last drop is the most dangerous due to pinning possibilities on the left. Egress here GR873156.

Dinas Mawddwy to Aberangell: 7 km II to III; one rapid III to IV***

Below the above egress point to the footbridge in Dinas Mawddwy the river should be easy enough but I haven't done this one kilometre or so. Access below this kilometre is by a footbridge below the confluence with the Afon Cerist GR861149.

A medium spate is a good level for this river whereas, in flood, it will be just that little bit harder. Grade I to two rapids lead under the main A470 bridge and then a beautiful little stone arched bridge follows.

Just after the Dugoed enters, is a sharp right-hand left-hand bend with a house on the right-hand bank. Here, there is a class III to IV fall which is easy to shoot, but there are a few spikes in this drop and these may be hidden at high water! Easier water leads to egress at Aberangell caravan park GR847099.

Aberangell to B4404 bridge: 8 km I to II***

Access as above. This is an easy and beautiful touring section suitable for Canadian canoes and beginners alike. In part it follows a dismantled railway track but this doesn't distract from the pleasures of bubbling down small rapids and carving around placid curves. Egress is by the public footpath, on the B4404, GR090043.

B4404 to Machynlleth: 8 km class I***

For those wanting a longer trip it is possible to continue down to Machynlleth on, once again, beautiful and bubbling water. There are no nasties on this section, apart from perhaps the two-legged variety! The river is topped up by the two Dulais rivers as it nears Machynlleth. Egress by the public footpath on the main A487 bridge. The parking is difficult here.

145

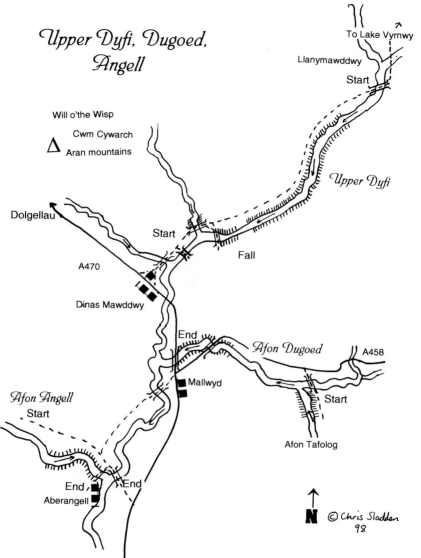

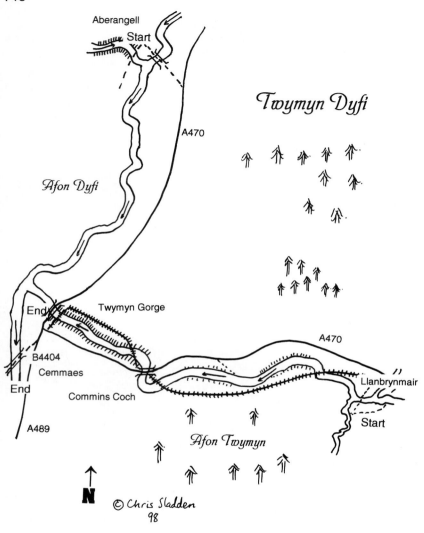

Aberangell
Start

Twymyn Dyfi

A470

Afon Dyfi

End
Twymyn Gorge

A470

B4404
Cemmaes

End
Commins Coch

Llanbrynmair

Start

A489

Afon Twymyn

N

© Chris Sladden
98

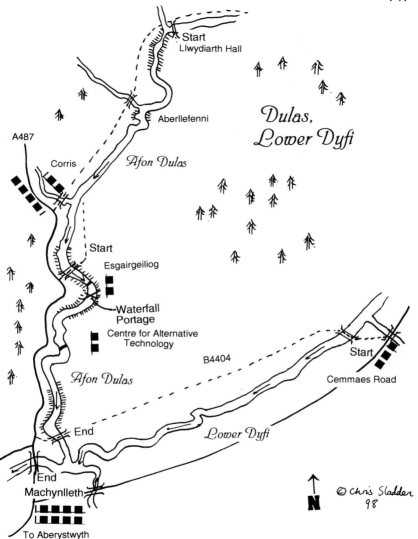

Start
Llwydiarth Hall

Aberllefenni

Dulas,
Lower Dyfi

A487

Corris

Afon Dulas

Start
Esgairgeiliog

Waterfall
Portage

Centre for Alternative
Technology

B4404

Start
Cemmaes Road

Afon Dulas

End

Lower Dyfi

End
Machynlleth

To Aberystwyth

N

© Chris Sladden
98

Afon L'Eri

Map:	Aberystwyth & surrounding area, no. 135
Grade:	II
Length:	4.5 km
Access:	A486(T)
Notes:	one weir
Quality:	****

A beautiful hidden gorge - fantastic for the grade.

Tal y Bont to Glanwern footbridge: 4.5 km grade II; one weir****

Tal y Bont is about 20 kilometres south of Machynlleth. It is a little hard to gain access to the river or get changed in Tal y Bont. The best approach may be to change out of the village and then drive in to opposite the pub where, by following the footpaths into the forest on the north of the river, it is possible to make your way down to the water's edge. This is well below two houses and a little footbridge! If you do manage to get on above this, there is at least **one unpleasant-looking weir!**

From here down, the water rushes through a class II(+) gorge on its way to the sea. Trees are the only potential hazard but, normally, the passage is clear. As you reach the first caravan park, there is an obvious weir with boxed-in sides. This is fine to shoot in medium water, though you should check it out on the day. Egress in Penybont is not easy, so it is best to continue down to the Glanwern footbridge and egress river left onto the public footpath by the caravan park. I have not paddled this last kilometre of water, but there shouldn't be any unpleasantries down here GR617888.

Afon Einion

Map:	Aberystwyth & surrounding area, no. 135
Grade:	V+
Length:	2 km
Access:	A487(T) Machynlleth to Aberystwyth coast road.
Notes:	various portages
Quality:	****

A hard and serious, but very beautiful, run dropping into the Dyfi valley.

Cwm Einion to Furnace Falls: 2 km grade V+; various portages****

There is an unwritten agreement that this river is big enough for groups of five or less experienced paddlers, but no more. Certainly, minibuses driving up the tiny access road would be sad indeed and I trust that paddlers will not use these notes to the detriment of others. That said, if you are prepared to portage, and want some hard and serious paddling, then you may care to check out this river.

About ten kilometres south of Machynlleth on the A487 is the village of Furnace. Turn off here up the Cwm Einion, or Artists' Valley. Drive up this for about two kilometres until the road drops down to join the river. Here access can be made above or below a class IV drop. The river needs to be in a medium spate - anything larger would be quite frightening and possibly unpaddleable.

A little way down are some irritating tree chokes which need to be portaged on the right. Below, however, a short class IV section leads straight into two of the *finest big class V+ hits in Wales*. The drops can be run on the left in medium flows though the stoppers are quite sticky and time spent setting up bank protection is sensible. The second drop is of questionable depth, but was ok on the left in short boats! The sculpture is fantastic. I have looked at these falls in big water when they looked class VI+!!

Easier water leads down to a footbridge where you can egress if all you came for were the waterfalls. Below, the river steepens again as it flows over and around large boulders and bedrock steps. The first rapid after the footbridge has a dangerous tree in it (in 1997) so be careful, as this could entrap a paddler!

The water eases off to about a IV during its passage through wonderful sculptured rocks with a few beckoning undercuts.

Just before the first houses are reached **lie two huge, class V+ rapids**. These are House Boulder and Bedrock Falls, respectively. Both are exciting but dangerous, and careful assessment and bank security is recommended. Pass under a pipe and finish the run on the right hand bank *above* the spectacular Furnace Falls - a little road just north of the river allows excellent access GR686952.

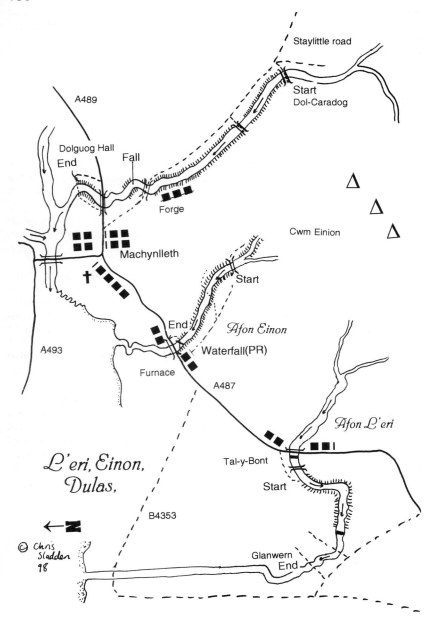

A489

Dolguog Hall
End   Fall

Forge

Machynlleth

A493

Staylittle road

Start
Dol-Caradog

Cwm Einion

Start

End   *Afon Einon*

Waterfall(PR)

Furnace   A487

Afon L'eri

Tal-y-Bont

Start

*L'eri, Einon,
Dulas,*

© Chris
Sladden
98

B4353

Glanwern
End

Afon Dugoed

Map:	Bala & Lake Vyrnwy & surrounding area, no. 125
Grade:	III+; lower gorge class V
Length:	4 km
Access:	off A458(T) Mallwyd to Llanfair Caereinion road
Notes:	trees are difficult portages
Quality:	***

The Dugoed is a tributary of the Dyfi (Dovey) River. It also runs in parallel valleys to the Twymyn and Wnion rivers and, as such, has an easier section to start, but with a closed-in gorge at the bottom. It needs to be in medium spate to do the top bit but at these levels, the Mallwyd gorge becomes a serious proposition. This gorge itself can be paddled a day or so after high water and is interesting in its own way.

Tafolog bridge to A470(T): 4 km class III; class V gorge; various tree portages***

Turn off by the Brigands Inn at Mallwyd and drive up the A458(T) for about four kilometres where a steep turn off right to Tafolog can be made. The road crosses the river at a little bridge where access can be made. A couple of kilometres of the Tafolog can also be done at III but isn't very inspiring. The river should have a reasonable flow to be worth doing. It is a moody little number. The first kilometre or so is grade III with hints of changing rock character.

Soon after the main road bridge the river changes more definitively, and begins to gorge up. At first some very beautiful, narrow drops are tackled. There are some good drops that follow but, at the time of writing, about three trees needed portaging. **These require class V skills in themselves** and are the main reason for the seriousness of the river. *The portages are damned difficult*. Picture yourself in a micro eddy, with sloping, green, smooth and slithery walls to hold onto, and just below is a solid tree choke. Some careful scouting and well pre-placed ropes from above are the answer. In truth, only the last drop in the gorge just before the road bridge reaches class V.

Don't be too put off with this as, combined with the tasty bottom gorge on the Angell, a good day out can be had.

152

Afon Twymyn

Map:	Aberystwyth & surrounding area, no. 135
Grade:	III to IV
Length:	9 km
Access:	A470
Notes:	no portages
Quality:	****

The Twymyn is a charming little river that allows a perfect warm up, through beautiful gorges, before a final flourish down the harder Glyntwymyn gorge.

Tafolwern to Cemmaes Road bridge: 9 km class III to IV; no portages****

At the S bend in the A470 turn off to Tafolwern (there is a new road since '98). Access may be made to the river just upstream of the first bridge where there is a convenient path. It is sensible to change discreetly so as not to upset the friendly locals. When the two rivers join just below, you are on the Twymyn proper.

The water is grade II to III depending on flow. Echoes abound as you pass under the first railway bridge and bounce happily along through excellent little drops and stoppers. However, I have it on very good authority that, in major floods, the grade of a few of these drops can suddenly crank its way up to a IV+ to V! That said ,don't worry too much, as this doesn't happen very often. The longstanding traffic lights have now gone and, halfway along the new road, there is a lane down to the side of the river by which is found a picnic site. This is an alternative point of access. The river continues at a similar grade all the way until Commins Coch. Here you pass under the road and a railway bridge, and then a second railway bridge with a small weir beneath it. This heralds the approach of the well-known Glyntwymyn gorge.

As the walls close in, you may want to inspect the gorge from the path on the right bank. The paddling is normally at the top end of grade III, but can be quite serious depending upon the amount of damage left by winter storms. When I last paddled this, the final fall in the gorge was partially made up of a huge tree trunk which was easy to shoot, but would certainly not have been nice to swim. Once the gorge finishes, continue downstream to below the main road bridge, where you can struggle up onto the left bank. Alternatively, continue down to the B4404 bridge over the Dyfi.

Afon Angell

Map:	Dolgellau & surrounding area, no. 124
	Bala & Lake Vyrnwy & surrounding area, no. 125
Grade:	IV to V
Length:	2 km
Access:	off A470(T) Dinas Mawddwy to Cemmaes road
Notes:	Jungle skills required
Quality:	***

Although some jungle warfare skills are required on the upper bit, the lower section is steep and exciting on this most unlikely of hill streams.

Cefn Gwyn to Aberangell: 2 km grade IV to V***

Turn off the A470 to the village of Aberangell and follow the steep road up out of the village until the river becomes visible. When the road comes very close to the river by a phone box and bridge, access may be had GR833104. "The first kilometre to the next road bridge is a bit like Vietnam" - was Franco Ferrero's description of the first bit of bramble-bashing. The fall under the next bridge heralds more exciting things. A small weir follows, before a final steep set of rapids of class IV to V which lead past a forest walk up the Angell. Egress between the two small bridges in the village. Combined with the Dugoed or the Twymyn, this makes for an excellent day out.

Afon Dulas

Map:	Dolgellau & surrounding area, no. 124
	Aberystwyth & surrounding area, no. 135
Grade:	III to IV
Length:	13 km
Access:	A487(T) Dolgellau - Machynlleth road
Notes:	possible portage in low water
Quality:	***

A beautiful river in a wonderful valley, with some good drops to boot.

Llwydiarth Hall bridge to Esgairgeiliog: 7 km grade III to IV; possible portage - low water***

Driving south to north on the A487, turn off to the village of Corris and continue driving up the small road to Aberllefenni. On the way, stop off to have a look at the falls below a small bridge, about one kilometre downstream of Aberllefenni. On our last run down the river (October '97) a tree was partially blocking the bridge arches. This could prove very dangerous in high flood. Even if clear, the stopper below the drop needs definite respect!

Access to the river is at the small bridge to Llwydiarth Hall and is next to a telephone box. The river is fast but easy until a sequence of three to four falls (depending on your definition of 'fall') is reached. Rhaeadr y Pwll Du, or 'The Falls of the Black Pool' are a committing class IV to IV+. The third fall and biggest drop, in particular, is much easier at higher flows and it is sobering to think that, at low flows, the bottom squeeze is less in width than that of a boat! The water eases off to an easy flow with occasional class III falls, but care has to be taken because of a few dangerous wires across the stream. About one kilometre below the slate mines of Aberllefenni are the aforementioned falls / weir which needs caution.

As the paddler approaches Esgairgeiliog heralded by a caravan site river left, a class III to IV rapid is reached just above the road bridge GR061755. An awkward boulder has a route that has caused one or two experienced paddlers to briefly tickle trout! Egress left if you've had enough.

Esgairgeiliog bridge to Glan Fechan bridge: 6 km grade III; one portage; one weir***

Below the bridge in Esgairgeiliog is a small weir with a surprisingly strong stopper. As the river begins to gorge up a little way below there is a major class VI fall that nearly all will portage. This is *immediately* below a rock island. Although this has been shot at high water a low water inspection of the sumps will put off most. *Portage* with care on river right. An excellent but easy gorge follows. Just before the stone bridge leading to The Centre for Alternative Technology is a large, but partially broken, weir. Inspect, but this can be shot down the large wave on the right in most flows (if you look at this in low flows it shows a left sided sump!). A few more good rapids follow before egress downstream river left of the bridge at Glan Fechan. Beware though, as strung below the bridge, was a dubiously placed barbed wire strand the last time I paddled this GR752024.

Afon Dulas

Map:	Aberystwyth & surrounding area, no. 135
Grade:	III; one fall IV; one fall V
Length:	7 km
Access:	Machynlleth to Llyn Clywedog road
Notes:	no portages
Quality:	****

When I first paddled this river it was one of those stolen moments; a last-minute thought after canoeing another local river. A brilliant run with no portages, although it has a test-piece drop to attempt. It goes for a few days after rain.

Henllan bridge to Garth campsite bridge: 7 km III; no portages; two harder falls****

Take the road out of Machynlleth towards Forge (part of Glyndwr's Way) and head upstream from the bridge for about five kilometres. Here a small road leads off right then right again down to a small bridge over the river, where access can be made GR795983.

From the bridge down, the water runs over bedrock steps and rushes down sculptured gorges. Between here and the next bridge are two drops that are easy in good flows but are too narrow to shoot in low water. Otherwise, the rapids are about grade II+ to III, depending upon water levels, but with a few extras thrown in. The first is a bigger drop about a kilometre and a half down from the next bridge, and found on a left-hand bend. Shoot the drop down the middle and then hard left or right. Where the road appears on the left with signs of habitation is the next noticeable feature. This double fall is best inspected for the line- firstly, over the first step, then around the corner and drop sharply down the exciting right-hand shoot. In big water this is quite a frightening fall. I last paddled this river a few days after the floods of March '98 when it was still quite easily paddleable. Three days earlier it was apparently above the plant barrels in the garden on the left bank of the drop - **some water!**

About 400 metres below Forge is a major class V fall that is very much of the same ilk as Brown's Falls on the Llugwy. This is on a left-hand bend in the river and just above some farm buildings also on the left. It needs a decent water level to be canoeable, and can be portaged on the right. Below here, the only real surprises are the grade III drops in the splendid little gorge above the egress point. This is reached by turning down the small road to Dolguog Hall, about a mile out of Machynlleth on the A489.

Afon Eunant Fawr

Map:	Bala & Lake Vyrnwy & surrounding area, no. 125
Grade:	V to VI
Length:	3 km
Access:	Bala to Llyn Efyrnwy road
Notes:	various portages around falls and fences
Quality:	**

A steep, outrageous and dangerous mountain stream flowing downhill at a rate of knots into Lake Vyrnwy. Not particularly appealing, but you may want a look.

Y Gadfa to Pont Eunant: 3 km class V to VI; various portages**

There are a few paddleable tributaries of Lake Vyrnwy, though I have only ventured onto one of them. They are all fairly radical and include various portages.

If you continue up the fantastic Afon Twrch, which drains into the southern end of Bala Lake, it is possible to take a small mountain road which leads down towards Llyn Efyrnwy. The stream can be seen raging alongside. The day after flood seems the best level as in full 'go' it would be even more frightening. Set off downstream where you will be faced with myriad drops, squirts, shakes and shoots to attempt to negotiate. At time of paddling, two fences and about five unpleasant drops were portaged. Egress in the lake, or well before if you have had enough.

Afon Banwy:

Map:	Bala & Lake Vyrnwy & surrounding area, no. 125
Grade:	I to II bouncy river
Length:	27 km
Access:	A458 Llangadfan to Llanfair Caereinion road
Notes:	no portages
Quality:	sections of *** and *****

The Banwy is a beautiful touring river with a few small rapids to negotiate. In off-the-flood conditions, it is a suitable and enjoyable trip for well-led beginners' groups. Best a few days after high water, when the levels have dropped and the Banwy turns a delightful clear colour as it winds its way down from the mountains to the lowlands.

Llanerfyl to Llanfair Caereinion: 12 km class I to II; no portages ***

The A458 crosses the Banwy at Llanerfyl and it is possible to put on the river from either the little road on the left, or from a public footpath on the right GR032097.
The river meanders its way around the obvious hill of Moel Bentyrch - worth climbing from the footpath found as the river turns back southwards. There are superb panoramic views on clear days. A calm gorge is enjoyably paddled before the next main road bridge is passed, just after the Afon Einion joins from the right.

Between here and Llanfair Caereinion, the rapids become more grade II than I, and certainly feel a bit heavier. One natural weir step - which can be seen from the road - reaches grade III in flood, and care should be taken in choosing a correct line through the stopper. Egress in town below the bridge into the car park, river left.

Llanfair Caereinion to Meifod Bridge: 14 km grade II (III); no portages *****

Access from the railway car park in town onto this lovely, lower section of river. Flood conditions are best avoided and, in fact, the river goes for a few weeks after heavy rain. Grade I rapids lead you out of town, and the only time you need to take extra care is at a small, broken step above the first railway bridge. There were few old wooden stakes here - best avoided.

A little way after the main road bridge is passed a caravan site appears on the left. In the next two kilometres are three grade II rapids. The last, Castle Earth Works rapid, just about touches grade III in high water and, in flood, has a good strong stopper on the left. The Vyrnwy enters from the left and it is best to continue down here, on a much more mature river, until the next bridge is reached. This is the Meifod Bridge. There is good access / egress here via the public footpaths   GR156128.

Afon Twrch

Map:	Bala & Lake Vyrnwy & surrounding area, no. 125
Grade:	III
Length:	5 km
Access:	small road upstream and on true left bank in Foel A458
Notes:	A few easy portages
Quality:	***

This little river, one of many with the same name in Wales, is a tributary of the Banwy. The lower gorge, especially in high water, is an exciting grade III. It is possible to put in at the halfway bridge thus avoiding most of the portages.

Dol-y-gaseg to Foel: 5 km class III; a few portages***

Turn up a small road in the village of Foel, found on the A458, and continue upstream. After crossing the river at the first road bridge (alternative access), work your way about three kilometres upstream, where it is possible to get on the river below a ford / sieve   GR9721146.

Set off down easy water until a second ford is reached about 500 metres downstream. This needs portaging unless in very high water conditions when it forms a weir-like stopper. The water is easy as it passes through beautiful mini-gorges on its way down to the halfway road bridge. This has a major fence underneath it and needs to be portaged. However, the family in the farm are delightful, and happy for access from the footpath below the bridge.

About a kilometre below here, and after an ancient stone bridge is floated by the fantastic Twrch gorge is entered. There are about four distinct rapids of grade III (or occasionally a bit more in big water) which require some manoeuvring. Just as the difficulties ease off there is an ***irritating wire*** across the flow that needs portaging. Get out below the A458 road bridge on to the council car park, GR988155.

Afon Gam:

Map:	Bala & Lake Vyrnwy & surrounding area, no. 125
Grade:	II to III; one rapid reaches III+
Length:	9 km
Access:	C road joining A458 - A470(T)
Notes:	trees deserve respect in flood; no portages
Quality:	***

An easy river that passes through a beautiful gorge.

Dolwen Bridge to Llanerfyl: 9 km grade II to III; no portages***

Turn off the small C road in Llangadfan. Cross the Banwy and head to GR011097, where a beautiful small stone bridge over the Gam is reached. The small rapid upstream should look vaguely exciting for the level to be worth paddling. Turn right and head upstream for six and a half kilometres where the river is crossed back to its west bank. Good access can be made a few hundred metres upstream, just above a small diagonal weir step (natural). In medium water the rapids are a good grade II. In flood they reach grade III and trees can be dangerous. The boats should be easily able to float at the put-in for the trip to be worthwhile.

Under this first bridge is **a fence** which can be sneaked on the left with care. The hardest rapid isn't in the gorges but is about 800 metres downstream, and is where the stream bends steeply around some tombstone-shaped boulders - grade III+. Easy water leads through small, picturesque gorges until a long section of bouncy water channelled through a long straight gorge is reached. This is in between the next farm road bridge and the first stone road bridge (suitable egress). As you near the Banwy, the stream opens out and easier water is reached. As you enter the Banwy, if it is in flood you will notice the feel of heavy water, but it is only grade I to II until the first road bridge and suitable egress at Llanerfyl GR032098.

160

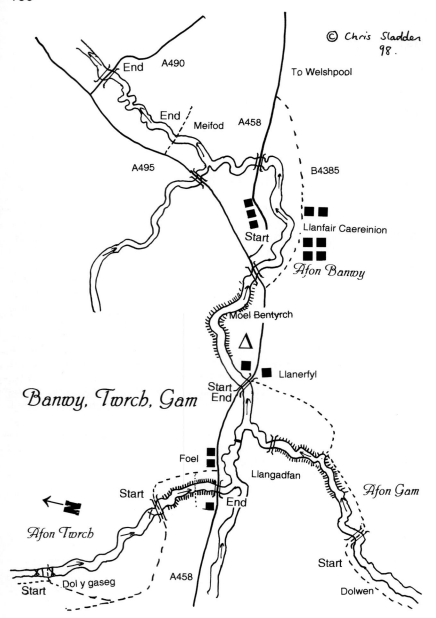

© Chris Sladden 98.

A490

End

To Welshpool

End

Meifod

A458

A495

B4385

Start

Llanfair Caereinion

Afon Banwy

Moel Bentyrch

△

Llanerfyl

Start
End

Banwy, Twrch, Gam

Foel

Llangadfan

Afon Gam

Start

N

End

Afon Twrch

Start

Dol y gaseg

A458

Start

Dolwen

River Vyrnwy / Afon Efyrnwy

Map:	Bala & Lake Vyrnwy & surrounding area, no. 125
	Shrewsbury & surrounding area, no. 126
Grade:	sections of II to III and IV
Length:	64 km
Access:	from Llyn Vyrnwy, B roads off the A495, and the A483
Notes:	one weir is a portage
Quality:	sections of*** and****

The Vyrnwy flows out of the bottom of the famous Vyrnwy dam, and follows a long and winding course before it joins the Seven at the ancient the village of Melverley. It is a river of marked contrasts, with excellent grade III to IV rapids in its upper reaches and a long gentle touring section lower down. Levels vary considerably depending upon flow out of, and over the huge dam, plus natural run-off.

There is an answering service at the dam which gives a coded message regarding the amount of release, but I haven't been able to work this out. However, I know a man who can:

The Vyrnwy is the domain of the enigmatic and gently-spoken David Proctor. He is the area's river adviser and has a wealth of local knowledge. Dave lives along a little side stream of the Vyrnwy (which I have never seen with water in, although he assures me that it is canoeable) in a converted chapel - an amazing place.

Capel Bethania is located at the following address: Llanwddyn, Nr. Oswestry, Powys SY10 0NJ Tel. 01691 870615. Dave is happy to help with group accommodation (near the pub), camping and river information and levels.

Lake Vyrnwy to Pontrobert: 21 km II to III; one section III+ to IV; one weir portage***

Work your way up the various winding lanes to the lake, where access can be made from the car park below the dam GR017192. The weir at the get-in is play-able if the water is within the central chute - any higher and it starts to get a bit worrying and it is best to get on below. Easy water leads down to between the following two road bridges. Here, by some mill workings, is a grade III to IV, partially natural fall. This is quite exciting. The Cownwy enters from the right and, between here and Pont Llogel, are some class III steps. In big water these can have quite sticky stoppers on them. Pont Llogel is reached where there is an alternative access point GR032153.

From here down to Dolanog are further natural weir steps. A little way below the bridge in Dolanog is the huge and nasty Dolanog weir. Although this has seen a few descents, there is little appeal to most canoeists. **_It is, therefore, best to portage with caution along the road._**

Below here, the walls begin to close in, and the best bit of white water on the river is reached - the Dolanog gorge. Continuous at its grade, which is a III plus or IV depending upon what the water levels are, the gorge can be inspected from Glyndwr's Way on the right bank. In big water, one or two of the holes deserve respect!

Easier water leads down to Pontrobert where egress can be made by the telephone box GR108127. Note the small easy weir below the bridge.

Pontrobert to A490 bridge: 13 km grade I; three weirs***

Pontrobert is about two miles west of the A495 just before it crosses the Vyrnwy. Access can be made as above.

Easy water leads down to a weir just above the next road bridge. Easy enough in low to medium flows, it becomes dangerous in flood. However, the best level to do this river is in low to medium flows. There is one further broken weir before the Banwy confluence. From here down, the river becomes much more mature as it cruises along to the Meifod bridge (alternative good egress / access). Rich rolling pasture and plentiful wildlife occur over the next few miles. Some while later a large and gloomy mill building is approached, which is on the right-hand bank at Cilmawr. This gives warning of the **_accompanying weir_**. In medium levels and below, the weir can be shot relatively straightforwardly on the left to centre. Continue to the next main road bridge, the A490, where a get-out can be made GR196155

Lower Vyrnwy: A490 bridge to Severn confluence: 29 km grade I

A beautiful touring section suitable for groups and beginners alike. It is best done whilst levels **_are well within_** the normal banks, as in flood it would be very frightening because of trees etc. In fact as a touring-type river it can be paddled in all but midsummer lows. The bird and animal life along this section is fantastic - you may be lucky enough to see otters, heron, kingfisher, mink and stoat, to name but a few as you drift lazily down. The sections can be broken down as follows.

A490 (GR197156) to aqueduct bridge (GR196253): 12 km
grade I****

Access from the A490 bridge via the footpath on river right. As you drift lazily down try and spot the **'crocodile tree'** on the left bank. A small white foot-bridge is passed under but, otherwise, the outside world is kept delightfully away until you approach Llansantffraid. There is a tiny broken weir before the road bridge which, at "surf-able water levels", gives a few play-able waves but you may not even notice its presence. After the Tanat joins (river left) the river sweeps around some huge bends known as 'the Islands'. Oxbows appear in the making, and this is a geographer's delight.

Good egress / access can be made at the B4398 road bridge, right next to where the Shropshire Union Canal crosses the river. For a further 17 kilometres it is possible to paddle down to the Severn confluence. There are no weirs or unpleasantries on this section with the only real obstacles being trees (in flood), and bridge stanchions if you paddle into them. Just below Llanymynech the line of Offa's Dyke Path is crossed. Over the last five kilometres the river strengthens up and the banks appear almost tidal - though I'm sure they are not. A little way past the amazing 13th century church at Malverley and, almost without warning, the Vyrnwy empties into the Severn (or is it the other way round?). Egress at the next road bridge GR329158. The choice is yours: Wales on the left bank, or England right, as the Vyrnwy has been separating both since Llanymynech.

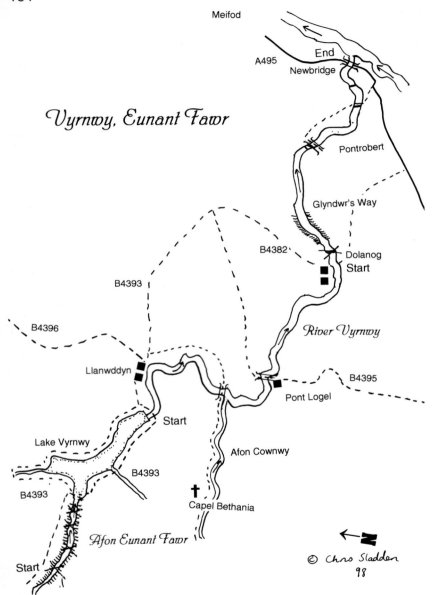

Vyrnwy, Eunant Fawr

Meifod

A495

End

Newbridge

Pontrobert

Glyndwr's Way

B4382

Dolanog
Start

B4393

B4396

River Vyrnwy

B4395

Llanwddyn

Pont Logel

Start

Lake Vyrnwy

Afon Cownwy

B4393

B4393

✝
Capel Bethania

Afon Eunant Fawr

Start

© Chris Sladden
98

Afon Cain

Map:	Bala & Lake Vyrnwy & surrounding area, no. 125
Grade:	I
Length:	8 km
Access:	Talwern bridge off B393 Llanfyllin to Llansantffraid-ym-Mechain
Notes:	an adventurous day out - but not much more to recommend it
Quality:	not recommended - snaggled with trees

Talwrn Bridge to Llansantffraid-ym-Mechain: 8 km grade I; various portages

From the A490 Welshpool to Llanfyllin road, it is possible to turn up the B4393 and take the first turn left, which leads to a little bridge crossing the flow GR174192. It is totally inappropriate, in my opinion, to paddle this river in flood or high water conditions! A few days after rain, or when the boat will easily float but you would be happy to wade or swim across the small stream with impunity, is the time to launch if you have to. Weave and turn, portaging the odd tree, fence and two low horse jumps (Bodynfoel Hall runs horse trials several times a year) on your way to the first village. Pass Llanfechain and the towers at Brongain, and continue bobbing and weaving, cursing and snarling!

Under a small brick bridge and, thankfully after only one further bridge, escape onto the road is possible. If you are a sucker for punishment like me, then the B4393 road bridge and its small following weir are next, before passing under the A495 where you eventually reach a white footbridge and can escape to the car park in town, get changed and go to the pub.

Afon Tanat

Map:	Bala & Lake Vyrnwy & surrounding area, no. 125
	Shrewsbury & surrounding area, no. 126
Grade:	II
Length:	24 km
Access:	off B4391 Bala to Pant road
Notes:	no portages
Quality:	****

A beautiful touring river thought to have been of inspiration to Tolkein for his wonderful Lord of the Rings.

Pentre to Llanyblodwel: 24 km class II; no portages****

Driving up the B4391 from Pant towards Bala, it is possible to put on the river at a footpath and bridge by a caravan park just downstream of Llangynog, GR059260. The river is often high enough here for a week or so after rain, and

navigable at lower levels from Brithdir ford. In a **big flood** the trees are dangerous and, for lower level paddlers, you will want to avoid these conditions. The
river is a delight for touring with grade I to II rapids, beautiful scenery and
crystal-clear waters. The first major tributary - the Afon Rhaeadr, rushing down
from the highest waterfall in Wales, joins just below the ford at Aber Rhaeadr
GR129246. This can produce a good wave in high water but also provides an
alternative starting point - shortening the trip by nearly half. From hre down the
lwrch swells the water even more as it passes under some very dubious (amusing) footbridges. There is a small weir of little consequence above the
Llangedwen Bridge, below which the river becomes the border between England and Wales. Another small weir below the bridge at Pen y Bont gives a bit
of excitement but nothing to worry about. The hardest rapid, grade II+ - with a
couple of play stoppers at medium level - exists above the bridge in the beautiful village of Llanyblodwel. Exit downstream of the bridge by the Horseshoe
Inn car park (after seeking permission) or above here from the right bank onto
a small road GR242228. Below here, just before joining the Vyrnwy, are two
large weirs. Although I haven't done this bottom two kilometres, I have it on
good authority that these weirs produce excellent play waves in medium levels,
but get nasty in flood.

Afon Rhaeadr

Map:	Bala & Lake Vyrnwy & surrounding area, no. 125
Grade:	IV
Length:	3.5 km
Access:	B4580 Llanfyllin to Llanrhaeadr-ym-Mochnant road
Notes:	numerous trees
Quality:	zero because of the portages

Pistyll Rhaeadr, Wales' tallest fall, is well worth a visit. It features one of only
two natural stone bridges over Welsh rivers that I have come across.

This river is included for completeness, but is fraught with portages. If the local
farmers ever decided to use the fallen trees for firewood, then the star rating of
this river would undoubtedly change from zero to four as, without the trees, the
gorge itself would be a really nice paddle.

Gorwallt bridge to Llanrhaeadr: 3.5 km grade IV; numerous portages

If you do want to paddle this river, then follow the waterfall signs for about three
kilometres, to where a rough track leads of on the left down to a bridge where
access can be had GR097279. Grade II water for one kilometre then a surprising weir, the first of many portages, appears. A gorge is entered with a few
good falls but many tree chokes, some filled with **enormous trees**. The portages are time-consuming and a long day is the likely outcome. Towards town
are three enormous pipes and a bridge that cross the river. These have to be
portaged so egress here GR122263.

Afon Iwrch

Map: Bala & Lake Vyrnwy & surrounding area, no. 125
Grade: lower II to III
Length: 3 km
Access: B4580 Llynclys to Llanrhaeadr ym Mochnant
Notes: few stock fences needed portaging
Quality: **

The Iwrch is far better than its tree-snarled neighbour, the Rhaeadr. The lower section is good and continuous at its grade. The upper section actually looked a brilliant and continuous class IV to V? However, I sooed this river late on a mid-winter's day and it was not sensible to run this stretch: **but it did *look good*!**

Cefnhirfarwr bridge to B4580 road bridge: 3 km II to III; few stock fences **

Taking the small C road out of Llanrhaeadr ym Mochnant (eastwards) it is possible to get on at a little bridge over the river GR134267. This is just before the road goes up a steep hill.

The river is immediately continuous II or III depending on water level and on the first bend is a small weir - to catch the unwary. The river continues at this grade under the next two road bridges and all the way to the get-out. The only hazards are low branches which need a few sharp manoeuvres, plus a couple of stock fences (one hanging from the first bridge) that needed portaging. However, this is a pleasant run that will be enjoyed at the grade. Egress at the B4580 via the footpath on the left of the river GR144248. Alternatively, continue on down the beautiful Tanat valley - featured in the recent film *The Man Who Went Up A Hill And Came Down A Mountain*.

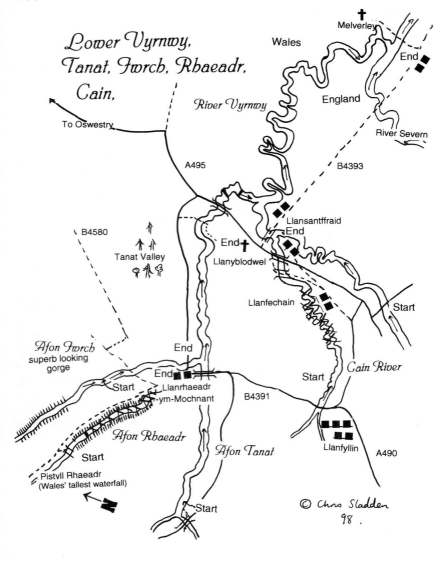

Lower Vyrnwy,
Tanat, Fwrch, Rhaeadr,
Cain,

To Oswestry

Wales

Melverley

End

River Vyrnwy

England

River Severn

A495

B4393

B4580

Llansantffraid
End

Tanat Valley

End

Llanyblodwel

Llanfechain

Start

Afon Fwrch
superb looking
gorge

End

End

Start

Llanrhaeadr
-ym-Mochnant

Cain River

Start

B4391

Start

Afon Rhaeadr

Afon Tanat

Llanfyllin

A490

Start

Pistyll Rhaeadr
(Wales' tallest waterfall)

Start

© Chris Sladden
98 .

River Severn / Afon Hafren

Map:	Newtown, Llanidloes & surrounding area, no. 136
	Shrewsbury & surrounding area, no. 126
Grade:	II to III; I to II; I
Length:	70 km
Access:	A470(T) and A483 trunk roads
Notes:	a few unpleasant weirs
Quality:	sections of* and** and***

The Severn is the longest river in Britain and has various touring sections plus harder stuff in its upper reaches.

Old Hall bridge to Llanidloes: 5 km grade II to III; one portage***

I haven't managed to get around to doing this pleasant section of water - either the water has been too low or I've been too exhausted. Anyway, having stayed at the beautiful Mount Severn Centre, I've had the river described by local experts. Coming out of Llanidloes towards the Severn Way, it is possible to take a left fork of a V in the road about a mile out of town. This crosses the river, which allows assessment of water levels. Take the first proper right after the bridge (50 metres) and head upstream. Access can be made from the various bits of land that lie adjacent to the river below the first bridge GR908846. The river needs to be clearly runnable at the inspection points but is best avoided in big spate. Grade II with the occasional III rapid leads down to the Mount Severn Weir. For people paddling at this grade, then the weir is a **definite portage** as it falls steeply onto rock, and then down the grade III slot. *George Novak, the Centre's director, told me with a wicked grin, "I'm not over-keen on guidebooks but we are definitely canoeist-friendly"!* **He is very happy for considerate paddlers to portage along the left hand bank.**

A grade II+ rapid leads under the bridge in town to the get-out downstream right of the bridge, just after the Clywedog joins.

Llanidloes to Caersws: 15 km grade II - no portages*

From below Llanidloes, the river winds its way down to Caersws. The only hazards are occasional trees that block the route - especially in high water. This section will go for a week or so after high water, or if the Clywedog is being released. Get out at the football ground in Caersws just before the railway bridge. I have to tell you that this is not the most inspirational of stretches.

Caersws to Abermule: 21 km grade I to II; one portage**

There is good access from the car park, found by turning off left immediately before the bridge as you head towards Caersws (on the main A470). From here, you can walk under the railway tunnel and turn right towards the river GR032916.

The Severn here is not a pretty river and, when I paddled it, there were copious quantities of rubbish in the river. Is this the best we can do for our returning salmon? The railway bridge is passed twice on a winding paddle towards Newtown. En-route there are some interesting trees to negotiate and, if you are a novice, your leaders will need to take care with these. There are really only two class II rapids on this part of the river; the first by the first footbridge in town, and the second towards the end of the golf course (found on the right bank at the other end of town). Those wanting a shortened trip may egress at Newport. There are footpaths travelling along much of both banks so just find a suitable place and park up. The major hazard is that a few of the local children like throwing stones - little rascals, time your visit before schools finish!

About three kilometres east of Newtown is **the large and dangerous Penarth weir**. This should be obvious from the river, and has some weir buildings on the left plus a steep bank on the right. There are various signs saying that it is illegal to trespass on the weir or the grounds nearby - but only a fool would want to shoot the weir with any kind of flow in it anyway. In anything above a low flow the stopper *would surely be lethal*. The choice is yours - portage with effort high above on the right bank or well before on the left, thus avoiding all the weir workings. Just after the next bridge to Aberbechan (possible egress) is a further grade II rapid. On the way down to Abermule there are the odd II rapids, one of which had some old wooden spikes in it - best avoided. There is good access/egress at the bridge in Abermule. This is found about eight kilometres downstream of Newtown on the A483 GR163952. This last five miles of river is far nicer than above!

Abermule to Buttington / Pool Quay: 28 km grade I to II; two weirs; one angry swan***

Occasional little rapids, in certain water conditions, give play-able waves on this winding section down to Pool Quay. First the Rhiw then the gentle Camlad are passed. In between the Camlad (a super little touring river) and the A490 road bridge is a left hand sweep, with five or six iron girders pointing out of the river bed - these could be dangerous if broached upon and, presumably, are part of an old weir structure.

Below the railway bridge and *just* past the A490 is a weir. The salmon steps mid-centre are best avoided (probably illegal) - but in low to medium flows is safely run on the left or *right*. Below the next road bridge (B4381) is an angled weir again, easily shot in these conditions. To the left is Welshpool.

Desperate moments with a swan:

It was on the section between here and the next road bridge that I had one of the most difficult and frustrating times on a Welsh river. It was all going well; I had paddled for miles "sussing-out" the Severn for this book, and was well in time to finish with plenty of daylight left for the hitch back to the car. I had seen many swans on the river and each time we had given each other mutual space. This time was different: a lone swan was determined to have me off his river or take me out on it. I got off the river and waited: he drifted downstream. I got back on and he raced back, wings flapping, neck writhing and definitely 'on for it'. The problem was that I couldn't easily get off the river, as I was boxed-in by muddy banks, thorny hedges and a railway line. I decided to hide: after ten minutes he floated off downstream and I put on again. Unfortunately, the small splash brought him immediately back upstream. Eventually, with nearly two hours of cat-and-mouse (paddler-and-swan?) I managed to trespass my way downstream to the next bridge - I never got to Pool Quay and had to hitch in the rain and the dark to Abermule. I had been totally seen off.

Egress can be had at this bridge at Buttington, GR250080, or Pool Quay three kilometres further downstream GR259115. Below here is a navigational right of way. It is described in a river Severn guide quite adequately. I was going to paddle it all the way down to the estuary, including its passage through England, but I'm afraid I simply ran out of steam.

The Severn Bore - By Paul Howells

The Severn Bore happens twice a day. This is because, with the uniqueness of the shape of the river's mouth, the incoming tide forces a great pressure wave to go roaring upstream and, of course, there are two tides daily. The Environment Agency publishes a Bore forecast for the year. This has star rating of one to five and gives dates and times and other useful information. 5 *bores being mainly on high spring tides.

However, 5 * bores are not necessarily the best bores to surf, with other factors including the amount of fresh water coming down the river, wind direction and times of the tide being of importance.

Suggested trips (OS map no. 162)**:**

Newnhorn GR120694	to Minsterworth GR755153	- ten miles' river distance
Minsterworth GR755153	to Gloucester GR817197	- eight miles' river distance

Short surfs on main wave:

It is possible to do combinations of short surfs, making the most of the fact that cars travel faster than the waves. Therefore, you can surf a short section, jump off the river , jump in the car, nip up the road and jump back on the water.

The short surfs can be done as follows:-

The first surf: on at Newnham, GR120694, to Broad Oak, GR703133 - a distance of one mile - then drive to the Severn Bore Public House, GR755153, get back on and surf to Minsterworth Church, GR773170 - a distance of one and a half miles. Then, drive to Over bridge near Gloucester, GR817197, get back on and shred to the weir, GR818217 - a distance of one and a half miles, followed by a paddle back to Over Bridge and 'Bob's your uncle'! Beware of the 'bounce-back' phenomenon from the weir. Between the surfs you normally get approximately 50 minutes to do the shuttle. A nice long paddle with the tide can be had from off Lydney Harbour GR014652, to Gloucester Over Bridge, where you can witness the second highest rise and fall of a tide in the world. Large waves firstly form just off the harbour: a 20-mile trip at 10 knots per hour!!

Play spots:

Maisemore Weir GR818217: can be a good site for the budding rodeo star. Local clubs make use of the site.

Severn Bridge Overfall GR555908: Hen-and-Chicken Rocks. Excellent playspot, with whirlpools, surf waves, large stoppers. The slip sides of the old Ferry produce excellent ender spots etc. This area produces some very strong currents, and is for experienced first time rollers only! This is certainly an exciting but dangerous area.

Hazards

Debris: I have witnessed a rear tractor wheel churning around in the wave next to me, and whilst trying to avoid this, a 45-gallon steel barrel was on the bank one minute and, the next, surfing on the waves beside me. This then bounced, hitting me on the head [author's note: lucky that "Foresters" have thick skulls, Owd Butt].

Sand banks: allow plenty of time and good river reading skills to keep off the sandbanks, or end up washing estuary mud out of every orifice.

Currents: very strong currents - not a good place to swim and lose your boat - first-time rolling essential. At Westbury Garden Cliffs be ready for a bounce wave off the cliff, as the wave can disappear here and re-form under you or in front of you!

Banks: the bank edges are a good place to surf on the edge!! However, this is only for the very experienced Severn Bore rider. Watch out for barbed wire fences, rocks, and debris which are all waiting for the inexperienced (or even the experienced).

River Camlad

Map:	Shrewsbury & surrounding area, no. 126
	Ludlow, Wenlock Edge & surrounding area, no. 137
Grade:	I
Length:	13 km
Access:	A490 Welshpool to Chirbury road
Notes:	three weirs, all shootable plus a few stock fences
Quality:	****

The Camlad and the Monnow are unique in this book in that they are the only two rivers that rise in England and finish in Wales. The Camlad is usually paddleable in the winter months for a few weeks, after heavy rain, but usually needs a bit of top-up during the summer. Apart from a few fences and three weirs, it is grade I in its entirety and is a superb run for those who enjoy wildlife, for here it abounds.

It was here I experienced one of those stolen moments when finishing the river at dusk, on a cold December day with the mist rising, that I was looked-upon with some amusement by a far more able river-man - **an otter**.

Chirbury to Hospital Bridge: 13 km grade I; three weirs with fences ****

Just south of Chirbury, situated on the A490, is a small road heading off east which crosses the river at a suitable access point GR272984. A flow without any exposed shingle banks is desirable, but in big flood it should not be, for in such conditions the trees become very dangerous. The first few kilometres weave their tortuous path through native woodland, with the only hazard being the current rambling into overhanging trees and branches.

Below the first road bridge is a small two-foot weir which, although difficult to inspect from the boat, is easily shot down the centre. A little way on are three consecutive sets of stock fences which, at time of writing and water level, were easily "sneakable". A few kilometres on is the next weir, a double-stepped affair, which is easily shootable in the middle of the left hand section. Passing under the Shiregrove Bridge the river twists and turns through steep and crumbly banks, out of which snipe, kingfisher and heron fly. The third road bridge also hides a small, play-able weir - shoot centre. A further railway bridge follows before egress at the old hospital bridge near the village of Forden (GR214999). If you desire, carry on down to the Severn, longest of all of England and Wales' rivers; otherwise take time to check out the ancient stone castle in Montgomery - just down the road.

Afon Rhiw

Map:	Newtown, Llanidloes & surrounding area, no. 136
Grade:	II; one fall III to IV
Length:	11 km
Access:	B4390 Berriew to New Mills road
Notes:	one small weir/ford has surprisingly strong stopper
Quality:	***

The Rhiw is a pleasant little of river, canoeable for a few days after heavy rain, and suitable for an intermediate group looking a for a new river to paddle.

Manafon to Berriew: 11 km class II; one rapid of class III to IV***

Turn off the A483 Newtown to Welshpool road at Berriew and head westward on the B4390. Passing through the village of Manafon, a pub and caravan park are reached where access onto the river can be made (after seeking permission), GR112023. The river is pleasant, the rapids easy and the trip value good. In Pant y Ffridd there is a caravan park which has a concrete ford, crossing the river at its downstream end. This produces a surprisingly strong stopper in flood and it needs to be a viewed with some caution in these conditions.

Below Felindre there are some interesting waves which bounce the paddler in towards town. The sting in the tail is the grade III to IV drop just above the bridge in town, which is surprisingly testing in high water. Egress downstream right of the bridge by the sculpture museum, GR188007.

Afon Mule

Map:	Newtown, Llanidloes & surrounding area, no. 136
Grade:	II to III
Length:	2 km
Access:	B4368 Abermule to Newtown road
Notes:	two large shootable weirs
Quality:	***

Who can resist canoeing a river with a name like "the Mule". I'm not sure as to the provenance of the name but would love to know. It has been suggested in previous literature that the Mule needs to be in flood to run. I would disagree with this, as a lovely little grade II paddle can be had, a few days after rain. In fact, during a medium flood run I found the trees to be a real nuisance.

Fron Fraith Hall bridge to Abermule: 2 km class II to III; no portages***

A short way downhill from the Llenmerewig turning (on the B4368) is a little bridge over the river GR164932. Here, access can be made from the left bank but check downstream as, at times of paddling (mid and late '97), there was an awkward tree about 30 metres below the bridge which could only just be sneaked under - or around. Below this you are shot down a miniature, class II gun barrel, which is exciting in high water. A little further on is a **large, sloping weir** which is shootable straight down the middle. A couple of bridges are passed, the second one of which has a blocked left channel but the right is clear.

The paddler passes a few more small bridges near some dwellings, and then enters a straight section with some picturesque cottages on the right-hand bank. *Here is a huge sloping weir* which can be shot in low and medium levels. If in a big flood, I have a sneaking suspicion that the bottom stopper could get a bit sticky - so be careful.

Abermule is reached and the first bridge has a large tree down, forcing a careful passage on the left. Pass the railway bridge and pull out on the left into the sewage works GR163946. Or, alternatively, carry on down to the next bridge over the Severn.

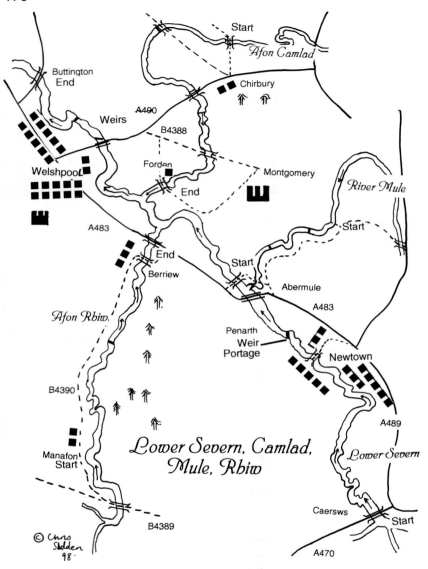

Afon Camlad

Start

Buttington
End

Chirbury

Weirs

A490

B4388

Forden

End

Montgomery

River Mule

Welshpool

Start

A483

End

Start

Berriew

Abermule

A483

Afon Rhiw

Penarth
Weir
Portage

Newtown

B4390

A489

Lower Severn, Camlad,
Mule, Rhiw

Lower Severn

Manafon
Start

© Chris
Skidden
98.

Caersws

Start

B4389

A470

River Lugg

Map:	Ludlow, Wenlock Edge & surrounding area, no. 137
Grade:	I
Length:	15 km
Access:	Presteigne to Monaughty road
Notes:	stock fences cause some ducking and diving
Quality:	**

The Lugg is a long river rising, as it does, in Powys from Pool Hill, and flowing eastwards and then southwards until eventually reaching the Wye at Hereford. It crosses the border near the little hamlet of Combe - a suitable place to end a trip.

Bridge end to Combe: 15 km class I; weirs - shootable; stock fences **

Driving up-river from Presteigne towards the little village of Whitton, there is a left-hand turn that crosses the river at Bridge End GR268669. Here, access to the little meandering river can be made. From here on down there are quite a lot of stock fences that need to be scraped, slithered, sneaked, creeped and cursed around. After a few kilometres is a weir, with an excellent right-sided newcomer shoot. Below the B4356 bridge is a large tree hanging by chains, that needs to be ducked. Before and after the next road bridge, a section of six or so weirs is reached - some of these are quite fun to play in at suitable levels.

There are four gauges at the tiny bridge in town. A level just below the bottom of all of them is a suitable flow. Passing under the picturesque bridge in Presteigne there is another **weir** that has a bar, or the like, suspended below it creating, I guess, an anti-scour effect. Though this is only small *it deserves caution*. One further small weir is left as the river meanders its way to the get out at Combe bridge GR348640.

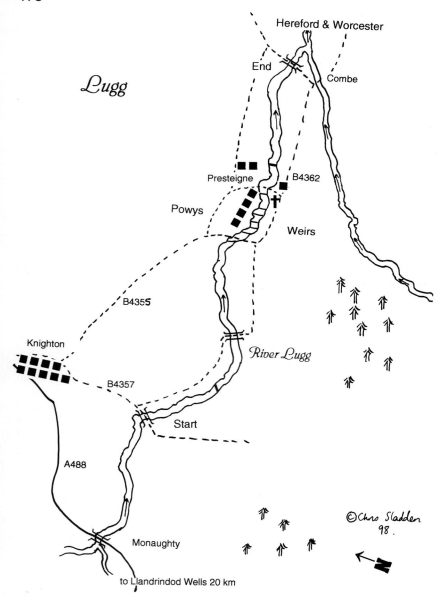

Lugg

Hereford & Worcester

End

Combe

Presteigne

B4362

Powys

Weirs

B4355

Knighton

River Lugg

B4357

Start

A488

©Chris Sladden
98.

Monaughty

to Llandrindod Wells 20 km

Afon Carno

Map:	Newtown, Llanidloes & surrounding area, no. 136
Grade:	II
Length:	6 km
Access:	A470 Caersws to Dolgellau road
Notes:	one dangerous weir
Quality:	**

The Carno is quite an interesting spate river running, as it does, in a small gorge alongside part of the A470. Easy enough, it has one particularly vicious weir to keep the paddler awake on the journey down to Caersws.

Maespandy bridge to Severn: 6 km grade II; one weir (portage)**

Just north of Clatter, on the A470, is a turn-off which crosses the railway line before reaching a small bridge across the river GR994958. There is a footpath along the right bank that gives acceptable access. Alternatively, but more tricky, is to start as I did about a kilometre upstream and via a short road, railway crossing and footpath.

The river needs to be in spate to paddle, though if over its banks will, undoubtedly, become unduly dangerous. Easy enough at first, there is a small weir with a surprisingly sticky little stopper immediately under the first railway bridge. Easy again, with attractive class II rapids running through 'semi-gorges', a footbridge and then a railway and road bridge are passed before you need to keep the eyes peeled for the approach towards a dangerous weir. This is about 100 metres after the small road bridge and just before the next railway bridge. You cannot see it from the road, but can pre-inspect the bend that it is on. It is a strange, boxed-in affair with ramps on either side. It is runnable in a medium spate but is not nice. In big water, the towback would, probably, become 'terminal' - I recommend a portage on the right. Below the next railway bridge is a further weir, but this is only six inches in height - a relief! By Pontdolgoch, things ease off, and occasional small rapids around carving bends take the paddler down to just above the Severn confluence. Egress can be made at the bridge GR026918.

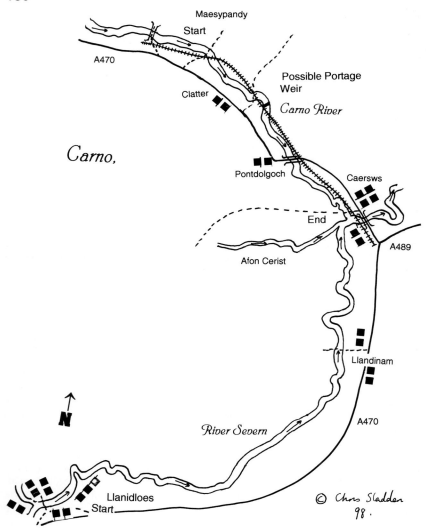

Maesypandy

Start

A470

Clatter

Possible Portage
Weir

Carno River

Carno,

Pontdolgoch

Caersws

End

A489

Afon Cerist

N

Llandinam

A470

River Severn

Llanidloes

Start

© Chris Sladden
98.

Afon Clywedog

Map: Newtown, Llanidloes & surrounding area, no. 136
Grade: II to III; one fall IV
Length: 6 km
Access: B4518 Llanidloes to Staylittle road
Notes: weirs demand respect at high flows
Quality: ★★★★

It a took me 15 years of canoeing in Wales, and only whilst running rivers for this book, to discover the Clywedog. A great shame really, as it is a superb run. The dams, out of which it flows, were constructed in the 1960s to provide water for the Midlands. They also provide flood limitation on the mighty Seven. Depending on water levels in the lake, releases are made all year round. The staff at the dam are extremely pleasant and helpful, and let you know what the release is and whether it is any good for canoeing. In full flood, with high release and natural run-off the trees will become quite problematic and the weirs extremely nasty. A release of between 450-800 Mega Litres a Day is ideal.

Bryntail lead mine to Severn confluence: 6 km class II to III; one class IV★★★★

Take the B4518 out of Llanidloes and drive to the dam where excellent access can be had from the car parking at the old lead mine workings GR913868. Put on above or below the footbridge weir, which is usually shootable via a central tongue through the stopper. The hardest fall begins immediately downstream and is an exciting class IV blast. In a very high water it may, perhaps, reach the top end of its grade. Things ease off to class III and then to superb continuous class II+.

The first road bridge is passed, which is an alternative access point if you don't fancy your chance with the first drop. About a kilometre or so below is a natural bedrock step that gives an exciting class III to IV shoot, depending on water levels. Below this are some great little playful weirs and steps. As you near the town a dilapidated bridge is passed, and there is an obvious weir by a caravan park. In reasonable flows this can be enjoyed down its centre channel or its edges but, in high water, the stopper can back right across, **necessitating a portage on the right**.

Further still, just before the confluence, are some nasty metalwork ridden weirs which demand respect for their size. Taking care with your line should ensure the canoeist avoids the grappling irons! If unsure then portage on river right. The very pleasant couple who live on the left bank like watching people enjoying their sport and have decided to clear out the weir for our benefit. Thank you. Once the Severn is entered good egress can be made onto a little track below the bridge, river right GR955847.

Afon Dulas

Map:	Newtown, Llanidloes & surrounding area, no. 136
Grade:	IV (IV+)
Length:	4.5 km
Access:	off A470(T) Llangurig to Llanidloes road
Notes:	tree portages
Quality:	****

I nearly didn't bother with the Dulas. I had seen it on the maps, but usually crossed it when there was no water in the rivers. I was also coming to the completion of the book and running out of steam. Luckily, I persisted and was treated to the narrow and dramatic Tylwch gorge.

<u>Tylwch to A470 bridge</u>: 4.5 km class IV (IV+)****

Turn off the A470 in Llanidloes and find the B4518 to Tylwch, up which you go until it crosses the Dulas in the village. The river needs to be in a medium flow for an optimal level. In full flood it would probably be quite frightening. Access can be made from the bridge GR970802.

Set off on bouncy class II, dodging the odd branch and ducking below an old girder. A little further on are the remains of an old bridge, where several iron girders stick out of the water. These need some care to pass and could be, potentially, quite nasty.

The river begins to narrow, and the grade rises to a good class III. This gives ample warning of the dramatic, sculptured and narrow Tylwch gorge, through which the river flows for the next kilometre. There was one big tree down (Feb. '98) that necessitated a portage in the class IV gorge. Just as you think the best is over, the gorge walls close in again and drop into a class IV+ chasm only a few feet wide - serious but wonderful.

Some enormous old bridge stanchions are passed and the best is over. Class II and III rapids, with an old weir to do, convey the paddler down to the main road bridge where you can get out GR951824.

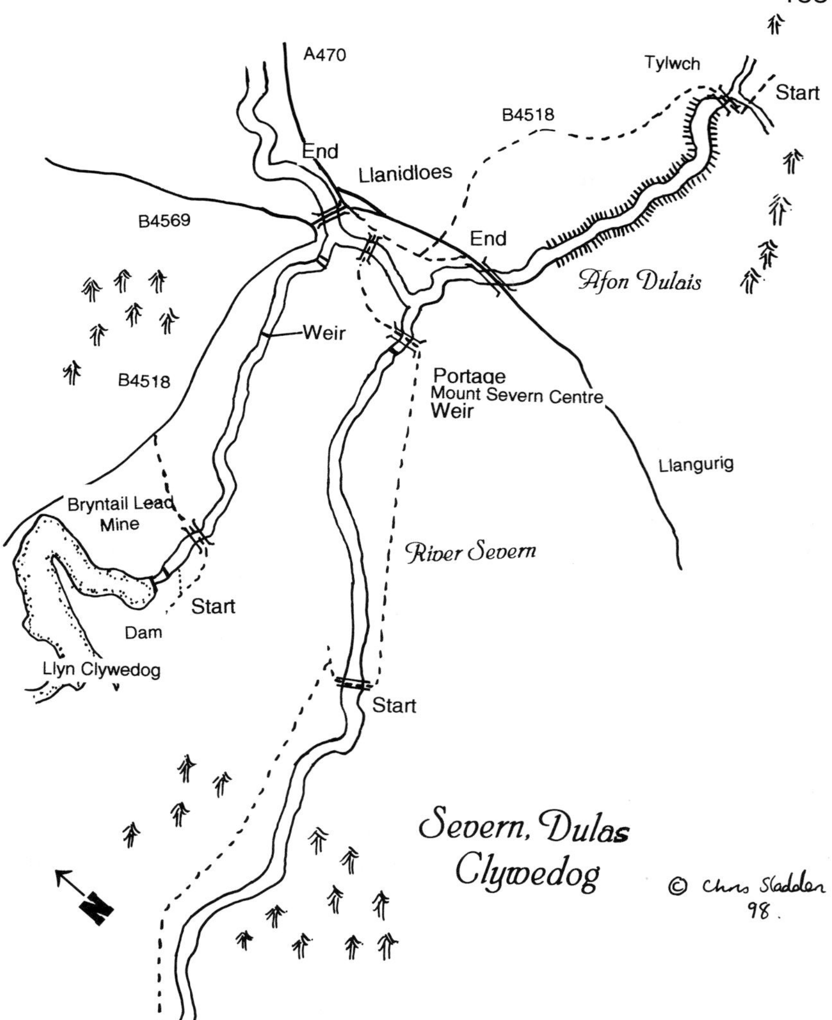

A470

End

Llanidloes

Tylwch

Start

B4518

End

B4569

Afon Dulais

Weir

B4518

Portage
Mount Severn Centre
Weir

Llangurig

Bryntail Lead
Mine

River Severn

Start

Dam

Llyn Clywedog

Start

N

*Severn, Dulas
Clywedog*

© Chris Sladden
98.

The River Wye / Afon Gwy

Map:	Several OS sheets, nos. 135, 136, 147, 148, 149, 161, 162
Grade:	sections of I, II, III (IV)
Length:	251 km (some 153 miles) of various sections
Access:	various
Notes:	no portages
Quality:	sections of*** and****

Along with the Severn and Rheidol, the Wye rises in Mid Wales from the Plynlimon mountain range. It is a long, majestic river flowing, firstly, through Wales over some good rapids, before mellowing out into broad, sweeping stretches in England. Finally, it empties into the longest river of all, the Severn, on the border in Chepstow. Managing to avoid most industrial centres, the Wye is a clean river with myriad wildlife along its entire length. Furthermore, there are no portages and no real weirs to disrupt its navigable beauty.

Steeped in history, too, is the Wye. Offa, the king of what was known as Mercia, built his dyke from the mouth of the Wye to join with another great Welsh river, the Dee, in the North. Traces of this rampart of old are still present on the Offa's Dyke Footpath. Navigation, too, began early on the Wye, with its lower stretches being used by great sailing vessels as far as Brockweir (Bigsweir) and, from here to Hereford, barges continued the journey, carrying various cargoes. So, since the 16th century, there has been a free right of navigation from Chepstow to Hay.

In the late 1700s, the Wye began its first recorded recreational navigation, with the so-called Wye Tour becoming a popular excursion for the wealthy. Today, touring on the river can be enjoyed by everyone, from young to old, and rich to poor. Sadly, the free right of navigation on the lower Wye is under dubious scrutiny from various quarters at the present time. Mr Wye himself, Paul Howells, is so passionate about this issue that, when talking about his beloved river, the eyes glaze over and acquire a far-away expression. For here at the Yat, on the waters of the Wye, countless people have made their first paddling strokes under his guidance and have been hooked for life. Surely though, like the air that we breathe, the waters of the Wye should be available to future generations wishing to explore the beautiful countryside.

The banks and river bed higher up are under private ownership, and are subject to fluctuating access agreements (check with WCA). *Whilst* these are working I would urge paddlers to adhere to them, for the river is a fine salmon stretch and the fishermen, too, have a right to share.

Published 108 years before this guide was Mr Stookes' *Tourist Map of the River Wye*. It is, to my mind, accolade indeed to him, that the right and the wish still exist to float the Wye.

Llangurig to Rhayader: 17 km grade III (IV)****

If you want to add an extra eight kilometres of class II it is possible to launch at Pont Rhydgaled (on A44T) but this is rarely done. In fact the Afon Tarennig that joins here is also a brilliant paddle. Above the bridge are, in fact, some class IV to V falls that require much water to be worth doing.

In medium to high levels this is a great section which, over the years, has seen its fair share of epics when in full-on flood. In these conditions, it is certainly not a beginners' river though many newcomers find themselves on it!

Access can be made at the small bridge in Llangurig GR908797. Grade II water leads down through a couple of kilometres of occasionally tree-overhung water. The first class III is on a sharp left hand bend, and has a boat-snatching right hand eddy. Easier water then down to the concrete bridge at GR922737. Below this the walls close in, and the river rushes down over a couple of good class III rapids. The aptly named rock garden, or letter box, gives some idea of the manoeuvring required to negotiate a particular section.

A footbridge and the Marteg are the next points of note. Below this, down to the town of Rhayader, are some excellent grade II and III rapids. A caravan park appears on the left a little way before the bridge. *Immediately* below the road bridge begins the well-known Rhayader Falls, grade III to IV. This double drop with its narrowing below has several choices of route. In huge water it becomes a solid and hard class IV with some notable stoppers to *avoid*. Egress can be made below on the right GR969676.

Rhayader to Builth Wells: 26 km grade II to III***

A well-known and popular run where an excellent day's paddling can be had. Easier rapids lead out of Rhayader until an old bridge just above the Elan confluence. Here is a good class III rapid weaving its way over bedrock steps with the occasional, stiff stopper. Between here and Llanwrthwl bridge are a few class II rapids. The good thing about all of these rapids, in high flow, is the excellent potential for playing on waves and small stoppers.

From Llanwrthwl to Newbridge is a further eight kilometres or so of paddling, with the occasional rapid. Newbridge is an alternative starting or finishing point GR014583. A little way down, the sizeable Ithon enters (another great touring river), soon after the Brynwern bridge. Easier rapids follow over the next few kilometres until below a railway bridge, where the bed becomes rocky again and an exciting class III rapid follows. Continue down to Builth past the, somewhat confusingly-named, Irthon which enters from river right. Excellent egress can be made at the obvious car park just above the bridge in town. Follow the one way system GR042512.

Builth Wells to Llyswen: 20 km grade II to III (IV); no portages****

In low to medium flows, this is a beautiful piece of water on which to launch your class II to III paddling. It is also a classic and justifiably popular section of the river. The river contains three sections of rapids with easier bits in between. They all have the character of bedrock reefs, with occasional channel constriction and narrowing.

Easy water leads down to the Duhonw confluence. The first, or Llanfared, set of rapids is class II to III depending very much on water conditions. The higher the water, the harder it is. These continue on and off for almost a kilometre and, towards the end, is a classic natural weir drop which is worth inspecting if in flood. There are also a few eddy-creating constructions built out from the banks - best for boaters to avoid.

Below these the **beautiful little Edw** enters from the left. After a few kilometres, and a little way above Erwood, a section of bouncy rapids begins - that stretches out for over a kilometre. In high water these rapids have fantastic waves for surfing. The B4567 is passed.

Below Erwood the adrenaline starts to flow and the mouth dries as the paddler approaches the infamous 'Hell Hole' rapids. Hard in their day, they can still provide a shock in high water with a poor line of descent! Warning is given as soon as the chain bridge at Llanstephan comes into view. The line lies far right though in higher water options over the central rock steps exist. In full spate the stopper middle and left takes on a vicious character - care should be exercised (IV). Below the bridge is a perfect surfing hole at low to medium conditions. Easier rapids follow, until a final flurry over a steep drop occurs about a kilometre above the Boughrood / Llyswen bridge. There is good access river right onto the small road upstream of the bridge GR128384.

Llyswen bridge to Hay on Wye: 16 km grade I***

Just north of Llyswen on the A470(T) is the access/egress point described above. From here to Glasbury are several small disruptions that can just about be described as rapids (rapid-lets, perhaps?). The funny **little Llynfi** enters from the right just above Glasbury. Alternate access/egress can be made river left, just above the bridge and onto the convenient car park GR179393. Over to the right are The Black Mountains with their accompanying series of rivers flowing south-eastwards. There are a few shallow rapids on the way to Hay that are soon washed out in any kind of water. Boats can be hired both in Glasbury and Hay. Just before Hay is a small, bouldery-type weir which is easily shootable right.

Hay is a border town and it is here that the Wye passes into England. It is, however, such an important river that I have described its lower reaches. Egress, if a little awkward, is possible on the public footpath left or right, below the bridge.

Hay to Bredwardine: 25 km grade I***

From the access in the book town of Hay (go look for yourselves), the river twists and turns through beautiful and rich countryside. The hardest rapid, if it can be described as that, is just below the bridge at the put-in. There is some debris from the old railway bridge just upstream of the B4350 toll bridge but otherwise the channel is usually clear. Whitney, about a kilometre below this, is a pleasant lunch stop. Egress can be made at the small bridge near Bredwardine GR336448, or this is reached by a small road off the A438.

Bredwardine to Hereford: 27 km grade I (II)***

Below Bredwardine the river sweeps majestically on down towards Hereford. A few islands are passed which, in low conditions, are great for sunbathing or lunch. The only exceptions to this tranquillity are the so-called Monington Falls - somewhat of an overstatement. On a left hand bend about six kilometres below the access, the river is forced against a left-sided cliff and, in doing so, produces a few little waves of grade I to II. You may even pass it without even noticing! Some way further on 'the weir' is passed - another misnomer. Egress in Hereford below the old road bridge river right.

Hereford to Ross-on-Wye: 49 km grade I***

This is a fairly long section which, although can be done in a day, is usually broken up by egressing at one of the various points en-route. Hereford is a reasonably large place but, once there, a bit of navigation will enable you to find the old stone bridge a little upstream from an old suspension bridge. Good access can be made here GR509397. At Hampton Bishop is the *Bunch of Carrots* public house. In days gone by it was simply *The Carrots Inn* - whatever the name it serves a good pint.

The river slowly meanders south-eastwards until, after about 12 kilometres, it is joined by the Lugg (a river of weirs). Three kilometres further on is the Holme Lacy bridge and campsite - possible egress.

If you are lucky you may see a kingfisher flashing its blue and red as it outpaces the paddler downstream. Occasional ripples, the odd island and banks with gnarled and ancient trees are passed towards Hoarwithy. This is about another 15 kilometres. Again, egress can be made near the bridge.

From Hoarwithy, the Wye takes a large swing back east towards the interestingly named Hole in the Wall, but there are no bandits here. Large parties of canoeists are probably from the PGL centre nearby. Swinging back westwards, the small village of Foy is passed before another large bend heads towards Ross. Perched high on a hill, the town is visible from some way off. The A40 bridge is passed under followed, in about a short kilometre, by the *Hope and Anchor Inn.* For those who cannot wait it is possible to land and find succour. Egress can be made at the old stone bridge of Wilton. Land left just below the bridge where there is excellent access GR596244.

Ross-on-Wye to Monmouth: 35 km grade I to II****

This section is one of the most popular touring stretches in Britain and numerous people have been introduced to the sport along here. The ten kilometres down to Kerne bridge pass through attractive countryside with occasional ripples here and there. Goodrich Castle can be seen perched high above the right hand banks. Kids (big and small) will enjoy this although scrambling up the steep bank is a trifle awkward. Access/egress can be made at Kerne, downstream left. The next section curving around in an enormous bend contains a few small rapids on its way towards the Huntsham bridge. This popular access point is just off the A40, along the turn signposted Symonds Yat East. In the small village of Welsh Bicknor along this section is a pleasant little Youth Hostel.

From the Huntsham bridge down to the Yat is the territory of the 'Owd Man of the Wye', Paul Howells. On the way, you will pass the seal-launching rock and see pleasure cruisers that motor up and down the river - watch out. At Symonds Yat East, the concrete steps of the Wye Dean Canoe Centre allow easy access and egress (river left). Here canoes and kayaks of all descriptions can be hired, as can top-notch instruction. The Yat cliffs loom up on the left. If you climb, go and check-out the super Prow on the prominent rock pinnacle.

At the time of writing, Paul and a group of Trustees (a non-profit group) are in the process of buying the well-known Yat rapids. These grade II rapids have given joy to countless paddlers over the years, but are under threat from fishermen wishing to dig out the river bed to make salmon-holding pools. The Trustees' plan is to buy the stretch so that it stays available to future generations of paddlers - *bravo.*

Below the Yat, a forested gorge is entered and passed. As you near Monmouth watch out for rowing boats training up and down the river. Good egress can be had via the rowing club steps on the right GR512128. By now you are back in Wales.

Monmouth to Chepstow: 33 km grade I to II***

From here down to Chepstow, the Wye is very much a border river. The Monnow enters from the right, followed by the delightful Trothy. There are occasional ripples and little waves from here on down. A gloomy old railway bridge is reached, with a pub on the right hand bank - good food here. The main road (A466) bridge is reached at Bigsweir bridge. Unless on big springs, this is the limit of tidal water and you may want to time your paddle. From here to Tintern the banks are of oozing mud, which even looked slimy whilst climbing on the limestone cliffs at Shorncliffe (a couple of kilometres away). At Tintern, it is possible to access/egress into the car park and visit this splendid old abbey. Or, if climbing is another passion, go try out the 'Big Green Meanie' on the cliffs above.

Certainly below Tintern it is useful to make good use of the tides. At low water, the river rushes through the remains of ancient weirs creating debris-strewn rapids. Having toured this section in the early days, I was somewhat dubious as to their existence until climbing on the cliffs above gave an excellent view of low water hazards! Therefore, for the trip from Tintern to Chepstow (a run of about 12 kilometres), leave within an hour of high water and continue straight on down. High water Tintern is approximately four hours after high tide at Dover.

Chepstow is fine Welsh border town with castle high overhead. There is good egress below the first bridge up the obvious slip way on the right GR535945.

Below Chepstow the Wye's currents become very dangerous as it swirls its way into the Severn estuary. For experienced experts only, there is a section on the estuary playspots and riding the famous Bore under the river Severn description.

Afon Marteg

Map:	Elan Valley & Builth Wells area, no. 147
Grade:	III; one gorge of V
Length:	2 km
Access:	A470 Rhayader to Llanidloes
Notes:	the gorge is a well-known one hit wonder
Quality:	***

The Marteg is a small, pretty river with a very well-known class V gorge to run. Tradition has it that, for many paddlers, this is one of the first class V sections they do - a bit of a one-hit wonder. Unfortunately, the access situation is at present rather unsatisfactory.

Gilfach y Rhiw bridge to Pont Marteg: 3 km grade III; one fall V***

Take the small road sign to Pont St Harmon. This runs alongside the Marteg. The road steepens and leaves the river - a sure sign of things to come. There is a cattle grid and gate by which is a steep road leading off to the nature area downhill and across the river. Access can be made here GR974723. The gorge is about 200 metres below and is heralded by an enormous house-sized boulder mid-river. Most people run right with a tight turn on the corner. Below this main drop the river has occasional class III falls as it winds its way past a couple of bridges down to the get-out at Pont Marteg GR953715.

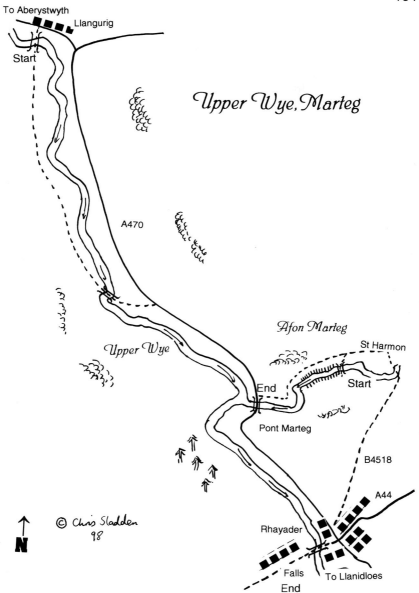

To Aberystwyth
Llangurig
Start

Upper Wye, Marteg

A470

Afon Marteg

St Harmon

Upper Wye

End
Start

Pont Marteg

B4518

A44

Rhayader

© Chris Sladden
98

N

Falls
End

To Llanidloes

Afon Claerwen

Map: Elan Valley & Builth Wells area, no. 147
Grade: III to IV; one fall V+; one class VI portage
Length: 4 km
Access: Rhayader to Claerwen Dam roads
Notes: one hard fall, plus one almost-certain portage
Quality: ****

In days gone by both the Claerwen and Elan rivers in their entirety would have undoubtedly been fantastic white water runs. If plastic boats and the 1990s urge had existed back in the old days then, no doubt, they would have been run. Both fall steeply with large catchment areas through a wild expanse of land. Being dam-released, the Claerwen often runs when other rivers are too low to paddle. It may well be worth the drive up if you have missed out on the rain - I've often found it up in the week after floods.

There are five great reservoirs within the Elan Valley system so, therefore, only small sections of river remain canoeable.

Claerwen reservoir to Rhiwnant bridge: grade III to IV; one fall V+ and one portage****

The river is easily assessed on the drive up for its canoeable potential. It is wise to check out the two possible portages as well, and make a good mental note for, sadly, a fatality occurred on the top falls a few years back. Either put on from waste ground below the dam and bridge, GR871633, and paddle the first, mainly flat one and a half kilometres down to this **horrendous fall GR884628**, or **put on below**. The whole of the this fall has, apparently, been run but would need extremely high water to wash out the horrendous boulder chokes, sumps and siphons. **Be warned**.
The next kilometre is fairly easy with occasional class III rapids and falls. A footbridge appears perched across two huge boulders. Immediately below, running out of the pool, is a hard class V+ double drop which is quite frightening to run. Most will want to **portage** and continue the next kilometre of grade III to IV in one piece. There is a good wave under the egress bridge at Rhiwnant but, be careful with the stanchions and pipes GR901606.

Afon Marteg: the main falls. Photo: Foxy

Touring at its best on the Upper Tanat. Photo: Chris Sladden collection

Colours of the Banwy. Photo: Chris Sladden collection

The end of the Edw in huge water, just before emptying into a
swollen Wye. Photo: Clare Jefferson

Descending the
Lower Sgithwen
Brook.
Photos by Clare
Jefferson and Dick
Renshaw.

In the Upper Irfon gorge. Photo: Clare Jefferson

Evening tranquillity at the bottom of the Iwrch. Photo: Clare Jefferson

Two views of the Lower Prysor. Photos: Phil Blain collection

Reflections on the Lower Dee. Photo: Chris Sladden collection

Flowing into Bala Lake, Paul Ross takes the last big hit of the Afon Twrch. Photo: Chris Sladden collection

The worst footbridge in Wales? Dave Evans watches his head on the Tanat. Photo: Chris Sladden collection

Afon Elan

Map:	Elan Valley & Builth Wells area, no. 147
Grade:	II
Length:	6 km
Access:	Elan Dam and village
Notes:	one small weir
Quality:	***

The Elan is a pleasant and entertaining trip for newcomers to the sport, or for those who would like a different start to the river Wye. For the river to be canoeable, water has to be either spilling *over* the immense Cabin Coch dam, or be released. A good level is around 6 to 7 on the gauge situated above the little measuring weir (this has a vicious stopper in flood!) and **above** the get-in.

Elan village to Junction Pool: 5 km class II; no portages***

Take the little road from Rhayader towards the Elan valley. After a few miles, the vast Cabin Coch dam is seen. Put on the water from the small bridge running across the river into the village, GR930648. The first rapids are a grade II, boulder garden, although this grade just about rises to a III in high water. A small weir in the middle of this is run down a shoot on the left. Easy rapids and beautiful swirls follow, as the river winds a way down to its meeting place at Junction Pool with that Queen of rivers - the Wye. A footpath just below the rickety footbridge allows good egress, GR967656. This is reached by the back road between Llanwrthwl and Dolafallen bridge.

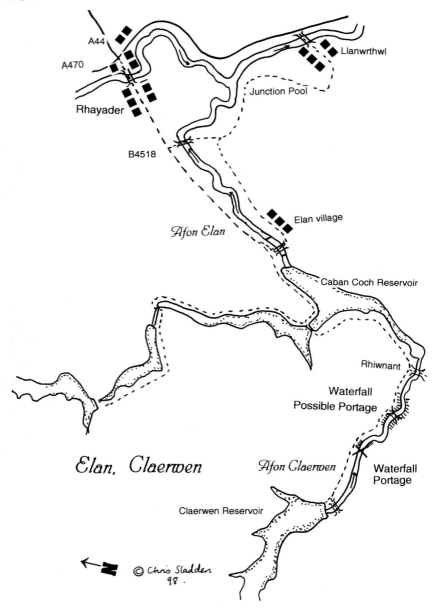

A44

A470

Rhayader

B4518

Llanwrthwl

Junction Pool

Afon Elan

Elan village

Caban Coch Reservoir

Rhiwnant

Waterfall
Possible Portage

Elan, Claerwen

Afon Claerwen

Waterfall
Portage

Claerwen Reservoir

© Chris Sladden
98.

Afon Ithon

Map:	Elan Valley & Builth Wells area, no. 147 Presteigne, no. 148
Grade:	II; with few sections of II+ to III
Length:	48 km
Access:	off A483 Builth to Newtown road
Notes:	weirs; one a definite portage in high flows; electric fences
Quality:	***

The Ithon is one of the longest tributaries of the Wye and, consequently, has a large catchment area. It needs to be in flood to become canoeable but, of course, there are floods, and there are floods. In a sizeable spate, some rapids certainly reach grade III and there are few meaty stoppers around. Otherwise it is a great easy grade river.

Upper Ithon. Llananno bridge to Shakey Bridge: 24 km class II; weir portage***

About 12 miles north of Llandrindod Wells is a turn off left, signposted to Bwlch-y- Sarnau, which immediately crosses the river GR092748. Access can be made onto the river from the main road. The river needs to be in a reasonable spate to paddle. Grade I to II rapids provide interest for those new to this type of boating and, because it is a flood river, it always has that added excitement to it. After about ten kilometres, the river passes under the A483 road bridge which allows alternative access. The paddling is pleasant down to the railway bridge at Dolau Jenkins, which is found immediately after a sharp right-hand bend in the river. There is a weir directly below the railway bridge, and this needs to be treated with great care. Although this is shootable (close to the right hand of bank), in low to medium flows *the towback becomes particularly dangerous in anything higher than this. It is easily portaged down the overflow tunnel on the right.* The river Aran joins just below.

About one kilometre downstream is a much easier weir which is just above the Penybont A483 bridge. From here, down to the get-out point at Shaky Bridge, the water becomes more exciting as it passes through the Cefnyllys gorge with its beautiful little Church on the right-hand side. Egress at Shaky Bridge GR084613. You may want to continue down the next few kilometres and get out at Crossgates: this is easy to do.

Lower Ithon -Shakey Bridge to Wye confluence: 21 km II, one section III***

Drive through Llandrindod where turning off by the All-Sports shop allows access, via a small series of roads (O S map useful), to a parking area by Shaky

Bridge church. Here is a memorial to a local doctor from the town (and also excellent access to the beautiful river)- what more peaceful place to rest?

The water starts off easy enough but, a couple of kilometres down, there is a sharp right-hand, left-hand sweep which leads into the Alpine bridge gorge. This is class II to III depending on water levels. At the bottom of the gorge just by the Alpine bridge, is a solidly-wedged tree right across the river GR0916832. This has been present each time I have paddled the river though, perhaps, a really big flood might rip it out. In high water a **sharp break out** right is required - **beware**. A small flood allows the paddler to sneak under the tree, where they are immediately faced with another grade II to III rapid. In the kilometre from here down to the main road bridge are some superb stoppers and waves in high water.

Below here is flat with just the occasional grade I to II rapids in small, beautiful gorges. However, it is a great training river especially with its objective hazards - it is the only time I have seen **electric fences** across any Welsh river. Between Disseth bridge and Pont ar Ithon is a good training weir - safe in a normal low to medium levels. Paddlers must use their judgment but, in the right conditions, it is an excellent place to learn stopper skills.

Egress just before the Wye confluence, at the obvious old railway bridge on the river right. A five minute walk allows the small road to be reached at GR102566.

Clywedog Brook

Map:	Elan Valley & Builth Wells, no. 147
Grade:	II
Length:	5 km
Access:	A483 Llandrindod to Newtown road
Notes:	fences!!
Quality:	**

The Clywedog Brook proved somewhat of a nuisance to me. I paddled it in the New Year floods of '98, got caught under a barbed wire strand, dislocated some ribs and put back progress of this book by a good few weeks. However, don't let me put you off as, when I re-paddled it in more sociable conditions, it was a pleasant spate grade II - with a few wires to dodge.

Henfryn bridge to A44 bridge: **

Driving north along the A483 from Crossgates, take the turn off left to Abbeycwmhir. About three kilometres along here is a 'phone box, followed by a small bridge, where access can be made below. The river needs to have enough water to clearly and easily float a boat. The main stock fences are all between here and the next small bridge. One of them has my name on it!

Small and attractive gorges are passed on the route down, with trees being the major obstacles. About halfway down is a small, old, brick weir. This is easily shot down its shoot or, with flood levels, over the left hand side. Further still and four enormous pipes and a footbridge span the river which, I guess, carry water to the Midlands. The next small bridge is a possible egress point and, indeed, in high water one is forced to duck to get underneath. Continue down to the A44 bridge, passing a couple of small weirs en-route - these shouldn't give you too much problem in suitable flows. Alternatively, continue down to the Ithon, though I haven't done this last 500 metres or so.

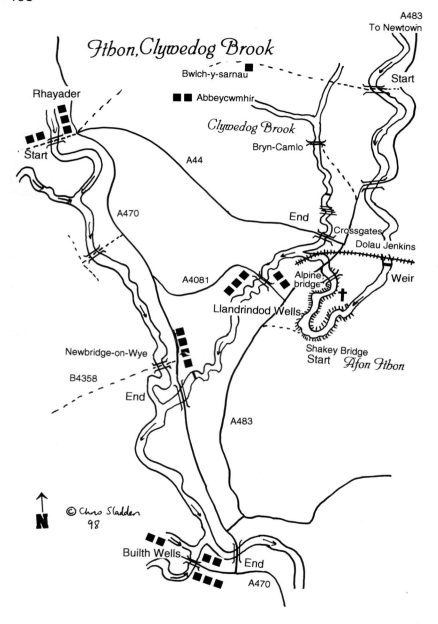

Afon, Clywedog Brook

Bwlch-y-sarnau

Abbeycwmhir

A483
To Newtown

Start

Rhayader

Clywedog Brook

Bryn-Camlo

Start

A44

A470

End

Crossgates

Dolau Jenkins

Weir

A4081

Alpine bridge

Llandrindod Wells

Newbridge-on-Wye

Shakey Bridge
Start   Afon Afon

B4358

End

A483

© Chris Sladden
98

N

Builth Wells

End

A470

Afon Irfon

Map:	Elan Valley & Builth Wells, no. 147
Grade:	IV (V), plus section of grade II to III
Length:	30 km
Access:	A483 Builth to Llandovery road
Notes:	few drops class V - may be prudent portages at certain water levels
Quality:	★★★★

The upper Irfon is a wonderful run through much unspoilt highland flowing, as it does, from one of the wildest areas in Wales. There are good testing rapids and falls en-route but nowhere is it desperate and all are easy to portage should this be desired.

Certain authorities state that, for paddling, the water levels should be near the pipe which crosses the river at the egress point. Unless the pipe has changed, and I have it on very good authority that it has not over the past 15 years, then I think this is a little inaccurate. The river does drop very quickly, but a very good run down the whole section can be had with levels anywhere from about four foot under the pipe plus, no doubt, bigger flows.

<u>Camddur Bleiddiad gorge to Llanwrtyd Wells</u>: 13 km grade IV to V; few potential portages★★★★

Follow the road to Abergwesyn out of Llanwrtyd Wells. On the way, near the Forestry area of Pwllbo, it is possible to look at two of the drops on the lower section - which are obvious from the road. Cross the river in Abergwesyn and turn left, continuing up this for about four kilometres or so. The river can be seen raging away down in the valley below, but is actually a lot easier than it looks!

Access below the awesome Camddwr Bleiddiad gorge (the Wolf's Leap') by walking down the grassy slopes. This has apparently been run, but I would be intrigued to know how the bottom sump was avoided in the five foot-wide gorge. Was it done in exceptionally high water ? - let me know!

In any case, this fabulous gorge has brilliant swimming holes in the middle of summer at low, low levels - I recommend it. Below the gorge down to the bridge in Abergwesyn are some excellent, wild rapids and drops. Most of these are runnable at a good IV at most levels. A few need inspection. One or two reach a V at certain levels and you may wish to portage. You can finish at the road bridge but there is good stuff below.

There are four major rapids in the section below, but only one is really grade V. They are all within one kilometre of each other. The first is below the forestry bridge about three to four kilometres down. In most levels it is a really stiff grade III though, occasionally, when low or very high, may reach an easy IV. The second is a beautiful tiered drop with a clear left line, in most conditions class IV. The third drop is the nasty one, with pinning potential at low water and a vicious central hole when high - *class V*. The fourth is easy, apart from two tree branches growing out to make the line awkward. These would both easily come off with a bowsaw!

Below these, flat water leads down under the road bridge before easy rapids reach the now infamous pipes (hanging below a bridge). Egress here if you wish, GR877472. However, an excellent kilometre and a half of grade II+ play stuff leads into town. Discreet egress can be made by the left hand steps or behind the public toilets near the bridge GR877466. The locals are extremely friendly, so let's keep it so by using the cafe and public house facilities, and changing out of sight!

The lower Irfon

It is possible to paddle the eight kilometres or so from Llanwrtyd Wells to where the Cammarch enters in Llangammarch Wells, though I haven't done this seciotn. I am told that it is class II with no portages. It is very pleasant to add the four kilometre section from here down to Garth either onto a Cammarch trip or onto a lower Ifron trip. This has nothing more than beautiful and quite exciting class II rapids and we have taken the Prospector down here a few times now.

Garth to Builth Wells: 11 km I to II; one rapid scrapes a III****

A pleasant touring river which is excellent for a first or second trip on moving water. The water is clear and often goes for a few weeks after rain. There are small rapids dotted along the way that reach up to grade II. About three-quarters of the way down is a tiny weir about six inches in height that you may not even recognise. As you round the sweeping bends in Builth Wells, and by a new estate appearing on the right hand side, is a slightly bigger rapid - which may, with a bit of imagination, just about reach grade III in big water. Finish on the Wye at the pay-and-display car park in Builth.

Afon Cammarch

Map:	Elan Valley & Builth Wells; no. 147
Grade:	I to II
Length:	5 km
Access:	A483 Builth to Llanwrtyd road
Notes:	piped bridge may need portaging
Quality:	***

In a medium flow this is a pleasant beginners' river which keeps its level for a good few days after heavy rain. However, it is best avoided in full flood.

Roman fort bridge to Irfon confluence: 5 km class II; one possible portage***

The A483 road crosses the river a few kilometres west of Garth. This is a convenient access point and the bridge even has seats built into it GR926504. The river is an excellent alternative start to the lower Irfon, or it can be paddled as a short trip in its own right. Paddle this water in a small group and you will see kingfisher, amongst other wildlife. At Dol-y-Gaer there is a piped bridge spanning the river, which is quite fun to plop through in a medium spate. However, in bigger water, this will almost certainly need to be **portaged** with care. There are a few, slightly bigger drops that just about hit the grade II mark as you enter Llangammarch Wells. There is excellent egress onto a small road that parallels the Irfon just below the confluence. Either finish here, GR934472, or continue down at grade II

Afon Dulas

Map:	Elan Valley & Builth Wells, no. 147
Grade:	II
Length:	5 km
Access:	A483 Builth to Llandovery road
Notes:	one easy weir; few fences - easy portages
Quality:	**

A pleasant, easy, spate tributary of the Irfon. The Irfon is an excellent touring river, but if you are paddling at this grade and the rivers are in spate, then this is a nice extra or alternative.

Glan Dulas bridge to Garth: 5 km grade I to II; one weir; few fences**

Turn off north in Garth; bear left and join the B4358. It is possible to access onto the river upstream from the left bank GR947532. The river needs to be at a good level, with no rocks visible at the put-in. The river is very pretty, with easy class I to II rapids as it winds down to Garth. A few fences needed portaging, but this was no great shakes. The wildlife is brilliant, and small groups will almost certainly see the flash of turquoise as the kingfisher leads off downstream. About halfway down is an obvious weir with a narrow salmon shoot on the right. This is easily shot in the middle of the main shoot. A few dilapidated footbridges are passed on the way to the egress - river right, above or below the two bridges in Garth GR949496.

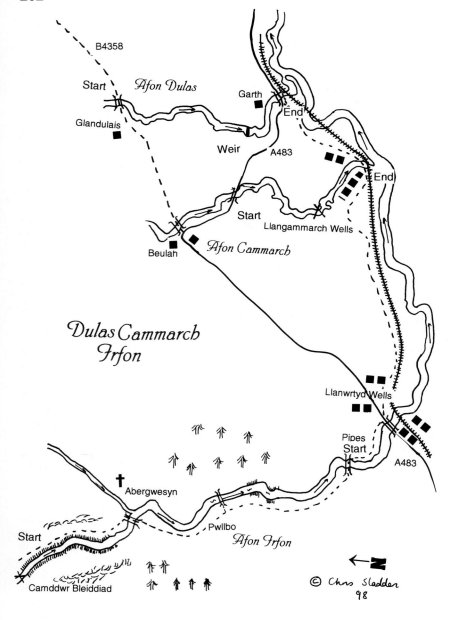

B4358

Start

Afon Dulas

Garth

End

Glandulais

Weir

A483

End

Start

Llangammarch Wells

Beulah

Afon Cammarch

Dulas Cammarch
Irfon

Llanwrtyd Wells

Pipes
Start

A483

Abergwesyn

Start

Pwllbo

Afon Irfon

Camddwr Bleiddiad

© Chris Sladder
98

Afon Chwerfri

Map:	Elan Valley & Builth Wells, no. 147
Grade:	II; one fall IV
Length:	10 km
Access:	C roads linking A483(T) Builth to Llandovery and B4358 Newbridge on Wye to Beulah
Notes:	one tree needed portaging at time of writing; one larger fall
Quality:	***

In big flood the river is undoubtedly dangerous at the grade. However, when in a reasonable flood and for a few days or so after heavy rain, the Chwerfri is a beautiful little river rushing, as it does, through a beautiful wooded valley.

Comin-y-Garth to Builth: 10 km II (one fall IV) ***

Turn off north opposite the public house in the little village of Cilmery, which is just along from Builth on the A483. By turning right, and then right again, it is possible to drive very close to the river at Comin y Garth GR980544. A convenient lay-by and short footpath leads down to the river where access can be had above a small footbridge. The river should be easily "floatable" but with a clear passage under this little bridge.

For the first kilometre or so the river winds around little bends and in between bowing branches before an excellent series of little rapids is reached. These carry on over the next four kilometres and at a decent water level there are plenty of little waves to surf on. A church on the right heralds the village of Cilmery (good alternative access/egress). Soon after Cilmery there was a large fallen tree blocking the river ('98) which needed a 30-second portage left.

A little while later Builth Wells Golf Course is reached. Here, a little surprisingly, perhaps, in between the two footbridges is a major double drop - **_a class IV rapid_**. If one were writing a guide book from the map only one might miss this! It is best to finish the run by passing under the bridge, joining the Irfon and soon the Wye itself to finish in the pay-and-display car park in Builth GR042512.

The Duhonw & Bach Howey

These are two tributaries of the Wye. On the maps both these rivers looked possibly excellent value. Both the rivers need good water; the Duhonw more than the Bach Howey.

We attempted the Duhonw river from a little side stream at Penllech GR016475. After **numerous** **portages** in the first kilometre, we pulled out leaving the gorge below well alone. From the get-out bridge at Llanddewi'r Cwm, where there are some exciting class IV drops, we checked upstream. There were four fallen trees in the first 150 metres. Enough said.

The Bach Howey is similar. It is a beautiful walk, but is fraught with fallen trees. Craig Pwll Ddu ('Crag of the Black Pool'), a beautiful waterfall, is about one kilometre up from the confluence with the Wye. Far better to wallow in the pool on a midsummer's night than to dodge tree after tree on a fraught river trip.

However, as this guide was going to press I was told there is a fishing group which is clearing the various tributaries of the Wye of all fallen debris. This is to encourage spawning salmon to ascend. And what salmon go up, paddlers come down - especially out of season!

Watch out for wildlife.

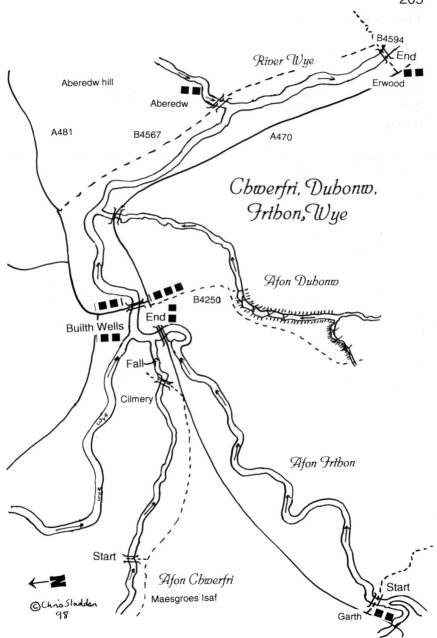

Aberedw hill

River Wye

B4594

End

Erwood

Aberedw

A481

B4567

A470

Chwerfri, Dubonw, Irthon, Wye

Afon Dubonw

B4250

End

Builth Wells

Fall

Cilmery

Afon Irthon

Start

© Chris Sladden
98

Start

Afon Chwerfri

Garth

Maesgroes Isaf

The Sgithwen Brook (a centre for the Wye)

Map:	Abergavenny & Black Mountains, no. 161
Grade:	IV to V (V+ to VI)
Length:	100 m (2 km)
Access:	A470(T)
Notes:	possibly a last, great challenge - possibly already run??
Quality:	***

The Sgithwen Brook roars its way into the Wye just below Hell Hole. On its right hand side is the beautiful Trericket Mill B&B plus bunkhouse. This is an ideal centre for groups visiting the Wye and bookings can be made via Alistair and Nicky Legge. Both Nicky and Alistair are particularly pro-young people, the environment and canoeing, so you can be assured of a relaxed and very comfortable stay (Trericket Mill, Erwood, Builth Wells, Powys LD2 3TQ, Tel. 01982 560312). The mill is on the left side of the A470(T) heading north towards Builth, just before Erwood bridge.

If you want more than relaxation and the Brook is 'full-on', then walk your boats up to below the little gorge and launch. The fence on the bridge can be lifted clear of the water by two ingenious ropes. This 100-metre section is a wonderful, photo-orientated blast. *Please note:* only go on here if the salmon have stopped spawning and the river is high.

No one, to my present knowledge (and local knowledge), has run the 'class VI' gorge above, though quite a few have enjoyed the lower thrills. It looks clean, but mighty mean in flood. Let me know if you know better!

Afon Edw

Map:	Elan Valley & Builth Wells, no. 147
	Presteigne & Hay on Wye, no. 148
Grade:	III to IV
Length:	12 km
Access:	A481 Builth to New Radnor and B4567 Builth to Aberedw road
Notes:	serious in high flood. At last time of paddling ('98) two trees needed portaging and one or two fences sneaking
Quality:	***

The Edw is a fine river that needs to be up to make it worth paddling. In flood it is dangerous as it piles down quickly over drops, stoppers, waves and, more importantly, through trees. Therefore, certainly in high water, it is not an intermediates river though when low it is quite pleasant. It is a surprisingly long river but has various escape routes should this be necessary.

Cregrina to Wye confluence: 12 km grade III to IV; few portages***

Work your way either upstream from Aberedw or via the A481 to the small village of Cregrina. Here, access can be made downstream right of the bridge and, indeed, this is the place to check-out whether you like what you see GR123521. Far from being grade II+, as it is in low water, the first drop, 50 metres downstream of the bridge, is class III+ to IV in big flood. There are two *meaty stoppers* to deal with - shoot far left. When lower it is **much** easier.

From below this awakening, the river rips off downstream for about 500 metres until a fallen tree is reached. In medium water this can be sneaked right and, in high flood, there is a sneak route far left. The water rushes down through low branches (easier medium water). A few kilometres further on, two static caravans and steepening of the water into a bouncy rapid give warning of a big drop approaching. This is just below a metal footbridge but by this time in big water you are well on your way, so get out above. Llanedw Falls is a reasonable class IV in medium water and a stiff IV in flood.

The water eases off to the next road bridge, under which is a good fall. A little farther on and a beautiful small gorge is entered with some exciting water. A few more bridges are passed along the way, with the odd drop you may want a quick look at. Below the picnic site are some fantastic stoppers and waves to shoot.

Aberedw bridge is next, after which a super gorge is entered. About 200 metres or so down this, the New Year storms of '98 have deposited a large tree that could at a pinch be sneaked on the left but is best portaged right (ask permission). Below this are some great III to IV rapids. The final flourish above the old railway bridge and the B4567 is worth inspecting for the right line as, especially under the bridge, there is no stopping. Egress river right just before joining the river Wye - roaring its way downstream GR077468.

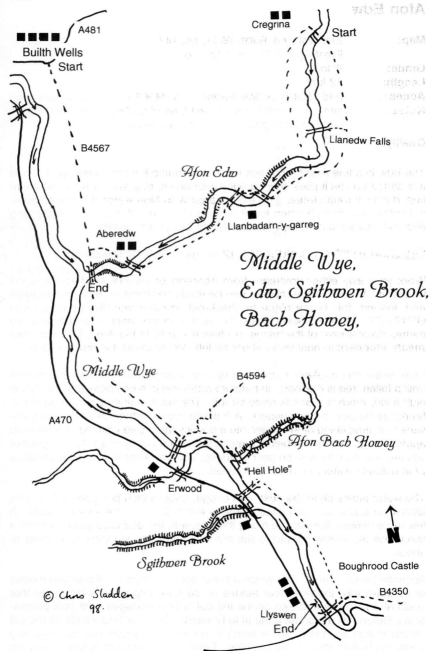

A481

■■■■ /
Builth Wells
Start

■ ■
Cregrina
Start

B4567

Afon Edw

Llanedw Falls

Aberedw
■ ■

Llanbadarn-y-garreg

End

Middle Wye,
Edw, Sgithwen Brook,
Bach Howey,

Middle Wye

B4594

A470

Afon Bach Howey

"Hell Hole"

Erwood

N

Sgithwen Brook

Boughrood Castle

© Chris Sladden
98.

B4350

■ ■
■ ■
Llyswen
End

Afon Llynfi

Map:	Abergavenny and the Black Mountains, no. 161
Grade:	I to II
Length:	7 km
Access:	A438 Bronllys to Talgarth road
Notes:	a few fences need care
Quality:	*

Natural weir-like falls towards the end liven up a pretty tedious trip. However, in the right water, these all provide excellent stopper waves.

Bronllys to Glasbury: 7 km grade I to II*

Start at Bronllys Castle bridge GR150346. The rapid above the bridge should be well-covered. The run is a fairly tedious grade I with a few fences to portage. However, towards the bottom half of the river are three partially natural weir drops that, in high water, have excellent playful stopper waves (you could start the run by getting on at the next bridge down, Pontithel). Thankfully you eventually reach the Wye, where you cross the river and egress on the left bank above the bridge in Glasbury.

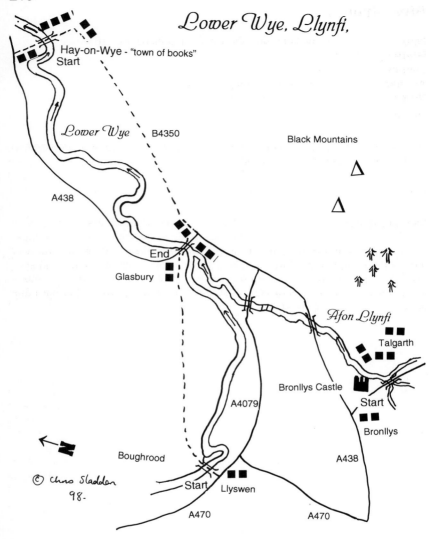

Lower Wye, Llynfi,

Hay-on-Wye - "town of books"
Start

Lower Wye   B4350

Black Mountains

A438

End

Glasbury

Afon Llynfi

Talgarth

Bronllys Castle

Start

A4079

Bronllys

N

Boughrood

A438

© Chris Sladden
98-

Start   Llyswen

A470   A470

Afon Rheidol

Map:	Aberystwyth & surrounding area, no. 135
Grade:	V +
Length:	7 km
Access:	A44 Llangurig to Aberystwyth road
Notes:	various portages
Quality:	**** for the adventure *not the paddling*

About eight years ago or thereabouts, when I was still a medical student, I got a placement out in Aberystwyth. Not many people from Cardiff chose to go there, - but at the time I hadn't paddled many of the local rivers so it was ideal for me. One day I persuaded Paul Howells, David Holloway plus a few other hapless individuals to come and do the mighty gorge. I had been told that it was a great paddle. Many hours, and much blood, sweat and tears later, the phrase, "you've been Rheidol-ed" was born!

To my mind, this is more a gorge walk with canoes - but most of the drops have been paddled. Indeed, in high water, some of the rapids would be brilliant but the portages would be fraught, if not impossible. I only know of low to medium level descents of the river. Still go there if you will, but take ropes, abseil harnesses, know-how, torches and time.

Ponterwyd to Allt y Gigfran footbridge: 7 km V+; various portages****

Heeding the above health warning, put on from the A44 road bridge. Just enough water in the channel is a suitable level for the adventure - enough to barely allow passage over the first rock strewn weir. Soon a steep gorge is entered via a rock bash of a fall which you may wish portage. If you are already starting to regret the day then it is not too late to bail out.

As you continue a further gorge is reached. The entrance rapid is a vicious, narrow, undercut chicane. With some ingenuity it is possible to do a sneaky portage and jump into the pool below therefore avoiding the unpleasantness of the drop. If the paddling isn't great then the rock sculptures most certainly are - this is a beautiful place to be.

Parson's Bridge is approached from where there is a possible escape - indeed, you may wish to trek in to here to get a feeling of the run GR749792. Over the next kilometre or so there are interesting manoeuvres to be made with two large and unpleasant drops to be negotiated. Tagged on to the end of one of these drops is a stunningly beautiful 30-foot waterfall. Far better to slide down the left hand rocks on your backside than to risk shooting it, as the plunge pool is deceptively shallow. There are just one or two places where it is deep enough to take a short boat but ankles break from this height so be warned. It has seen a few descents though. Below this are a few good rapids but more potential portages on the way down to a major waterfall. Gyfarllwyd falls are a certain portage even for the brave of heart. Abseiling ability is a plus here as you try and work out the best way to get into the pool below. However, from experience it was amply deep enough to jump into and certainly a lot quicker than using ropes. However, the water does run out of the pool and immediately **sump badly under the rocks below**. So don't get swept over. It is possible to scrape up the steep wooded banks on the right and pick up an escape footpath - but this is a real effort.

Below this, the river eases off with just the occasional grade III to IV rapids over the next two kilometres down to Allt y Gigfran footbridge GR726782. This is reached by a minor road which parallels the true right hand bank of the river. On the way down this section you will pass the stunning Mynach Falls cascading below the Devils Bridge. The lower section of the river is also canoeable at around grade II to III but I have not ventured onto here.

Afon Diliw / Afon Ystwyth

Map:	Aberystwyth & surrounding area, no. 135
Grade:	IV to V
Length:	9 km
Access:	via Aberystwyth, or via the Elan Valley from Rhayader
Notes:	top-notch sections in flood
Quality:	*****

The combination of the Diliw and Ystwyth, or upper section of the Ystwyth is a brilliant spate run. In big water, the upper parts will put most paddlers to the test; this run is of superb quality.

Afon Diliw / Afon Ystwyth to Cwmystwyth: 9 km grade IV and V*****

Access can be made either by taking the small Elan Valley road from Rhayader, or by making your way towards Cwmystwyth from the coast. At Blaenycwm, it is possible to take a rough track up to the access on the Diliw GR843773. There is a ford here but, in conditions of spate when the run is on, it is unlikely you would want to take a vehicle through. It is possible to trek upstream from the ford where there is a big but canoeable drop, but most will start the run at the ford. The run starts off easily enough until **Author's Boat Gorge is reached**. The name tells a sad tale; the water is grade V until the confluence with the Ystwyth.

Alternatively, put in on the Ystwyth above this confluence, as high as you dare. There is one kilometre of serious grade V paddling, with various pinning possibilities. A little way below the confluence there is an old stone arch, where the water sumps on the right. Run this left. There are certain blind bends on this river, though all rapids go in the right place. Inspect if in doubt. Egress is at Cwmystwyth bridge, before which a small weir and gorge are negotiated GR789739 - brilliant - I bet you'll be back! Below here are two gorges, **neither of which I have got around to trying, and therefore the information is second hand**. The first is grade IV to V, depending on water levels with a possible portage at a dam through which the water flows. The second is an altogether more torrid affair and has only been attempted at low water with a lot of tedious portages. From the second gorge down to Aberystwyth is a class II to III run. There is at least one weir in the harbour but I know little else about this paddle.

214

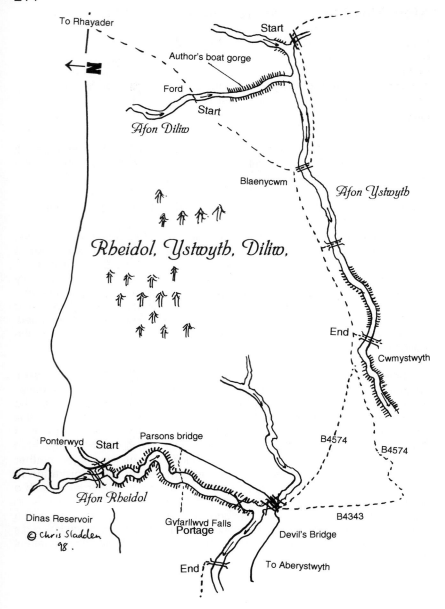

To Rhayader

N

Author's boat gorge

Ford

Start

Start

Afon Diliw

Blaenycwm

Afon Ystwyth

Rheidol, Ystwyth, Diliw.

End

Cwmystwyth

Ponterwyd   Start   Parsons bridge

B4574

B4574

Afon Rheidol

Dinas Reservoir

© Chris Sladden
98.

Gyfarllwvd Falls
Portage

Devil's Bridge

B4343

End

To Aberystwyth

SOUTH WALES

Jon was a bit surprised to find that he hadn't done the first descent of Cenarth Falls.

Afon Aeron

Map:	Lampeter, Llandovery & surrounding area, no. 146
Grade:	sections of grade I and II to III
Length:	24 km
Access:	A482 Aberaeron to Lampeter road
Notes:	four potentially dangerous weirs
Quality:	***

The Aeron is a beautiful river flowing, as it does, through rich pastureland before steepening during its final journey towards Cardigan Bay. The upper section is fine for touring and beginners, whilst the bottom grade II to III sections have more play and white water potential.

Llangeitho to Ciliau Aeron: 15 km class I; no portages ***

By taking the A482 Aberaeron to Lampeter road, and turning off in Temple Bar towards Llangeitho you cross the river on the B4342, in Llangeitho itself GR618598. Access can be made from this little bridge or, indeed, any of the other bridges that cross the Aeron further down and have public footpaths leading from them.

Once on water, the paddling is a gentle grade I through an open and picturesque valley. The only real problems are occasional bushes to dodge or fences to sneak. Below Trefilan the river feels canalised and the canoeist is constantly on the guard for weirs - which, thankfully, never appear. Get out either on the left bank and onto the old dismantled railway at Ciliau Aeron, GR503592, or at the next bridge down via the right hand footpath GR500597.

Cilau Aeron to Aberaeron: 9 km class II to III; four weirs in Aberaeron (portages) ***

Choose an access to the river from one of the above choices. In spate, this is a great run with little stoppers and weirs to play in as you travel on down to town. The eddies are well-defined so this is a great training run for those paddling at the grade. The section is really enjoyable, with the only real hazard being the possibility of a tree down.

Between the two bridges in town - in fact just upstream of the (lower) A487 bridge and just out of sight of the road - are **four unpleasant weirs**. Nasty even in low spate, they become **potential killers in flood** and I recommend a portage. Fortunately, this is very easy and only takes about one minute along the right-hand footpath. The angling club don't seem opposed to paddlers so I would urge all canoeists to keep off this river during the fishing season. In fact it was a local fisherman who told me the story of the **Aeron raft race** which ended in near disaster in one of these weirs - **beware**. Egress in the harbour by the convenient slipway on river left, just before the Aeron empties into the sea GR454629. If the sea is rough then this can be a wild finish! When the tide is on the flood take care not to get washed out to sea!

Afon Arth

Map:	Lampeter, Llandovery and surrounding area, no. 146
Grade:	IV
Length:	5 km
Access:	A487(T) Aberaeron to Aberystwyth road
Notes:	Trees
Quality:	*

"The river would be a brilliant run but it is ruined by fallen trees": this is what I wrote in the *White Water Runs* series back in '94. I gather that during the winter of '97- '98 things much improved. I look forward to a return journey when I am next out west.

Pennant to Aberarth: 5 km class IV*

Take the B4577 Aberarth to Pennant road where access can be made onto the spate by a little bridge, GR513631. This is by a particularly pleasant little pub. The run is a classic class IV paddle full of drops, falls, slides and shoots. However, be cautious, because when I ran it in '94 many trees crisscrossed the river which certainly dampened the spirits and darkened the gloom. Egress above or below the excellent Corsica-like falls in town GR479638.

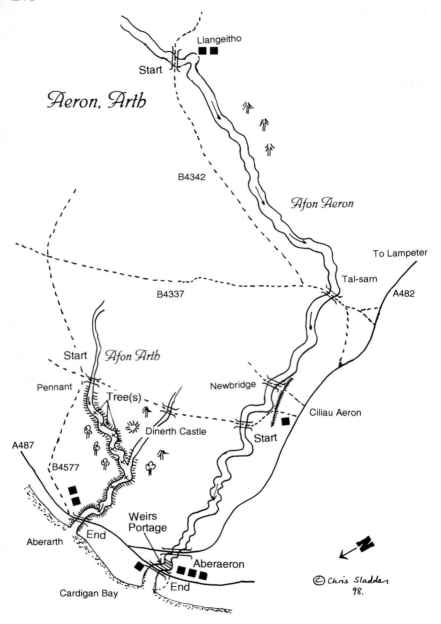

Aeron, Arth

Llangeitho

Start

Afon Aeron

B4342

To Lampeter

Tal-sarn

B4337

A482

Start

Afon Arth

Pennant

Newbridge

Tree(s)

Ciliau Aeron

Dinerth Castle

Start

A487

B4577

Weirs
Portage

End

Aberarth

Aberaeron

End

Cardigan Bay

© Chris Sladden
98.

Afon Teifi

Map:	Cardigan & surrounding area, no. 145
	Lampeter, Llandovery & surrounding area, no. 146
	Elan Valley & Builth Wells area, no. 147
Grade:	sections of II, III, IV and V
Length:	79 km
Access:	Cardigan to Tregaron roads
Notes:	one dangerous weir
Quality:	sections of*** and****

The Teifi is of one of the longest rivers found entirely in Wales. Its source is from the Teifi pools high up on a plateau of barren moorland known as the Elenydd. It is one of the finest areas of high-lying wild grasslands left in Britain, especially so for Wales as parts have escaped the ravages of the forestry people. Ravens, buzzards and kites may be found, in addition to the various rare bog plants. Theoretically, it should be possible to paddle the whole river from source to sea, though I haven't done this.

It is a delightful river, excellent for touring in Canadian canoes and kayaks alike, with some sections great for play-boating. It is also one of Wales' finest salmon rivers and, as such, is best avoided in fishing season unless prior arrangements have been made. Saying this, there is a long tidal section finishing in Cardigan, which really shouldn't cause many confrontations.

Pont Gogoyan to Lampeter: 14 km grade I to II (OS sheet no. 146)***

Drive out of Lampeter on the A482, before turning off left on the B4343. Just before the quaint village of Llanddewi Brefi there is a sharp left hand turn that crosses the river at Pont Gogoyan. Access can be made just downstream of the bridges on river right GR643544.

The section down to Lampeter is a beautiful touring stretch with nothing harder than a few easy grade I or II rapids. Egress onto the main A482, via a public footpath, where the river sweeps next to the road just before town. The King's Head pub in town serves some of the best bar meals in West Wales.

Lampeter to Maesycrugiau: 17 km grade I***

I haven't done this section, but have had it described as a fine grade I touring stretch. However, it is important to note the one grade III at the egress/access point to the next section.

Maesycrugiau to Newcastle Emlyn: 25 km II to III (one III to IV); one weir - portage (OS sheets 146 & 145)****

Maesycrugiau can be reached from either the A475 or A485, but either route will probably require a road map to help. It is possible to park up in the village near the inn without causing too much disturbance to the villagers but this is not a good spot for mini-buses! There is a small church room nearer the bridge than the pub, but it would be impolite to park here without first asking. After walking down the road to the bridge a footpath can be seen bearing off right, which allows access above or below a grade III fall. GR473411. This is Maesycrugiau Falls, a one-hit wonder which becomes easier in higher water.

From here to Llandysul the river weaves and meanders, with the occasional good surfing wave. In town the river picks up to give just under one kilometre of grade II to III water. This is better in low to medium flows and the last drop known, amongst other things, as the Cauldron, can become quite tricky. In higher water the section becomes somewhat washed out. Just by the bridge, which allows alternative access and egress, is one of the previous sites of *White Water Consultancy* - this has now moved to the banks of the Gwili.

About four kilometres below town the river passes under a railway bridge. A 100 metres further on is a right hand, left-hand swing of the river passing under the road bridge at Pont Allt y Cafen, GR386392. **The weir immediately below the bridge is dangerous at medium to high flows, and has unfortunately already caused the death of a popular South Wales canoeist.** It is best portaged on the right just before, or with great care, just after the bridge. The rapids below the bridge are excellent surfing territory, which are far better fun than this vicious weir above.

Some three kilometres further on are the classic grade III(+) Henllan Falls. It is as well to be aware of trees here, as I have seen one, in particular, cut and chained to maintain its position blocking off much of the rapid! There are one or two unfriendly people hereabouts!

Received on a postcard was the following anecdote:

If chased for about ten kilometre down the river Teifi by an irate fisherman, how about using the excuse that you are writing a guide book for canoeists to pacify him!!

The river eases off apart from the odd good surfing wave on its way down to the egress point. Get out a 100 metres or so above the Newcastle Emlyn salmon ladders into the convenient car park on river right. This is by the rugby grounds GR313409.

Newcastle Emlyn to Cardigan: 23 km II, one fall IV to V (OS sheet 145)****

A few hundred metres along the A475 from Newcastle Emlyn is a small turn off into a car park serving the local rugby grounds and playing fields. This offers excellent access onto the river at the above grid reference point. Just below are the Newcastle Emlyn salmon ladders. Awesome in major flood, they are usually safer to run on the right. The stoppers can be great fun for playing in or being played with. However, this needs to be assessed on the day. The chicken shoot far right offers an alternative line. From here on down to the main road bridge are some excellent surfing waves.

From here to Cenarth the river is flat. Cenarth Falls, an inspiration to many artists, is reached. They can be heard roaring and a rumbling a little way upstream. Many clubs come here, just to run the falls at medium to low water levels. Although reputedly runnable at any level, at certain flows the stopper on the main left-hand route looks decidedly unpleasant. A chicken shoot is available far right but choose your line carefully as, in places, the water falls into a V-shaped ledge. Some may wish to end the run here, and there are excellent egress amenities.

The section below is effectively flat but fast-moving and is particularly suited to families or those wanting a lazy afternoon paddle. Below Llechryd, the river enters a solemn gorge. This almost feels prehistoric as you wait for the rumble of mighty cataracts around the next bend. Fortunately, or unfortunately, depending upon your viewpoint, these never come. Cilgerran Castle sits rather moodily on the left-hand bank as you drift by. This is well worth visiting with the children later on.

Below the old bridge in the picturesque town of Cardigan is a council pay-and-display car park that provides an admirable egress on the true right hand bank GR176460.

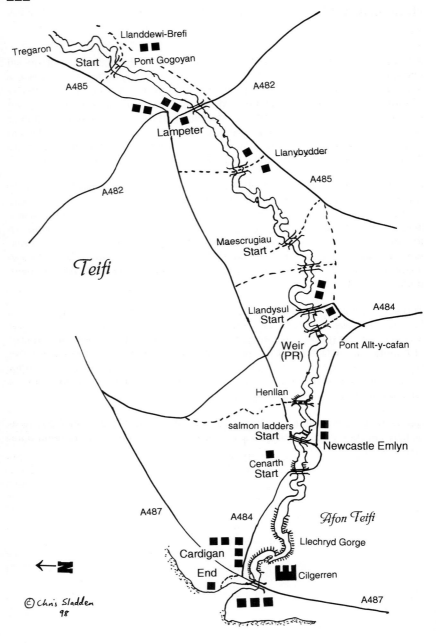

Tregaron

Llanddewi-Brefi

Start

Pont Gogoyan

A485

A482

Lampeter

Llanybydder

A482

A485

Teifi

Maescrugiau
Start

Llandysul
Start

A484

Weir
(PR)

Pont Allt-y-cafan

Henllan

salmon ladders
Start

Newcastle Emlyn

Cenarth
Start

A487

A484

Afon Teifi

Llechryd Gorge

Cardigan

End

Cilgerren

A487

© Chris Sladden
98

Afon Cothi

Map:	Lampeter, Llandovery and surrounding area, no. 146
Grade:	II to III
Length:	35 km
Access:	A482 Llanwrda to Lampeter road
Notes:	trees are a problem. Abergorlech gorge used to have a large tree strainer but this wasted away in '94 or thereabouts.
	However, the storms of '97-'98 ...
Quality:	***

An excellent touring river through pleasant surroundings with the odd surprise in store. Unusual in having no man-made weirs.

Brynteg to Tywi confluence: 35 km grade II to III***

Take the small right hand turn off the A482 (coming from Llanwrda) just before crossing the river at Pumsaint. Follow this to the bridge at Brynteg GR684433, where access may be had from the footpath on the right bank. The river needs to be fairly high to make the run worthwhile. A wire slung low and fallen trees needed some careful negotiating but they were fairly obvious (apparently just before the storms of '97/'98 the channel was clear of trees) . A short distance on and you may be surprised (especially so in flood) to see vehicles driving through the river. This is only the Landre fording point (*the best thing about river fords is trying to ride the bow waves behind Landrovers* - an old South Wales proverb!). In point of fact, fords are common on many Welsh rivers, but don't try them crossing them by vehicle when the water is up!

The Pumsaint bridge (A482) has barbed wire slung from it and needs caution in high water. Tributaries swell the river but make it no harder than the odd grade II as it flows towards Abergorlech. As the banks close in and significant afforestation occurs, the Abergorlech gorge is approached. This is similar in formation to the Sawdde gorge, in as much as the rounded rocks make access and egress slippery. It is wise to get out on the right hand footpath and inspect the next few 100 metres or so, if you are new to paddling. During my first run of the Cothi, I remember a tree choke that blocked the whole river requiring a difficult portage. This had gone in '94, but could always be blocked again.

The river opens out for a while, but the banks close in again after the bridge at Ynysowen. There are some good playspots and swirls here. Egress is best river right by the B4310 road bridge just after the confluence with the Tywi, GR493203.

224

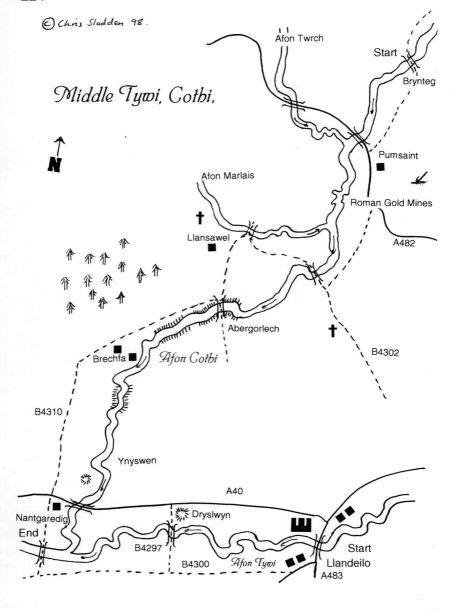

© Chris Sladden 98.

Middle Tywi, Cothi,

N

Afon Twrch

Start

Brynteg

Pumsaint

Afon Marlais

Roman Gold Mines

A482

Llansawel

Abergorlech

B4302

Brechfa

Afon Cothi

B4310

Ynyswen

A40

Dryslwyn

Nantgaredig

End

B4297

B4300

Afon Tywi

Start

Llandeilo

A483

Afon Doethie

Map:	Lampeter, Llandovery and surrounding area, no. 146
	Elan Valley & Builth Wells area, no. 147
Grade:	IV with two grade VI falls
Length:	10 km
Access:	needs OS map
Notes:	isolated possible portages
Quality:	***

There are two rivers, tributaries of the Tywi, that make great adventures. Both require long shuttles but give paddling in a true wilderness situation.

Blaendoithie to Junction Pool: 10 km grade IV with two grade VI falls (possible portages)***

The shuttle is awesome, by British standards, and it is best to use a driver who doesn't paddle. Access is onto the Doithie Fawr at GR742543 where the river should be in good spate. The river has various grade III and IV drops with flat sections between them. In the middle are two waterfalls which have now both been paddled. Egress at Junction Pool GR778466.

Afon Pysgotwr

Map:	Lampeter, Llandovery and surrounding area, no. 146
Grade:	V to VI
Length:	7 km
Access:	requires OS map
Notes:	various portages
Quality:	***

I have get to get around to doing the Pysgotwr and these notes have been handed down by a few paddlers - make of them what you will.

Bryn Glas to Junction Pool: 7 km grade V to VI***

Probably the least boring access into the Pysgotwr Fawr is via the small roads from Llanddewi Brefi GR738515. The first three kilometres will be a flat scrape at suitable levels to do the gorge ie. a low flood level is probably the best level for the gorge.

Though rumours abound, much of this wild chasm is probably still to be paddled. Between Craig Pysgotwr and Cribyn Du there are many hard falls and combinations of drops. A kilometre or so before the Doethie confluence, the river eases off to numerous excellent grade III and IV drops. Egress at Junction Pool.

Afon Tywi

Map: Elan Valley & Builth Wells area, no. 147
                      Lampeter, Llandovery & surrounding area, no. 146
                      Swansea, Gower & surrounding area, no. 159
Grade: Sections of I, II, III, and IV to V
Length: Over 80 km of paddling
Access: Off A40(T) Llandeilo to Llandovery road
Notes: Various portages in upper gorge
Quality: sections of*** and**** and*****

The Tywi is one of the longest rivers in the Wales and has something for every canoeist. It is truly a great river with hard rapids and challenges on its upper reaches, and with beautiful touring sections further down. Kayakers and canoeists, hard men and families will all find something to suit them on this lovely river.

<u>Llyn Brianne to Junction Pool</u>: 3 km IV to V; several portages in lower gorge****

From Llandovery take the small road signed posted to Llyn Brianne dam. The river tends to flow quite a few days after heavy rain when the pipes will be releasing, or when flood water is still running over the spillway. It is, therefore, common to be able to do the river at good flows and with the sun shining. It runs through one of the most beautiful valleys in Britain. Occasionally, a large release is made from the dam in the summer months to allow passage for migrating fish. This makes for one of those stolen moments - a midsummer British flood.

Access to the river is down the steep track below the dam to the bottom of the spillway, GR792484. Canoeing down this spillway is great fun (allegedly) but is highly illegal and shouldn't be done. Legend has it that this was first run by an Irish navvy on a shovel - who apparently received significant burns to his nether regions!

The first gorge is entered with a rapids being grade III to IV depending upon water release. If you find this hard going, then it is possible to get out above the nature trail weir and make your way up to the road. Whether the meshwork and weir are shootable depend very much on the water level. The second gorge is in two parts. The first half is grade IV to V, and has the infamous undercut rock rapid halfway down. Many a paddler has found their way under this large boulder, but there has never yet been a tree jammed in it: ***Beware***. The second part, after the left hand sweep, has various portages that need to be made. Some parts can be run at grade IV and V. In a huge flood there is a line down all of it, yet to see all the sheep stuck under rocks at low water has put off everyone to date. In addition to the sheep, there has been a succession of boats that have also found various places to spend time out!

Egress at Junction Pool or at the next bridge down, GR773460. Junction Pool itself is a beautiful place for picnics but, just occasionally, as stated above, the dam gives a big release so don't let the children play in the river bed.

Burial chamber bridge to Dolauhirion Bridge: 16 km class II to III*****

About three kilometres before the dam, and just before the road becomes very steep, there is a bridge across the river which gives good access to the water. Or, by following the track on the other side of the river, it is possible to reach the aforementioned Junction Pool. This is one of the best grade II touring sections in the country. It run us through a stunningly beautiful valley. In full flood the grade goes up a notch, but normally it runs with a blue hue and this is the time for kayaks and Canadian canoes alike.

The river is best done when all three pipes are spilling and the overflow is running, which gives a normal high but not flood condition. The character of the river is of sweeping grade II bends with various gorges where the water swirls myriad blue and green. Above the first gorge at Penrhyn there is a stopper guarding the chasm entrance. This is easily missed or, if you like, played in. There are only two rapids that make the paddler stop and think. The first, on a sharp left-hand bend below the bridge to Cilycwm, consists of a drop either side of large boulder. In big water this has a large hole behind it. The second, a longer rapid, is right at the get-out at a Dolauhirion bridge, GR762361.

Dolauhirion to Llandeilo: 25 km II (one III); no portages*****

Dolauhirion bridge is about two kilometres north of Llandovery and can be reached by a road on either side of the river. Access can be made to the next beautiful touring section of the river from here. Again, this stretch is suited to kayaks and Canadian canoes alike.

The Tywi starts to lose its gorged-in feeling as the river opens out. There is one bouncy rapid with a great play stopper on it, just below the bridge in Llandovery (class III in high flows). The water is fairly fast down to Ashfield where alternative access or egress can be had. A further alternative access for the lower part of the river is to get on at the Llangadog Common bridge, GR706277, and bounce down the last few broken weirs on the Afon Sawdde.

From here to Llandeilo, the water loses its haste and it begins to drift more lazily towards the sea. The Cennen then enters from the left, and the splendid old stone bridge in Llandeilo is reached. Egress can be made river left, downstream side of the bridge, though parking is difficult. Alternatively, although it adds to the trip (or shortens the next one), egress and access are easier at the next bridge down, GR589214.

Llandeilo to Nantgaredig bridge: 21 km I to II; no portages***

Access as above, GR628219 or GR589214. This is superb for family canoeing and holidays. At one point I was able to see three ancient castles, an 18th century tower and the best of the RAF roaring overhead. From old to new in one moment of time. An alternative access or egress spot is to pull out up-stream right of Dryslwyn bridge. The castle is excellent, which kids both young and old will love. With the Cothi entering on the right the river swells in volume, and you hurry down to Nantgaredig bridge where there are some small waves to play upon. Egress downstream right via the public footpath, GR493203.

Nantgaredig bridge to Gwili confluence: 9 km class I

For some reason I haven't got around to tackling this nine-kilometre section of river, but I have it on good authority that it is a pleasant a class I run with no nasty surprises. Perhaps another year.

A40(T) Gwili bridge to Llanstephan Boat House: 19 km grade I***

The access point to the lower section of the river is somewhat up in the air at the moment. The old get-out point to the Gwili may well need to be revised because of the building of a new bypass. At the moment it is possible to get on the last 500 metres of the Gwili from the A40 trunk road, or from the series of public footpaths and the old railway embankment that run from it. This section of river is tidal and you may well want to time your paddle, though this isn't always necessary. As with any other tidal river mentioned in this book it de-serves respect in its lower reaches. An alternative start can be made from the quayside in Carmarthen itself.

From here on down the river meanders through pleasant countryside with the odd bubbly rapid here and there. It is an excellent place to observe estuarine bird life. It is best to try and coincide paddling the last five or so kilometres, with the high tide. As the tide turns it will quicken your speed tremendously but still allow egress onto the right bank at the boating house in Llanstephan, GR362113. However, take care not to get shot out to sea! At lower water you will have to wallow through the mud banks to get off.

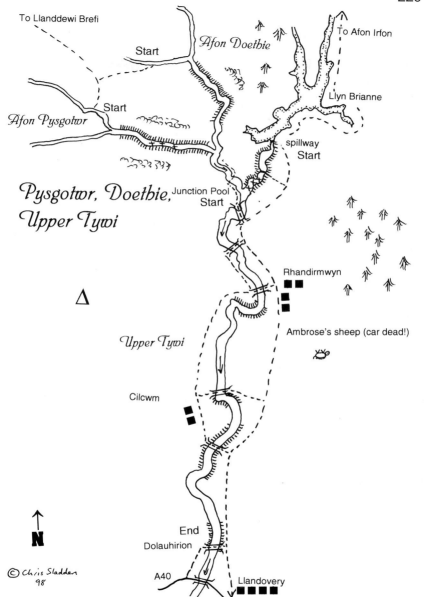

To Llanddewi Brefi

Start

Afon Doethie

To Afon Irfon

Llyn Brianne

Start

Afon Pysgotwr

spillway
Start

Pysgotwr, Doethie, Junction Pool
Start

Upper Tywi

Δ

Rhandirmwyn

Upper Tywi

Ambrose's sheep (car dead!)

Cilcwm

End
Dolauhirion

A40

Llandovery

N

© Chris Sladden
98

Afon Bran

Map:	Brecon Beacons, no. 160
Grade:	I to II
Length:	8 km
Access:	off A483(T) Llandovery to Builth road
Notes:	portages - one fence
Quality:	**

A beautiful little river with crystal clear water only somewhat spoilt by a few low trees and fences. One, usually shootable weir just below egress that needs care in high water.

Cynghardy to Llandovery: grade I to II (one portage - fence)**

Take the A483 Llandovery to Builth road up to the small village of Cynghardy where a left-hand road crosses the river at GR806400. Access can be had over the bridge arch itself onto the river bank. The water is only a gentle grade I but beware fences en-route down to the two small bridges about one kilometre below - I portaged one. Trees, too, can be a nuisance but improve greatly below the second bridge. A few broken boulder weir steps liven up the proceedings en-route to the road bridge. The wildlife is excellent. Below Maesllydan Hall bridge there are a couple of broken weirs which can be safely shot en-route down to egress on the right bank, just above the A4069 road bridge, GR772343. Alternatively, finish further down the Tywi - but be careful of the weir just below the bridge - which is nasty in big water.

Afon Gwydderig

Map:	Brecon Beacons, no. 160
Grade:	II to III; one fall of III to IV
Length:	11 km
Access:	A40(T) Llandovery to Brecon road
Notes:	one fence and one grade IV fall
Quality:	**

Following the main A40(T) into Llandovery, the Gwydderig is an excellent paddle and, despite the road's closeness, the paddler is soon hidden in the little gorges.

Halfway to Cwm Rhuddan bridge: 11 km grade II to III**

On the A40(T), just upstream of Halfway, there is a small layby on the true left hand bank GR837324. Like many other rivers of this type, there needs to be good flow at the access for the trip to be worthwhile. Three bridges down, there is a gauge that reads 7-8 on the lower scale at excellent levels.

A little way down, a shabby tin footbridge is reached. A little way further is a tasty little gorge with the first drop being grade III to IV. So long as no trees are down, both routes are fine. At time of writing, no trees required portaging, though one fence required care just down from the fall.

Further on, near Pentrebach, is a small weir shoot under a bridge. Further on under the bridge to Babel is a fast grade II to III fall which will be savoured by those new to the grade. The river changes character as it gets ready to join the majestic Tywi below Llandovery. True to the Tywi's character, Llandovery Castle is passed on the right (well worth a visit) and the River Bran, another grade II run, enters.

A few little weirs lie between here and the egress at the Cwm Rhuddan bridge GR760330.

Afon Dulais

Map:	Brecon Beacons, no. 160
Grade:	III
Length:	6 km
Access:	A482 Llanwrda to Lampeter road
Notes:	trees are a nuisance
Quality:	***

The Dulais is an excellent river full of surprises not seen from the road. Good fun can be had a few days after rain. The trees can be a bit of a nuisance, but all portages are easy and do not detract from a great little paddle.

Hafod Bridge to Llanwrda: 6 km grade III***

Take the A482 Lampeter road which follows the river through a wooded valley. Access can be made at the fifth crossing of the river which is just below the actual Hafod bridge GR698356. There should be ample water at the get-in for easy passage around the rock-strewn river bed. In flood the river becomes dangerous because of the tree hazard. A small grade II to III gorge just below the bridge gives a feel of this paddle. Grade II rapids, interspersed with grade III-type gorge enclosed drops, follow, and this is the essence of the river nearly all the way to Llanwrda. Two trees required portaging at time of writing and there were two fences that needed careful negotiating.

Egress is best by the War Memorial on river right, though some will want to shoot the small weir in Llanwrda and clamber out below. If you do, you should ask permission before clambering over any gardens to egress! GR713317.

Afon Dulais (The Halfway Dulais)

Map:	Lampeter, Llandovery and surrounding area, no.146
Grade:	I
Length:	5 km
Access:	A40(T) Llandovery to Brecon road
Notes:	one weir
Quality:	**

A gentle, lazy, summer afternoon paddle. Suitable for well-led newcomers.

Pyllau-cochion Bridge to Brynwgan Bridge: 5 km grade I; one weir**

A couple of miles to the east of Llandeilo is a turning off towards Talley, the B4302. There are two turnings within 50 metres of each other on the right, about six kilometres upstream of Rhosmaen. The first of the two provides good access onto the river GR656288. From here down peaceful meanders pass through beautiful countryside and under several small bridges. As long as the boat will float this can be done most times during the year and is an excellent beginners' trip. *It is best avoided in flood*.

There is one weir, strangely out of place, which is safe to shoot anywhere at low to medium level. This is just above the get-out and is obvious from the river. Egress just below the little broken step just beneath the following road bridge, reached by turning first right up the B4302 from Llandeilo GR645254.

233

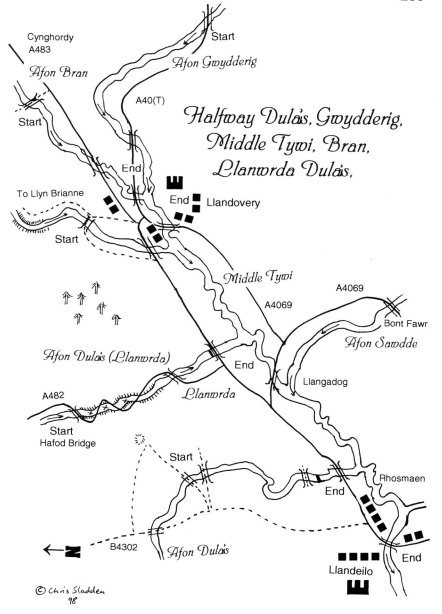

River Usk

Map: Brecon Beacons, no. 160
                 Abergavenny and the Black Mountains, no. 161
                 Cardiff, Newport and surrounding area, no. 171
Grade: sections of I, II, III (IV in spate)
Length: 104 km
Access: various points: A40 Abergavenny to Llandovery road
Notes: in high water, several of the natural weir steps can produce
                 dangerous stoppers and towbacks. If in doubt, portage.
Quality: *** and ****

Along with the Wye, the Usk is one of the most popular rivers in South Wales. It has sections to please most paddlers from bouncy upper rapids and beautiful lower touring stretches. It descends from the northern foothills of the Black Mountains range. Interestingly enough, when full to the brim, it normally shows a wild, red colour derived from the sandstone beds over which its numerous tributaries flow. There is an ongoing access agreement on the Usk, though this seams to be in a state of flux at the present. There appear to be fewer days available for canoeing every time I look, so I wait with bated breath. Extra permission is required to canoe through the Glanusk Estate. This is partially for the paddler's own good so as not to be peppered by shotgun pellets from the regular shoots held here. Seek advice from the access officer, WCA.

Pantysgallog to Brecon: 19 km grade II to III (map no. 160) ****

Passing westwards on the A40(T), four kilometres from Sennybridge, there is a small road on the left which crosses the river GR904292. Just above is a four-foot drop that can be shot (with care in high water). The river bubbles gently at grade II through pleasantly wooded banks towards Sennybridge. There is alternate access off the small road to the Sennybridge training camp GR919286. There are three main, natural weir drops on this section. The first, on a right hand bend, is fairly straightforward, although trees on the far right can be a problem. The second, a short distance after, needs to be inspected in high water as it forms a big stopper. The third, and biggest, drop is a little way on after some easy rapids. In spate, it forms a dangerous towback in its horse-shoe-shaped, left hand side. Portage if in doubt. In point of fact all of these drops can get a bit weir-like in high water and need to be run with care.

Grade II to III rapids take the paddler down to Brecon. Even in low water, there is a superb play stopper on one of these. In big flood much of the river is a big grade III roller coaster with numerous waves to shred. Egress may be made at the Aberbran bridge GR987292. The farmer is quite amenable when asked for permission. Better still is easy egress on the left hand bank into a car park on the outskirts of Brecon GR038289.

Brecon to Talybont: 14 km II to II+***

This excellent, gentle section is popular for beginners' groups and coach assessments! There is a shoot on the left of the large, sloping weir in Brecon which saves scraping over elsewhere. In flood this should be treated with care. Trees on bends are the only problems as the canoeist winds down gentle rapids, the Brecon Beacons overlooking you from the right. There is a small, broken weir a little way beneath the aqueduct, carrying the Monmouthshire and Brecon Canal. The river eases off more and meanders its way through gentle farmland. Egress is at the Llansantffraid to Talybont-on-Usk road bridge, reached by turning off the A40(T) road GR123233. Details of the access agreement may be seen here on the right.

Talybont-on-Usk to Llangynidr: 7 km grade III (IV)****

When full to the brim, this section rages down, usually with a brick red hue. It stays up after other rivers have dropped and, as such, is excellent at the grade. When in condition there are excellent play waves.

Grade I to II rapids lead into the Mill Falls, which begin soon after a church on the right bank. The falls are probably best run right to left to avoid a large stopper on the right, halfway down. In very high water, these falls may reach grade IV. In low water, a series of steps and pools exist. Please keep to the right banks if you have to get out. Bouncy water leads the paddler down to Llangynidr bridge where egress can be made on the left hand banks GR152203. Parking has to be on the far outskirts of the village and the people are friendly so don't upset them please!

Llangynidr bridge to Crickhowell: 11 km grade III (IV) - map no. 161****

Below the bridge there is a ledge which, in high water, forms a boat- and person-gobbling stopper from which many pub stories have originated. This is best avoided. A little way further is the so-called Spuhler's Folly ledge. This is best inspected for, at higher water levels, it can form a dangerous stopper. Portage if in doubt. This is the best of the river from the white water paddler's point of view. Egress is about a half a kilometre below Crickhowell on the right hand bank, where a suitable layby is found (A4077) GR218178. Alternatively continue for about four kilometres to the next bridge where there is easy access on the right hand bank GR241160.

Crickhowell to Caerleon: 71 km grade I to II - map nos. 161 and 171***

The trip can be shortened at will simply by choosing one of the many alternative get-on/ get- off points: an excellent section for those who enjoy touring the gentler river. Scramble down the steep right bank (egress for the previous section) at GR218178 or, perhaps better, the next bridge down. Trees are the only real problem on a river like this, especially where they hang over bends. The rapids never reach more than grade II and decrease in frequency en-route to Caerleon. Passing the Sugar Loaf on the left, Abergavenny is reached, where there is a small, broken weir directly below the main road bridge. The easiest route is through the right arch. If time permits, the castle and museum on the left are well worth a visit. Some way after Abergavenny, footpaths of the pretty Usk Valley Walk run alongside the river. Where the B4598 comes close to the river, some six kilometres short of Usk, is a small, boxed-in weir. This is obvious from the river with the weir buildings left. The stopper is quite fierce at high flows but, at normal levels, is no problem providing the canoe punches straight through without being caught sideways! Portage if in any doubt. A few broken steps take the paddler to Usk. The grassy banks by the main road bridge in Usk provide an alternative egress, thus saving 20-odd kilometres to Caerleon. Usk is a beautiful, small town full of pleasant watering establishments and is well worth a stop regardless.

The next stop is at the small road bridge at Newbridge-on-Usk GR385948. Egress is a bit scrambly up the left bank but the Newbridge Inn is very friendly and a beer feels good at this stage. The remaining section to Caerleon is tidal and is hard work if a big tide is on the flood. However, if you can time high water slack, or just after, it is possible to egress river left at the B4236 bridge and straight up into the Ship Inn GR342903. Low water is best avoided although the trudge up the steep mud bank isn't too grim. If you really want you can continue further to Newport docks but it isn't very inspiring.

Afon Crai

Map:	Brecon Beacons, no. 160
Grade:	II+ to III(+); one fall III+ in spate on Usk
Length:	7 km
Access:	off A4067 Swansea to Sennybridge road
Notes:	one bridge is a definite portage
Quality:	***

This is clearly a salmon-spawning river and should only be done when the water is high enough to amply cover all shingle beds, and also only when the fish have finished spawning. It is suitable for groups of three to four paddlers only. An excellent little river for the lower grade paddler, with a lively gorge to finish on.

<u>Felin Crai to Sennybridge</u>: 10 km grade II+ to III(+); one bridge portage***

Turn off the A4067 about two kilometres downstream of Cray reservoir and drive to the small bridge at Felin Crai GR882236. This is not suitable for large groups or those leaving minibuses - the locals are friendly - so let's keep it so. As stated above, this is a spawning stream for salmon and the river needs to be just below bank full to **ensure all beds are well covered**. *Salmo salar* has one of the most interesting of all nature's journeys. From its feeding grounds over the deep ledges of the Atlantic to its home rivers, the journey is fraught with dangers. From net to rod and gaff, the salmon is hunted by man on its passage home. Like the salmon, the canoeist is excited by the spate but must surely pass each others paths with equanimity.

The rapids barely touch grade II on the way down to the second (double) bridge at Tanyfedw. Trees are the only problem until now but this piped low bridge must be portaged (*left*). There are two more road bridges and then a smaller bridge which heralds the approach of the Crai gorge. A right hand bend leads excitingly into a kilometre of grade II to III drops (III+ in high water). Excellent play stoppers cry out for attention for most of the way until the paddler joins the Usk at Pantysgallog. Above the bridge is a four-foot drop III to III+ which can be shot (with care in flood) until easy water leads down to good access on the left bank in Sennybridge, GR920287.

Afon Cilieni

Map:	Brecon Beacons, no. 160
Grade:	III - with one fall of IV
Length:	3 km
Access:	A40T C road from Sennybridge to put-in
Notes:	trees are again a challenge but none needed portaging at time of paddling
Quality:	***

A medium grade spate tributary of the river Usk.

Pentre'r Felin to Park Farm bridge: 3 km class III (one rapid IV); no portages***

Turn off in Sennybridge northwards from the A40 trunk road up towards Pentre'r Felin. Access can be made (discreetly) in the village itself GR9020305. The water needs to be clearly in spate to be worth doing. Once on, the canoeist is immediately faced with a fast, tree-lined, class III torrent which requires some weaving to descend. There are some excellent waves and holes which fortunately lack the viciousness of the ones found on the Nant Bran. As you quickly reach the first proper road bridge at GR920305 there is a solid class IV rapid, which is exciting to shoot. This deserves inspection for the right line, though at time of paddling it was best run on the right-hand side because of an irritating tree growing from the sweeter, left-hand side: a wild buzz. It is better to continue on down through more fast water, join the Usk which will be really big and bouncy and finish one kilometre further down at the next bridge GR947296.

Afon Senni

Map:	Brecon Beacons, no. 160
Grade:	II+, plus two falls of grade III
Length:	7 km
Access:	A4215 Sennybridge to Merthyr road
Notes:	one weir; no portages
Quality:	***

An excellent river with good grade II+ rapids plus a harder section at the end. There is one weir which is shootable with care.

Heol Senni to Usk: 7 km grade II to III***

Turn off the A4215 Sennybridge to Merthyr road at the sign to Heol Senni. Access can be had at the bridge over the river. The river should be in at least a small flood to paddle. The clay lands it drains lends a brick red colour to the main flow, with certain streams adding a variety of chocolate browns to oranges. The river meanders down to under a farm bridge to the next road bridge, with trees being the only probable difficulty. Immediately under this bridge though is a sloping weir - **shootable with care left or right** avoiding central debris. There is a gauge on the left wall - good levels are between two and seven. If the gauge is covered, it is big water! Below are some excellent rapids leading down to Defynnog. Before the next road bridge is a particularly good set of stoppers and waves - which can certainly hold boats sidewards as you surf back and forth.

The water has now increased since after the addition of the Treweryn (no, not that one!) and there is a steep, good class III drop with a big bouncy run down middle to left. As you near the A40T road there is a powerful rapid right on the confluence with the Usk. *This is unnervingly difficult* to inspect or portage and is, therefore, best "sussed out" when you set up the shuttle. In flood there is a strong stopper across much of the flow but, at most levels, there is a route through on the far left if you don't fancy your chances on the charge. Egress 100 metres down the Usk at the "MOD access point", on the left bank, GR920286; or, continue further on down the Usk.

Nant Bran

Map:	Brecon Beacons, no. 160
Grade:	III - medium flows IV in spate
Length:	4 km
Access:	off A40(T) Brecon to Sennybridge road
Notes:	in spate trees are a major fright; the weirs become dangerous
Quality:	**

The river is grade III in medium spate but solid IV in flood conditions, when a certain amount of expertise is required to get down in one piece. In these conditions it is testing at the grade!

Tir y Felin to Aberbran: 4 km of grade III (IV)**

Turn off the A40 west of Brecon and cross the Usk at Aberbran. Take the small road up to Tir y Felin where access can be made to the river at GR965321. The river needs to be in at least 'medium flood' to be paddleable but, if over the banks, becomes highly dangerous. Trees are clearly a problem as you weave your way down this fast funnel of water. After about a kilometre there are a series of weir steps and drops. *In high flood the towbacks of a few of these become quite frightening* and you will want to carefully pick your line. The river gets better further down, and there are some superb waves to surf on, and stoppers to get thrashed in. Egress at the arched stone bridge and footpath just above the Usk GR987294.

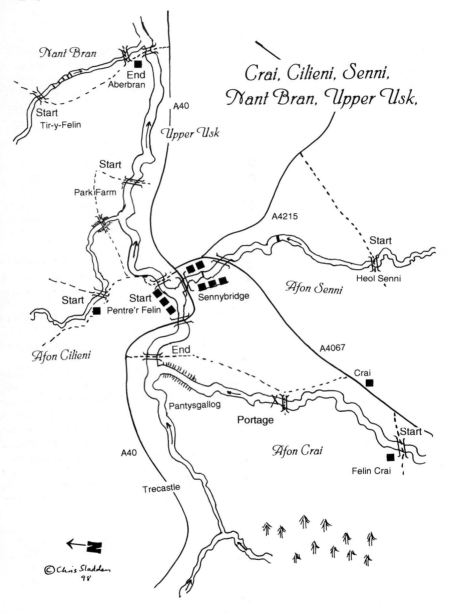

Nant Bran

End
Aberbran

Start
Tir-y-Felin

A40

Upper Usk

Crai, Cilieni, Senni,
Nant Bran, Upper Usk,

Start
Park Farm

A4215

Start
Heol Senni

Afon Senni

Start
Pentre'r Felin

Start

Sennybridge

Start

Afon Cilieni

End

A4067

Crai

Pantysgallog

Portage

Start

A40

Afon Crai

Felin Crai

Trecastle

© Chris Sladden
98

Afon Ysgir

Map:	Brecon Beacons, no 160
Grade:	III
Length:	11 km
Access:	back roads west of Brecon
Notes:	two weirs - one best portaged; trees and wires a problem
Quality:	**

The run can be shortened by getting on just above the confluence of the Ysgir Fawr and Fechan and Pont Faen. From here down is the best of the river. The Ysgir Fechan can be canoed at tree-ridden grade III from Yscirfechan Farm - but I haven't done this section.

Ty du Bridge to Pont ar Yscir: 11 km grade III; one portage**

Taking the small road west out of Brecon towards Cradoc (and the golf course) it is possible to reach the **egress** point at Pont ar Yscir GR003303. It is worth inspecting the small weir under the bridge, but more especially the large, boxed-in affair about 100 metres upstream. This forms a dangerous towback and is **best portaged** on the left at most levels when the river is worth doing. Using a large-scale map work yourselves upstream to Merthyr Cynog and take the road to Upper Chapel where it crosses the river at GR992382.

The first four kilometres are fraught with tree and wire dangers which may require portage depending on your herbiculture and barbed wire-dodging abilities. Below the small farm bridge at GR007356 the river begins to improve but even so, it may be best to access at Pont Faen from the convenient footpath. Below the little weirs in Pont Faen, the river alternates between grade II and III **natural** weir-like steps enclosed within a wooded gorge. Some of these provide excellent surfing waves and holes, and a good few hours can be spent in Beech Tree Gorge. After passing under the next footbridge, the above-described boxed-in weir is reached - **portage left**. Either egress right above the bridge, or take the *left* shoot of the small bridge weir and egress via the stile just below Pont ar Yscir.

Afon Tarell

Map:	Brecon Beacons, no. 160
Grade:	III (one fall III+ to -IV)
Length:	10 km
Access:	A470(T) Cardiff to Brecon road
Notes:	one weir - possible portage; one or two harder
Quality:	***

Not a bad river. Can be combined with one of the sections of the Usk to make a good day out. Like the other tributaries, the river needs to be in a medium spate to be a runnable.

Old Glanrhyd Bridge to Usk confluence: 10 km grade III; one weir ***

Opposite the A4215 turning off the main Merthyr to Brecon road is a small lane which crosses the river at a small bridge, GR984240. The river is best run in a medium spate, as when over its banks it becomes a bit hectic.

Almost immediately, a steep drop has to be contested with before the first of several mini-gorges is entered. Just above the road bridge, opposite the old people's home, is a steep horseshoe weir - the so-called "Zimmer Falls". It can be shot on the left of the main shoot in medium flows, but inspection is advised. If in doubt portage. Below here are some excellent step-like rapids and small broken weirs. If you pick your stoppers and waves, there are some that are excellent for surfing in. With the addition of the Nant Cwm Llwch the river swells and a little further on an island is reached. Island Falls is probably best taken on the left and reaches a good class IV in big flows. Visible from the bridge to the industrial estate is a stiff slot, the stopper of which has extracted one or two good paddlers from their boats over the years! Egress by the little road that parallels the river below the next-but-one bridge down, GR034284 or, if you like, on the Usk itself.

Afon Honddu

Map:	Brecon Beacons, no. 160
Grade:	III
Length:	6 km
Access:	B4520 Brecon to Builth road
Notes:	one brick weir above Brecon; canalized section with few weir drops as river enters Brecon
Quality:	**

The river needs to be in a reasonable spate to make it worth paddling. If *exceptionally* high there is one weir step below the B4520 road bridge in Brecon itself that is worth checking out. In exceptional conditions it produces a potentially nasty towback. The river has been paddled from Upper Chapel in big flows giving a further ten kilometres of II to III but I have not done it.

Llandefaelog to Brecon: 8 km grade II to III; a few weirs**

Turn off the B4520 in Llandefaelog where access can be made easily onto the flooded river. The river is grade II for the next three kilometres with small twists, turns and the odd tree to negotiate. A little way before the bridge at Llanddew is a sloping weir. This is an odd affair with vertical brick segments splitting the river into three channels. At most conditions there is a route straight through the centre or shooting the towback left and right. The river steepens and some bedrock steps with grippy stoppers have to be negotiated. As the river enters Brecon, there is an exhilarating kilometre of grade III over shoots and small weirs. Below the B4520 is one small, vertical step that requires caution in **exceptional flows** and, just below the next bridge, is an angled weir best taken by a right hand shoot. Egress with a sneaky beaky break out on the right hand bank, by the public toilets and car park right by Aber Honddu (the mouth of the Honddu) just under the next bridge, GR043286.

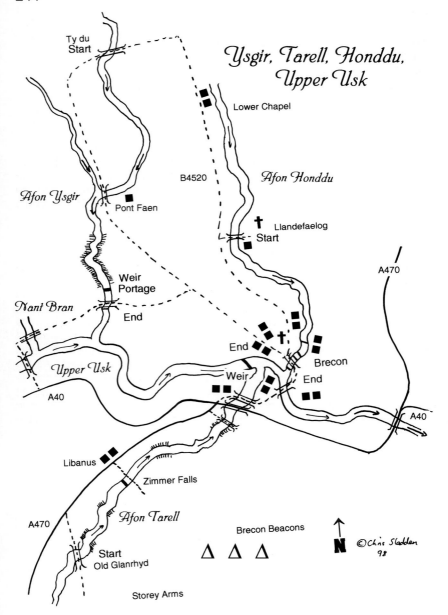

Ty du
Start

Ysgir, Tarell, Honddu,
Upper Usk

Lower Chapel

B4520

Afon Honddu

Afon Ysgir

Pont Faen

✝ Llandefaelog
Start

A470

Weir
Portage

Nant Bran

End

Upper Usk

End

✝

Brecon

A40

Weir

End

A40

Libanus

Zimmer Falls

A470

Afon Tarell

Brecon Beacons

Start
Old Glanrhyd

Storey Arms

△ △ △

↑
N

©Chris Sladden
98

Afon Caerfanell

Map:	Brecon Beacons, no. 160
Grade:	II to III
Length:	4 km
Access:	from the C road linking Talybont-on-Usk to Pontsticill
Notes:	three fences needed portaging
Quality:	*

A small spate stream worth doing if you happen to be passing. The upper section is apparently a great class V run but I haven't managed to drag myself upstream with a boat. The river eventually flows into the Usk at Talybont-on-Usk.

Forest Walk bridge to Talybont-on-Usk Reservoir: 4 km II to III*

This small stream is included for completeness and is probably only worth doing if passing. Three large deer fences spoil what otherwise would be a good spate run for its grade.

That said, if the water is brown and the rocks covered, start at the bridge about four kilometres above Talybont reservoir GR063170. The water is fine and fast enough but I found the fences a nuisance. Three portages were required at time of writing. Deer fences cannot be sneaked under. Take out at the reservoir and head down to the Star in the village for some sustenance.

Afon Grwyne

Map:	Abergavenny and the Black Mountains, no. 161
Grade:	II to III
Length:	6 km
Access:	A40 Abergavenny to Crickhowell road
Notes:	one possible weir portage if high water
Quality:	***

This is an excellent little river - one of the many canoeable tributaries of the Usk. Only paddleable after rain, the river rises and falls quickly after a downpour onto the Black Mountains.

Lower Cwm bridge to Glangrwyney: 6 km grade II to III; one weir possible portage***

Turn off the A40T, just Abergavenny side of the river, and make your way up the small roads towards Grwyne Fawr Reservoir. Good access can be made by a public footpath at Lower Cwm bridge onto the Grwyne Fechan GR245200. At times of writing, there was a single barbed strand swinging merrily over the flow exactly at the confluence with its bigger sister. From here down there are exciting little grade II and III shoots and drops. In the half-kilometre before Llangenny are some excellent little broken weirs, with only the trees being a possible annoyance. A little way downstream of Llangenny is a triple-stepped weir which *should be inspected on the way up* as it is obvious by the road. **In flood** it becomes very dangerous. Check out the bottom towback in particular, before committing yourself to the run. Far better to watch the occasional enormous salmon trying to loop out of the stopper rather than you, if the water is very big. He can hold his breath for far longer. Below are some excellent waves and shoots down to 'Dicky Valentine's' bridge in Glangrwyney. This is the main A40 road bridge and is named after a well-known comedian of yesteryear who sadly lost his life in a road crash here. Egress left a little way upstream GR238164.

River Clydach

Map:	Abergavenny and the Black Mountains, no. 161
Grade:	very water-dependent: III in low water; III to IV in medium; up to IV to V in flood
Length:	5 km
Access:	off A 465(T) head of the valley road
Notes:	a real adventure; very serious in flood; *several portages necessary*
Quality:	***

When I first paddled this river I took along a relative newcomer to paddling (albeit an extremely experienced and hardened outdoor man), in a low flood condition. In these conditions, there was enough water to float but, if push comes to shove, it would be possible to jump out of the boat and head to the side. Although I had never met anyone who had actually paddled this river, rumours suggested a reasonable run: what an adventure we had!

<u>Clydach Gorge park to River Usk</u>: 5 km of grade III (low water); III to IV in medium water; and IV to V in flood; several portages***

At the bottom of the steep Clydach Gorge hill (A465T), turn off sharply towards Llanelly Hill. Just before the road heads uphill, turn off right down to a small bridge where access can be made onto the beautiful little gorge. Easy enough for the first part, after which the gorge begins to deepens and a rumbling may be heard. A brown bridge comes into sight (about two kilometres from the start), directly under which is a large 20+ foot fall. The line in low water is horrible. In high flows, it can be run down the guts middle to left and straight over onto a huge boat- and paddler-gobbling stopper - ***class V+***.

Further down, the river piles down a dark tunnel over which the Monmouthshire and Brecon Canal passes. Directly below this is a nasty class IV to class IV+ drop. In low water it is possible to just about stop on the lip. In flood, you can only run blindly down the centre - *this is worth inspecting beforehand by nipping along the towpath* westward from the bridge in Gilwen GR244145. Again, immediately below, is a nasty little shoot which is more dangerous than hard. This is undercut. A little way on are two large weirs, before and after the A4072 road bridge. These are shootable depending on the amount of rubbish stuck in the shoots. Below, are a few pleasant drops, which are the last of the difficulties as you relax on the way down to the Usk. Get out 500 metres below on the right bank just before Glangrwyney bridge GR241159.

248

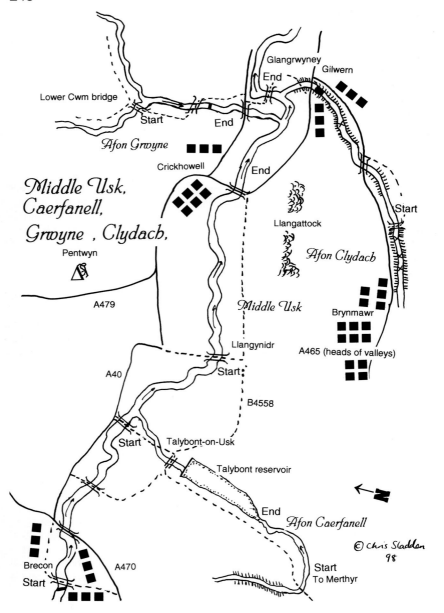

Lower Cwm bridge

Start

End

Afon Grwyne

Crickhowell

Middle Usk,
Caerfanell,
Grwyne , Clydach,

Pentwyn

A479

A40

Glangrwyney

End

Gilwern

End

End

Llangattock

Afon Clydach

Start

Brynmawr

A465 (heads of valleys)

Middle Usk

Llangynidr

Start

B4558

Start

Talybont-on-Usk

Talybont reservoir

End

Afon Caerfanell

© Chris Sladden
98

Brecon

A470

Start

Start
To Merthyr

N

Afon Honddu

Map:	Abergavenny and the Black Mountains, no. 161
Grade:	II
Length:	16 km
Access:	off the A465(T) Abergavenny to Hereford road
Notes:	fences, fences and more fences; one nasty weir
Quality:	none - because of fences

A waterway through a beautiful part of the land that is pretty well spoilt by the numerous fences that crisscross its way.

Llanthony to Monnow confluence: 16 km of grade II; various portages

Turn off the A465 at Llanvihangel Crucorney and head towards the trout farm signs which takes you up the Honddu river. Better still, stop off for nutrition at Wales' oldest inn, the Skirrid, instead. We started the run at the bridge at GR290273. It would have been an excellent grade II spate run apart from the numerous barbed wire strands that cross the river rather like the Checkpoint Charlies of the bad old days of the Cold War. The other dubious quality is that the Honddu rises from Lord Hereford's Knob! Many fences later, you come into the small village of Stanton where there is a nasty, wreckage-choked weir even sporting some upwards-facing, open, metal barrels stuck in the weir face - *an extremely odd finding and not at all pleasant*. Most of the following bridges have more wire slung from here on down to the get-out point at Brynhonddu bridge GR333226.

River Monnow

Map:	Abergavenny & the Black Mountains, no. 161
Grade:	I to II
Length:	49 km
Access:	off B4347 Monmouth to Grosmal road
Notes:	weirs - runnable at most levels
Quality:	****

A beautiful touring river. Can be run when lowish levels - a few weeks after rain. Excellent for groups and beginners. Probably best avoided in fishing season as is a classic salmon river. I found this to be a perfect river for drifting down after a hard night on call!

Longtown to Great Corras bend: 19 km of II; one large weir - usually shootable ****

Turn off the A465 in Pandy and make your way northwards to the small village of Longtown GR327281. Here, providing there is enough water, access can be made onto the Monnow proper, just before its confluence with the Escley Brook. A small, safe weir in the first village (Clodock) livens up the pleasant journey down to the confluence with the Honddu at Alltyrynys. Here, alternative access via the footpath can be made for a shorter journey if, for instance, the upper section is too dry. By this stage, the river has left its beginnings in England and has become very much a border river as it starts its journey towards the Wye. There is something special about the river despite the close proximity to the A465. In only one place after a right then left hand bend, close to the road, does any rapid exceed grade II - and only then at grade II and a bit - so this is a river for all touring and intermediate paddlers. There is one tiny broken weir hardly recognizable as such before the main road bridge at Monmouth cap.

The next weir is a classic demonstration of inaccurate OS map weir location - or one simply being missed out. There is a large, easily-angled, sloping affair which occurs about one kilometre after the Dore enters from the left. This is about 300 metres before the B4347 road bridge. This is obvious from the river by the clear horizon line and the sensation of the water slowing down for a good 500 metres or so above it. Unless in big water, this is safely shootable in most places, but probably best far left. After the Dore enters on river left, a pleasant run remains down to the get-out at Great Corras bend - river left GR419252. The lower sections of the Monnow are equally good - do them!

Great Corras bend to Monmouth: 30 km grade I to II; two weirs****

The B4347 crosses the river at Cupid's Hill, which is between the villages of Ewyas Harold and Grosmont. It is possible to turn off eastwards towards Kent Church, where, by following the road, it is possible to reach a good access point by the river banks GR418250.

The river is a beautiful meandering run with the occasional grade I and II ripple. One small natural weir step about halfway down is a little bigger than the rest and gives a good wave at high flows. The appearance of the majestic Skenfrith Castle gives warning of the **Skenfrith Weir**. This large, sloping affair can be shot at most water conditions but is best avoided in big flood. It is possible to access/egress below the bridge on the right for a shorter trip GR459202.

From here down the water is much the same - a few surfable waves and shoots (ideal for learning the art) pop up now and again. Below an old bridge is a small broken weir - easily shootable. As the river enters Monmouth, there is another **_huge sloping weir_** that, again can be shot in **_off-flood conditions_**.

The finish below the walled ramparts of Monmouth bridge is surely not to be missed. Egress up the convenient steps on river left _above_ the final broken weir GR504125. Those wishing to play in the waves below can easily egress into the market area 100 metres further down.

River Dore

Map:	Abergavenny and the Black Mountains, no. 161
Grade:	I
Length:	8 km
Access:	off A465(T) Abergavenny to Hereford road
Notes:	a few low trees; one weir on Monnow
Quality:	*

The Dore is actually an English river in its entirety, though it empties into the Monnow which forms part of the border. I was intrigued to explore it after the *Shadowlands* film only to discover that, although Anthony Hopkins may have explored the Golden Valley (through which the Dore flows), C S Lewis certainly did not.

Abbey Dore to Great Corras bends: 8 km grade I; one weir*

Turn off the B4347 at Abbey Dore where access can be had at the Court Gardens bridge GR386309. The river is grade I as it weaves down its narrow course between gnarled and ancient tree roots. A fantastic place this for the flash of blue and red of the kingfisher, despite the proximity of MOD fencework. After the addition of the Worm Brook and then the Dulas Brook, the trees take a step back and the channel becomes much clearer. About a kilometre after the confluence with the Monnow, Cupid's Hill weir is reached - safely shootable unless in high flood. Egress by the little ford and footbridge at the Great Corras bends. See Monnow notes.

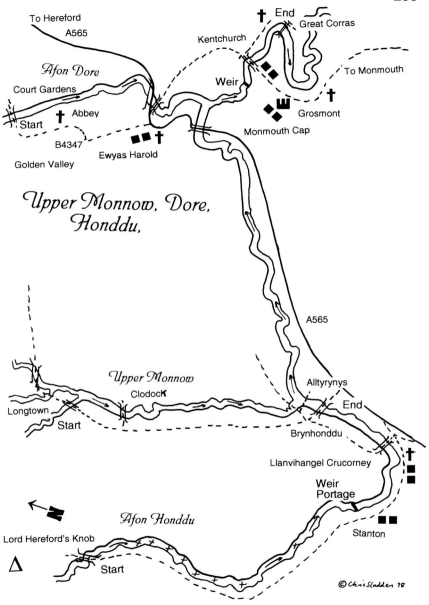

To Hereford
A565

Kentchurch

† End

Great Corras

Afon Dore

Court Gardens

Weir

To Monmouth

Start † Abbey

Grosmont

B4347

Monmouth Cap

Golden Valley

Ewyas Harold

Upper Monnow, Dore,
Honddu,

A565

Upper Monnow

Clodock

Alltyrynys

Longtown

End

Start

Brynhonddu

Llanvihangel Crucorney

Weir
Portage

N

Afon Honddu

Stanton

Lord Hereford's Knob

△

Start

© Chris Sladden 18

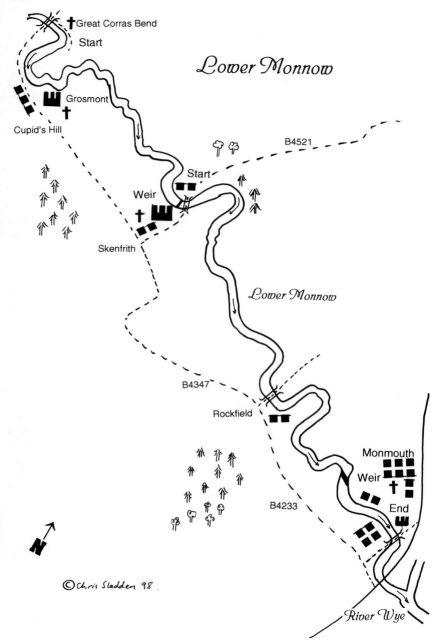

† Great Corras Bend

Start

Lower Monnow

Grosmont
†

Cupid's Hill

B4521

Start

Weir
†

Skenfrith

Lower Monnow

B4347

Rockfield

Monmouth

Weir †

B4233

End

© Chris Sladden 98.

N

River Wye

Afon Lwyd

Map: Cardiff, Newport and surrounding area, no. 171
Grade: II
Length: 17 km
Access: Newport to Pontypool road A4042(T)
Notes: trees to be portaged, one weir to be respected in high water
Quality: **

An easy but quite attractive river teeming with animal and bird life. It ends in a tidal stretch.

Pontypool to Caerleon: 17 km grade II; a few weirs**

A good access point is from waste ground by a small road and bridge leading into the village of New Inn GR298995. The river is best paddled after reasonable rainfall, when the canoe will float down the shingle rapids. This is a pleasant run, although nowhere reaching greater than grade II. Trees may require portaging depending upon recent storm damage, but this is a pleasant paddle finishing up, as it does, in estuarine water. There are two easy, small weirs in Llanyrafon. The first produces a surprisingly strong stopper in times of high water. The greatest danger on this part of the river is being hit by golf balls from the course on the left. However, the golfers and, for that matter, the fishermen seem extremely friendly here!

There is one weir in between the railway and road bridges in Ponthir that requires caution. It consists of three boxed-in sections, the middle one of which is best avoided. The left is ok (although boxed) at normal river flow (in huge flows the stopper backs across the whole of the weir face - a typical occurrence on this type of weir in very high water). A good egress point is after the Lwyd joins the Usk (described elsewhere). The bridge at Caerleon is suitable, with a pub each side. This section is strongly tidal and you may, therefore, wish to time your runs GR342903. In point of fact, if you really time your run it is possible to egress at the river and be sinking a pint of Brains' best with the minimum amount of effort.

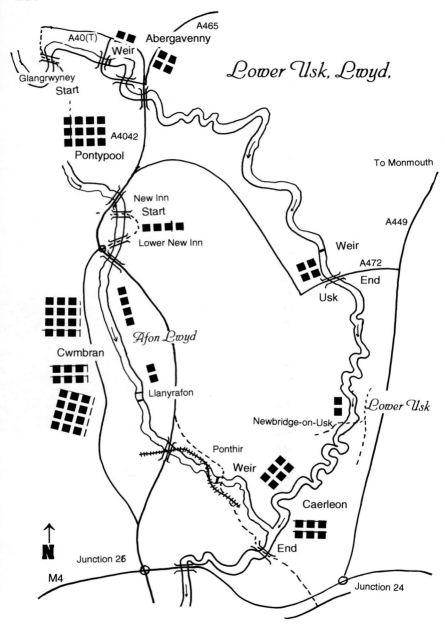

A465

A40(T)   Abergavenny

Weir

Lower Usk, Lwyd,

Glangrwyney
Start

To Monmouth

A4042

A449

Pontypool

New Inn
Start

Lower New Inn

Weir

A472

End

Usk

Afon Lwyd

Cwmbran

Lower Usk

Llanyrafon

Newbridge-on-Usk

Ponthir

Weir

Caerleon

N

Junction 26   End

M4   Junction 24

Afon Ebbw

Map:	Cardiff, Newport and surrounding area, no. 171
Grade:	II
Length:	17 km
Access:	Risca to Newbridge road A467
Notes:	weirs may require respect; low wires (more accurately big thick cables)!
Quality:	**

A pleasant easy area excellent for training.

Cwmcarn to Newport: 17 km grade II**

Access is best made above the Sirhowy confluence by a small bridge that crosses the river in Cwmcarn GR216937. Two small weir steps occur soon after the start. Easy but interesting water is doubled in volume with the Sirhowy entering from the right. By a sports ground, with obvious floodlights, care should be taken as low wires cross the river. These may be covered in high water! There are two weirs just before and after the power station (on river left). Both can produce strong stoppers in times of flood and the second, although small, is boxed-in. If in any doubt, portage left or right.

There is one more weir just before the main road bridge in Bassaleg. It is a large, sloping affair, broken down in floods, especially on the left. Inspect to assess stopper and debris. Portage over the road if necessary. Egress by the road bridge at Maes Glas GR298857. This is about a kilometre or so after the M4 is passed. If, for some strange reason you wish to continue into Newport Docks, I think there are some further weirs to negotiate or portage.

Afon Sirhowy

Map: Cardiff, Newport, and surrounding area, no. 171
Grade: I to II
Length: 14 km
Access: off A4048 Newport to Tredegar road
Notes: one weir *portage*
Quality: *

The Sirhowy is not a beautiful river. It flows through some quite pleasant land, especially in the Sirhowy Country Park, but is lined with rubbish thrown in from various places upstream - a great shame. When I first paddled the Sirhowy some years back, I put in much higher and ran down a long tunnel - somewhere above Pochin House - below which were some very unpleasant weirs so, beware, if you run this section.

Argoed to Watsville: 14 km I to II; one weir portage*

North of Blackwood turn off in Argoed to a little bridge over the river at GR179998. Access can be made here to the stream which should be well covered to make it worth canoeing. There is one small weir after the second road bridge and then a large weir - after the A472 - which is probably sensible to portage. It shows an obvious horizon line and consists of a central salmon slot which contains eagerly-waiting concrete teeth. Far better to take the short portage on the left and take a look to see if any fish are jumping. The following bridge offers an alternative access point. The next eight or so kilometres are grade II interspersed with small, broken weirs to shoot on the way down to the egress - at the small footbridge at GR214915. This is reached by taking the first turning off right just after the A4048 bridge just south of Watsville. Do not leave valuables in the car!!

Afon Rhymney

Map:	Abergavenny and the Black Mountains, no. 161
	Cardiff, Newport, and surrounding area, no. 171
Grade:	sections of III to IV and I to II
Length:	54 km
Access:	A489 Caerphilly to Pontlottyn road
Notes:	one weir needs to be portaged, as does one tunnel
Quality:	**

The upper Rhymney is an exciting paddle at high water. There are quite a few hazards which, from personal experience, require and deserve respect. A serious undertaking at the grade!

Pontlottyn to Llanbradach: 24 km grade III (IV); two portages**

The river needs to be in spate to run from Pontlottyn. Put on by the bridge below where the river comes spurting angrily out from the confines of a tunnel GR117063. Bounce down on fast grade II to III water, the only problem being low fences which require care. Craggy outcrops are passed on the left and, some kilometres further on, the river passes down a dark tunnel. One of the things we've always planned to do, and never got around to, is to walk this tunnel with head torches at low levels - maybe another year. This must be **portaged on the right 100 metres before**. The river is fast but easy here, although not a place for beginners. An excellent section of rapids follows.

As the river approaches Bargoed, *extreme care* must be taken due to a **dangerous weir** on a boxed-in section of the river. This should be inspected beforehand. Turn off the main A469 down the steep road to Gilfach railway station GR153992. A steep track goes off left, crossing the river and giving access to a power station-like building. Park here and walk 500 metres upstream, where the weir can be seen above a bridge and boxed-in between 30-foot, sheer, brick walls. *You must break out 400 metres or so above* where it is possible to climb out up crumbly banks. This is just below another bridge - not a place to swim. In high water, I have seen large objects recirculate from 20 feet downstream - ooh, horrible! In low water this weir shows its unique construction - bricks, wood and underwater pipes. *A definite portage*.

The easiest place to put on is above the power station. The rapids flow under some large, concrete slabs crossing the river. The next few hundred metres are grade III to IV. A pipe under the road bridge requires care. There is another broken weir a kilometre or so downstream, which can be shot. Below this is an excellent mini-gorge through which the water swirls at grade II to III. One more fall at the bottom of the gorge reaches III (just below a small road bridge).

After an impressive viaduct, the water eases off with weirs being the only problem. At high water spate, the ones by the egress in Llanbradach form powerful stoppers and towbacks. At lower water these look totally innocuous. Portage left or right if in doubt.

Egress by these weirs onto the estate roads which are right next to the river GR155915.

Llanbradach to Cardiff: 26 km grade II; a few weirs**

A pleasant paddle as the seriousness of the upper section relaxes on its way to the sea. Access is below the above mentioned weirs. The trees are the only problem on this first section. At off-flood conditions there is an excellent beginners' surfing wave that can be found a little way down. A few kilometres further, and an obvious weir needs to be inspected. This is between Bedwas and Machen. If in doubt portage. The river meanders as it follows the attractive Rhymney Valley footpath walk. There are several bridges en-route that make easy egress points for those not wishing to go the full way to Cardiff. Under one small bridge before the motorway crossing, there is an entertaining stopper lurking in the right-hand arch. Just before A48 bridge is a measuring weir and there is another about three kilometres further on in Llanrhymney. Both stoppers can get sticky, especially in high floods. Egress at one of many road bridges towards the estuary.

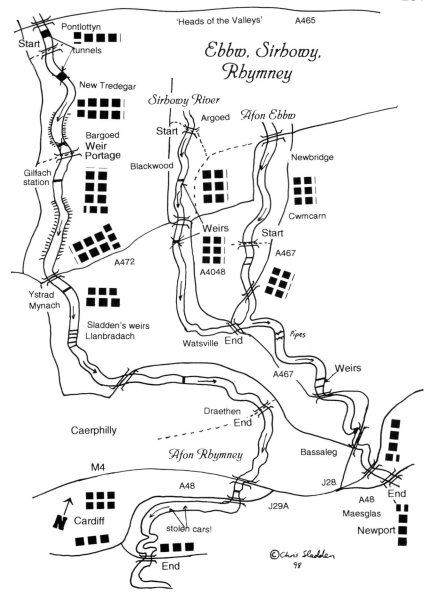

'Heads of the Valleys'   A465

Ebbw, Sirhowy, Rhymney

Pontlottyn

Start

tunnels

New Tredegar

Sirhowy River

Argoed   *Afon Ebbw*

Start

Bargoed
Weir
Portage

Blackwood

Newbridge

Gilfach
station

Cwmcarn

Weirs

Start

A472

A4048

A467

Ystrad
Mynach

Sladden's weirs
Llanbradach

Pipes

Watsville   End

A467   Weirs

Draethen
_ _ End

Caerphilly

Afon Rhymney

Bassaleg

M4

A48

J28

J29A

A48

End

stolen cars!

Maesglas

N

Cardiff

Newport

©Chris Sladden
98

End

Afon Taf Fawr

Map: Brecon Beacons, no. 160
Grade: II to III
Length: 2 and 3 km
Access: A470(T) Merthyr to Brecon road
Notes: fences may need portaging
Quality: not recommended

Two fast stretches of stream paddling. However, the water authorities are not keen on people paddling these sections so these notes are for information only - the sections are not recommended.

Beacons Reservoir to Cantref Reservoir: 2 km grade III

The Merthyr to Brecon road shadows the river and the various sections can be run from off here. Put on below the A4059, road bridge GR989182 for a fast spate run to the next reservoir, where it is best to egress. Care needs to be taken because of trees and wires crossing the water.

Cantref to Forest Centre: 3 km grade II to III

Take the drive down to the waterworks and put on just above a small weir GR999152. A huge overflow shoots water in just above. This has been run, not by me, but incensed the water authority bailiffs - not recommended for a repeat. The first rapid is a good grade III with the only problem being overhanging branches. At time of writing, there were three fences to negotiate between this and the next reservoir. A good egress point is at the bridge crossing the river just above the reservoir GR005132. The weir below is best portaged.

Afon Taf Fechan

Map: Brecon Beacons, no. 160
Grade: IV; one fall IV+ to V
Length: 7 km
Access: A470(T) Merthyr to Brecon road
Notes: undercuts in the various gorges make this a serious run for the grade
Quality: ***

By far the better of the two tributaries this is an exciting run over steps and through shoots and narrow gorges. In big water it is quite testing at the grade! A word of warning - **don't leave valuables in the car around here.**

Pontsticill to Merthyr: 6 km grade IV (one fall IV+ to V)***

When the river is up, it is possible to put in at the little bridge across the river at GR060107. This is reached by turning right off the A470 just past the Brynmawr turning. Carry on up to Pontsticill where there is a right hand turn in the village, leading to the bridge. Grade II to III water rushing between bushes and eddying behind cars (thrown in the river) is your first taste of the Taf Fechan. Many, therefore, will prefer to put in above or below Pont Sarn. Just above here an old viaduct, which is often used for abseiling, spans the river. A grade V mini-gorge and following 15-foot drop is found at the road bridge. The shoot is more straightforward than it looks but several undercuts make it potentially dangerous, and you will want to take a careful look before paddling. The water eases off before picking up to pass through several rocky gorges on its way to Merthyr. Undercuts make swimming potentially dangerous, and there is always the chance of trees being jammed in the river. Some may require portaging. Egress is at the A470 road bridge - a bit of a scramble up on the right GR038077. If you do carry on below here, there is at least one weir to contend with. Overall, the river in full spate is an exciting and bouncy ride by anybody's standards.

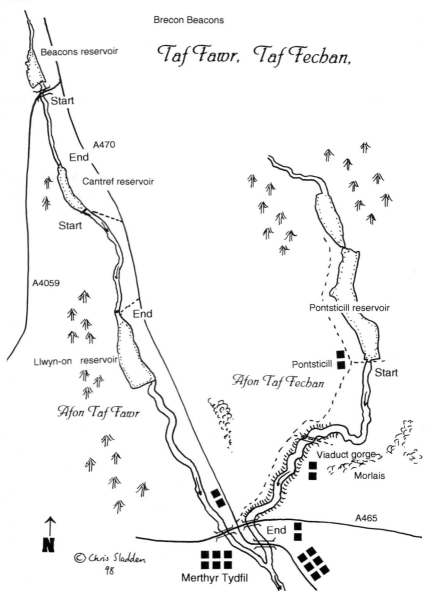

Brecon Beacons

Taf Fawr, Taf Fechan,

Beacons reservoir

Start

A470

End

Cantref reservoir

Start

A4059

End

Llwyn-on reservoir

Afon Taf Fawr

Pontsticill reservoir

Pontsticill

Start

Afon Taf Fechan

Viaduct gorge

Morlais

A465

End

© Chris Sladden
98

N

Merthyr Tydfil

Afon Taff

Map:	Cardiff, Newport and surrounding area, no. 171
Grade:	sections of I to II and II to III, one rapid V plus weirs
Length:	39 km
Access:	A470 and A470(T) Cardiff to Merthyr roads
Notes:	one unpleasant grade IV to V fall. Many of the weirs need portaging
Quality:	***

If pollution is ever solved then the Taff will lose its major stigma and become a great touring river. Although, at first, a seemingly gentle Welsh river, a few surprises undoubtedly exist for the paddler to find. Just occasionally, due to its massive catchment area, the Taff has a correspondingly massive flood. In these conditions, it is far better to go and paddle one of the tributaries described elsewhere in this book, than to risk a hammering in one of the many weirs.

Aberfan to Pontypridd: 18 km grade II to III (one fall IV+ to V); weirs***

This section is usually good for up to a few days after heavy rain. Take the B4285 turning to Aberfan off the old A470. Where the road crosses the river it is possible to put in below a two-stepped weir GR072002. The first mile through the town is best passed quickly, after which an excellent wooded section is reached. At good river levels the rapids are an entertaining grade II to III with numerous playspots. This is a superb area for kingfishers!

Care needs to be taken when approaching Quaker's Yard where **a nasty grade IV+ to V** rapid awaits. This can be easily inspected during the drive up. An unpleasant plug of rock awaits at chest height in the first of the two drops on the right. Tricky in any conditions, it becomes a serious V in spate. Portage right if in any doubt. This rapid has seen its fair share of epics over the years.

Below Quaker's Yard are two weirs. Both are obvious from the river. The first is best portaged because of shallow landings and debris. The second can be run down the large central tongue, although high flows can iron this out - ***inspect!*** The Cynon and Nant Clydach entering from the right swell the river. This section is excellent for playing. Two stoppers, formed by pipes crossing the river bed, provide some amusement. There is one rapid of note just before an old bridge on the outskirts of Pontypridd; best taken on the left to avoid upstream-pointing rock slabs - class III. Egress is on a small road, river left GR074906.

Pontypridd to Cardiff: 21 km grade I to II - weirs definite portages***

Access at the above egress point for this pleasant paddle to Cardiff. There are five weirs on this section and two are best portaged, with one being a **definite portage**. The first, about a kilometre from the start should be obvious from the river and is a *certain portage*. This was always a fairly nasty weir with a potentially holding stopper. In 1996 and 1997, I watched the local authority effectively re-building the weir - an interesting spectacle - and I had great hopes that it would be made safe. Instead they turned it from a dangerous weir into a **totally lethal weir!** *Beware and portage*.

The second is below the main road bridge to Treforest. This is a large, vertical, horseshoe affair and is best portaged with some scrambling on the right.

The third is at Radyr just after the M4 road bridge. This can be shot with care at normal river levels. The fourth at Llandaff Rowing Club is another large, angled affair, shootable with care, which has a good stopper a little way below the main weir. A good egress point is by Tal y Bont halls of residence GR170783 just off North Road, Cardiff. Far better to watch salmon jumping the huge, sloping Blackweir below, than to shoot it. In a massive flood - one where it is impossible to walk along the foot paths alongside the river - there is an enormous wave in part of the Blackweir. This is about 10 feet in height and offers an awesome surfing session, but with disastrous consequences if you were to drop off the sides of the wave and into the stopper or eddies on each side. The purist may wish to paddle to the sea and egress up mud banks in Grangetown. En-route, you will pass the Castle (well worth a visit) and, on International Day, hear the roar from the old Arms Park or the new National Stadium being presently built for the 1999 Rugby World Cup. If you do decide to paddle to the docks you will have to choose your own egress point as, at the moment, the area is in quite a state of flux. I cheated the last time I was on the lower Taff. On a high spring I drove a speed boat up past the stadium with Roger Heslop amazing me with his barefoot water skiing ability being towed behind.

Afon Cynon

Map:	Vale of Glamorgan and Rhondda area, no. 170
Grade:	II
Length:	8 km
Access:	A4059 Abercynon to Aberdare road
Notes:	three weirs and trees
Quality:	* JUST

This is an odd one to recommend, because of the valley through which it flows. However, the Taff into which it flows, and the last couple of kilometres of the Cynon provide entertainment.

Mountain Ash to Taff confluence: 8 km grade II*

Put on, if you dare, in this incredibly used Welsh valley at a small footbridge that crosses the river upstream of Mountain Ash. This is found just before the large, industrial workings spurting forth flames and fumes, two kilometres upstream of the town GR037997.

There are three weirs on the river. The first, below a railway bridge in Mountain Ash, is difficult to inspect or portage. A climb up a crumbly bank on the right some 100 metres before is best. Although broken, it forms a strong stopper. However, the worst danger is probably being bricked by the local kids having fun.

The second is obvious from the river a few kilometres downstream and is broken in nature. The third, as the river nears the Taff, usually consists not of a stopper but a superb standing wave, which is great for surfing. It is just below a footbridge. It is best to continue into the Taff and egress a couple of kilometres downstream where the river nears the road GR080933.

Nant Clydach

Map:	Vale of Glamorgan and Rhondda area, no. 170
Grade:	II to III plus one gorge of IV
Length:	8 km
Access:	B4273 Pontypridd to Ynysybwl road
Notes:	two definite portages: one fence; one low bridge. A tight gorge in the lower section.
Quality:	****

I love this river and the surprises it holds. It's only big enough for a group of about three people, and the locals are friendly so please don't abuse this!

Porthcelyn bridge to Taff confluence: 8 km grade II to III; bottom gorge IV; a few portages****

The Nant Clydach needs to be in spate to run. Get in at the road bridge crossing the stream at GR048967 (Ynysybwl to Miskin road). An alternative for the adventurous is to run the Y Ffrwd some two kilometres downstream. This enters the Clydach via some fast, big drops.

If the river is brown and over the banks at the get-in, then the run will be a hectic grade III. Slightly lower, the river is more manageable at II to III. Continual grade II takes the paddler through a tunnelled bridge. Shortly after the bridge a fence needs to be portaged. Trees and two more sets of wires after this need to be treated with caution, but generally can be sneaked. A fording bridge at the Ynysybwl Inn needs portaging (unless in big spate when the water goes over!) GR055951. The river, now bigger in volume with the entry of the Y Ffrwd, passes through Ynysybwl where it rushes down a 70-metre tunnel hewn out of the rock. The roar gets louder as the paddler bounces out of control and in the dark through this, and over the small weir at the other end. This is best taken on the left to avoid metalwork in the centre. It should be stressed that, although it is tremendous sport to run this tunnel, it is difficult to know if any debris has been left inside from the last storm! Portage if in any doubt.

A grade III slot and a small weir follow. The weir buries you in the stopper below. A pipe crossing the river, thankfully over a quiet pool, needs to be sculled under or portaged. In massive floods this becomes covered! As the river nears the road and Glyncoch is approached, there is an excellent grade **IV to IV+ gorge**. This is a very popular run as it gives consistent and technical paddling within 20 minutes drive of Cardiff. In early '97, I spent six months at the hospital in Pontypridd and it was only five minutes up the road to this great little river. There were no trees blocking the gorge during this time. In big water it is **one continual frothing class IV+**, (or even harder rapid), all the way to the finish. The rapids ease off until a final rush just before the small road bridge. Beware of metalwork debris in this last rapid. Egress on this road, GR080928, reached by turning off right from the B4273 just before Glyncoch.

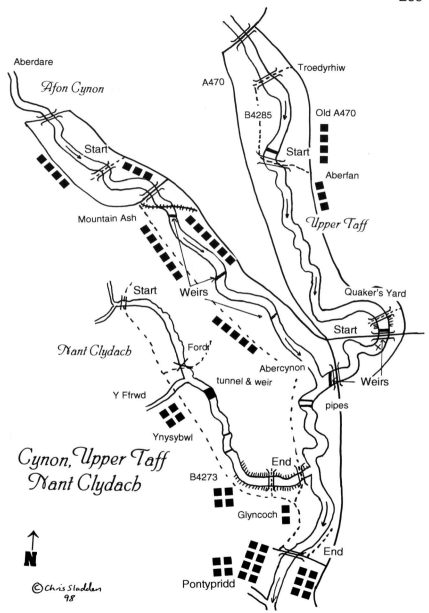

Aberdare

Afon Cynon

Start

Mountain Ash

Start

Nant Clydach

Weirs

Ford

Y Ffrwd

Ynysybwl

Cynon, Upper Taff
Nant Clydach

B4273

N

© Chris Sladden
98

A470

B4285

Troedyrhiw

Old A470

Start

Aberfan

Upper Taff

Quaker's Yard

Start

Weirs

Abercynon

tunnel & weir

pipes

End

Glyncoch

End

Pontypridd

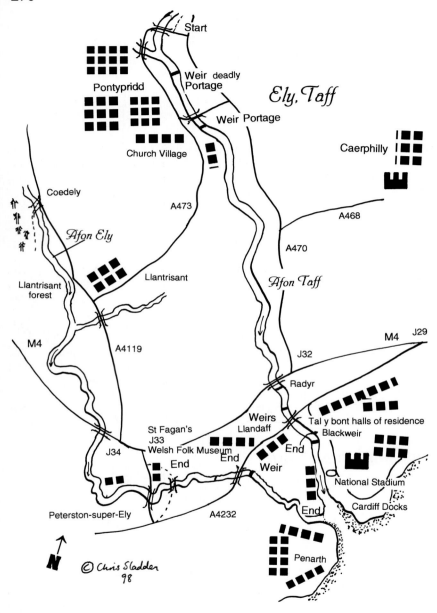

Start

Weir deadly
Portage

Weir Portage

Ely, Taff

Pontypridd

Church Village

Caerphilly

Coedely

A473

A468

A470

Afon Ely

Llantrisant

Afon Taff

Llantrisant
forest

M4

A4119

M4   J29

J32

Radyr

Weirs
Llandaff

Tal y bont halls of residence

St Fagan's
J33
Welsh Folk Museum

Blackweir

J34

End

End

End

National Stadium

Peterston-super-Ely

A4232

Weir

Cardiff Docks

End

N

© Chris Sladder
98

Penarth

Afon Rhondda Fach

Map:	Vale of Glamorgan and Rhondda area, no. 170
Grade:	II; one rapid grade III
Length:	5 km
Access:	B4277 Porth to Maerdy road
Notes:	two pipes crossing the river - one a definite portage
Quality:	***

The Rhondda Fach would be a beautiful river if the rubbish adorning its banks were removed. There is plenty of wildlife, however, which seems to flourish despite this. The locals are also very friendly. For some time, I worked in East Glamorgan Hospital and got to know many Valleys people, and they are lovely folk.

Pontygwaith to Porth: 5 km grade II (III)***

Start the run at the main road bridge crossing the river in Pontygwaith GR012939. There is a convenient parking space just by the bridge where you can also put in. A few hundred metres down and a pipe needs to be either squeezed under, or portaged, depending on river height. Grade II water follows, passing quickly down a short tunnel and over a few weir steps towards Porth. Here a pipe spans the river and needs to be portaged. Since the publication of the first book, this pipe has seen *much carnage* - so beware. Just before the confluence with the Rhondda Fawr some man-made steps under a road bridge give a grade III rapid.

Exciting enough at its grade, the trip is best finished by carrying on down to Hopkinstown, described under the Rhondda Fawr section.

Afon Rhondda Fawr

Map:	Vale of Glamorgan and Rhondda area, no. 170
Grade:	II to III plus two rapids grade III to IV
Length:	26 km
Access:	A4058 Pontypridd to Treherbert road
Notes:	three low pipes - one portage
Quality:	***

Canoeing through the Valleys has a charm of its own and, although strange as it may seem at first, there is an abundance of wildlife including kingfishers. This river, since the publication of *White Water Runs and Touring Rivers of South Wales,* has become very popular and, when in condition, there are paddlers on the river most weekends.

Blaencwm to Porth: 20 km grade II to III; pipe portages***

Turn off the A4058 in Treherbert towards Blaencwm and pass through the village of Tynewydd, where you turn left under a bridge. Access can be made on the Nant y Gwair, just above the confluence with the Rhondda GR928991. There should be ample water to float the canoe on this small stream. Start off on fast grade II, with sharp eddies that are exciting for those new to this type of paddling. Soon a small weir with measuring gauge is reached. This should read at least 3 to make the run worthwhile. At 9 or 10 the grade will be III. The gauge is visible just behind the bus stop GR935985.

There are so many bridges on this river that one loses count very quickly and makes it pointless describing them! However, they do provide alternative access and egress points. Care should be taken at the first of the pipes crossing the river some four kilometres from the start. **Portage right** if the water is high.

The urban is forced back by the rural as the river passes through woods before Llwynypia. The next problem is a small weir below which another pipe spans at chest height. It can just be squeezed under on the left, *but not in flood, so beware*. Below the large road bridge in Tonypandy is a pipe which **needs to be portaged** left or right. Since my 1990 guide, this Tonypandy pipe has had its fair share of epics. Approach with care! Bouncy water, including a broken weir step takes the paddler to the confluence with the Rhondda Fach.

Porth to Hopkinstown: 5 km grade III to IV***

This section acts as a surprising finish to the upper stretches. The river doubles in volume after the confluence and, shortly after the first main road bridge in Porth, is a weir step with a surprisingly strong stopper.

About two kilometres below Porth, in between the two crossings of the A4058, a railway bridge spans the river. The river here surges over a series of partially man made, partially natural, steps. The middle channel through the bridge is the best entry to avoid concrete structures on the left. It is best to inspect from the pipe in the right arch, for some of the ledges in high water carry large stoppers - best avoided (certain old sea dogs from Cardiff CC have tested their buoyancy here - and this is often known as Colin's Rapid!). Some good waves are found under the next road bridge, after which the river eases off until just before Hopkinstown. Here, under a small bridge, the river is compressed to give a short grade III (IV) rapid. Egress is river left just before the town GR061904.

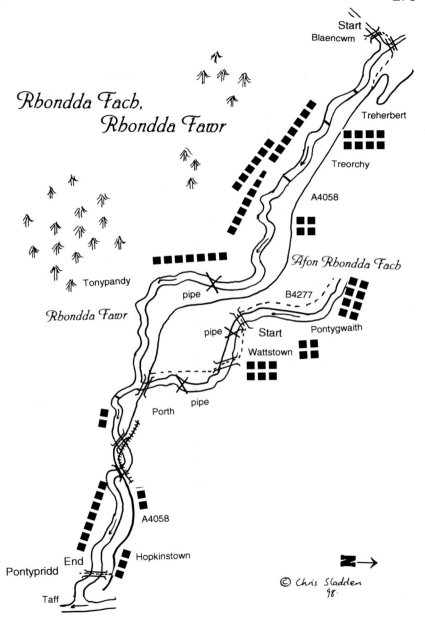

Start
Blaencwm

Treherbert

Treorchy

A4058

Rhondda Fach,
Rhondda Fawr

Afon Rhondda Fach

B4277

Pontygwaith

Tonypandy

pipe

Rhondda Fawr

pipe

Start

Wattstown

Porth

pipe

A4058

Hopkinstown

End

Pontypridd

Taff

© Chris Sladden
98.

Afon Ely

Map: Vale of Glamorgan and Rhondda area, no. 170
Cardiff, Newport and surrounding area, no. 171
Grade: II
Length: 30 km
Access: M4 junction 34, A4119 to Tonyrefail
Notes: low trees require care
Quality: **

A gentle, relaxing touring river which lazes by the Welsh Folk Museum.

Dyffryn to Cardiff: 30 km grade II**

Start the run at the small bridge that crosses the river on the edge of Llantrisant Forest GR023852. From here, the river bubbles along under bridges, over small weir steps and around trees towards the M4, under which it passes. From here, it meanders in large, slow loops with deep, crusty banks towards Peterston-super-Ely. An excellent place, this, to see wildlife.

After Peterston, the river straightens out and some steering is required, especially in high water, to avoid overhanging trees. A small measuring weir near the Welsh Folk Museum and a couple of broken weir steps are the only other disturbances before Cardiff. Egress may be made at the small bridge in St Fagans GR119770, or at the next major road bridge at Ely, Cardiff GR146768 (a weir after this is difficult to portage should you fancy a trip to the sea - I haven't done this). In point of fact, it is far more pleasant to finish this trip at St Fagans where the egress, parking and open mouths are far more benign.

Afon Ogwr Fach

Map: Vale of Glamorgan and Rhondda area, no. 170
Grade: III
Length: 7 km
Access: A4093 Blackmill to Tonyrefail road
Notes: fences need to be portaged; trees may require portaging
Quality: **

This is the smallest tributary (within reason) of the valley and one many would laugh at. However, when full to the brim, it gives a tremendous run albeit serious at the grade due to trees and fences. An unorthodox type of break-out called 'grabbing the banks' is needed on this type of river!

Evanstown to Blackmill: 7 km grade III; fences **

Turn off the A4093 on the B4564 to Evanstown. Access may be made where the road crosses the river by putting on below the tunnel through which the river rages GR979893. This tunnel may well have a grill within it and so would have to be inspected before any attempt to paddle through. This stream wants to be over the banks for an exciting run. A hanging fence a short way down needs to be portaged. Two further fences between the next farm and road bridge need portaging (asking permission useful here!). Just after these fences is an excellent set of weir steps to bounce through to just past the road bridge.

The river continues under an old railway bridge and accompanying farm bridge. Soon after these, two huge concrete tunnel pieces thrown into the river need to be carefully steered around. From here to the Ogwr Fawr confluence the only problem is trees, depending upon recent storm damage. During my last trip in '96, this was clear, storms or perhaps wood gatherers having moved the previous trees.

Egress just before the main road bridge at the confluence onto the left bank GR933867. Better still, continue down the Ogwr Fawr where you will be in for a bouncy ride at this water level!

Afon Ogwr Fawr

Map: Vale of Glamorgan and Rhondda area, no. 170
Grade: II to III
Length: 20 km
Access: A4061 junction 36 of M4 to Ogmore Vale
Notes: one pipe after the confluence of all the rivers requires
                 portaging
Quality: ***

A good run. If you can turn a blind eye (and maybe other senses) to the sewage works at Merthyr Mawr then an excellent trip will be had. Actually, finishing a run down to the dunes at Merthyr Mawr is quite special.

Ogmore Vale to Merthyr Mawr: 20 km grade II to III***

When the water is up it is possible to start the run up in Ogmore Vale. Take a small road, first on the right, on entering the town from the M4 side. This runs through football pitches to a small bridge across the stream GR934896. If the water is very high, a railway bridge 100 metres downstream needs to be **portaged**. There are three fences slung from railway bridges, and one other, that needed to be portaged or dodged. Take care.

After the confluence with the Ogwr Fach things improve dramatically and, indeed, you may wish to put in here. Between here and the Garw confluence is an excellent series of steps which, in big water, have powerful waves to negotiate. After the Garw confluence, and around a left hand bend, is a metal-banked section with a double-stepped weir at the bottom end. This forms boxed-in stoppers that need to be treated with respect if the water is high! Portage if in doubt. If the water is one metre below the top of the gauge then the river is well up, although it can be run at much lower levels.

After the confluence with the Llynfi, and just before passing the motorway, is a pipe spanning the river that needs portaging. This is covered in extremely big water and forms a good wave but to swim would be **potentially** very dangerous! Bouncy waves and closed-in banks take the paddler through Bridgend to a weir with a good stopper in high water. For six months I worked in a doctor's surgery that overlooked the section of the river. Sometimes I would see paddlers and, once, a raft bouncing their way happily along. A slipway on the right and low banks on the left allow escape if needed. The weir is fairly obvious from the river although difficult to find as you drive, hopelessly lost, around Bridgend. Far better to buy some cream buns rather than trying to find it, and inspect from the river. Extremely pleasant touring water takes the paddler under ancient stone bridges to Merthyr Mawr. Egress by a footbridge into a car park on the right GR883772 or further down the estuary. The dunes at Merthyr Mawr and the castle are well worth a wander. With a good flood and the right stage of tide there are some good waves to be found along below here to the sea - take care of the current as Merthyr Mawr has a notorious reputation.

Afon Garw

Map:	Vale of Glamorgan and Rhondda area, no. 170
Grade:	II
Length:	9 km
Access:	A4064 junction 36 M4 to Pontycymmer road
Notes:	several portages around low fences and trees
Quality:	*

An easy, pretty river teeming with bird life, but with the odd surprise in store.

Braich y Cymmer to Ogmore confluence: 9 km grade II*

Start the run at the railway crossing just by the Braich y Cymmer public house GR905898. This fast-running stream takes the paddler into a wooded valley where trees may be a problem. Barbed wire spans the river twice before the next road bridge. This is passable with care. Just after the next road bridge, the river bends sharply to the left and the paddler must crash through over-hanging bushes (in Llangeinor). The river bends back to the right and a fence needs to be portaged river right. Further on, just before a railway bridge, another fence requires portaging on the right. The next two low bridges need squeezing under at normal water levels. Wooded banks and, therefore, trees will always keep the paddler on his toes as Brynmenyn is approached. Rhodo-dendron bushes begin to mark the journey's end, and a wooden adventure playground on the right makes for amusing respite. Only one fallen tree, over which the river pours, remains. Egress at the main road bridge in Brynmenyn on river left GR907848 or continue down the Ogmore.

Afon Llynfi

Map:	Vale of Glamorgan and Rhondda area, no. 170
Grade:	II
Length:	9 km (16 km)
Access:	A4063 Bridgend to Maesteg road
Notes:	one pipe just after the confluence may require portaging. A few small weirs are present
Quality:	**

An easy touring river, good for groups.

Pont Rhyd y Cyff to Bridgend: 9 km grade II**

It is possible in high water and entertaining enough in its own way to start the trip above Maesteg adding a further seven kilometres to the run. A small bridge in Nantyffyllon GR853930 marks the start. Break-outs behind (or even into) shopping trolleys, a couple of short tunnels, and a passage between debris caught on the pipe, are amusing if not taxing. A more reasonable place to start is by the Tyler's Arms pub at Pont Rhyd y Cyff GR873892. The river flows gently with trees on bends being the only problem. A weir found on a left 90-degree bend just by the obvious buildings on the right bank provides entertainment for those needing it. Further on is a small measuring weir.

The confluence with the Ogmore makes the river more bouncy, but no more difficult. Continue down, if necessary portaging the pipe described in the Ogwr Fawr section. Egress may be made by the bridges near the hospital GR903822 or up the steep banks to the nearby small roads. Alternatively, carry on down the Ogmore. If you are shouted at by a large and angry, but somewhat well-spoken, fisherman in a Barbour jacket, I may know your aggressor:

As a student I was present in an out-patients clinic when one of the local GPs (assisting with the clinic) started to berate canoeists to the consultant, totally ignoring my presence, I may add. He concluded by saying that someone had dared to write a guidebook to the area - I didn't let on and simply smiled happily to myself.

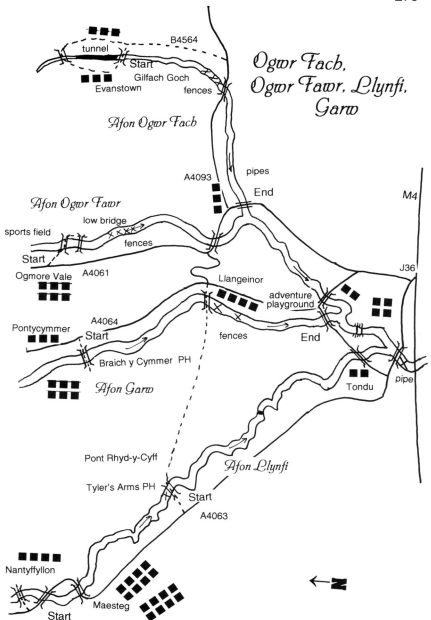

Ogwr Fach,
Ogwr Fawr, Llynfi,
Garw

B4564

tunnel

Start

Gilfach Goch

Evanstown

fences

Afon Ogwr Fach

pipes

A4093

End

M4

Afon Ogwr Fawr

low bridge

sports field

fences

Start

J36

Ogmore Vale

A4061

Llangeinor

adventure
playground

A4064

Pontycymmer

Start

fences

End

Braich y Cymmer PH

Tondu

pipe

Afon Garw

Pont Rhyd-y-Cyff

Afon Llynfi

Tyler's Arms PH

Start

A4063

Nantyffyllon

Start

Maesteg

N

Ewenny

Map:	Vale of Glamorgan and Rhondda area, no. 170
Grade:	I to II
Length:	12 km
Access:	A473 Pencoed to Llantrisant road
Notes:	no fences or weirs; two small, playable weirs; numerous small steps
Quality:	***

An excellent night paddle for competent groups, though you can also paddle it during daylight hours if you wish.

Pencoed to Ogmore Castle 12 km grade II; one portage***

From Junction 35 of the M4 drive towards Pencoed for 500 metres. Turn left where there is a bridge over the Ewenny and access to the river can be made over playing fields on the left bank. There should be enough flow here to *easily* float a boat. Lower down below the main A48(T) gives alternative access.

The tunnel under the motorway is clear and good fun to bounce along. There is a small weir a little way after the A473 bridge on a sharp right hand bend - excellent for playing in. Lots of interesting little steps follow. At Moor Farm there is a bridge over the river that needs to be **portaged** - this should be obvious from the river. Pass the following factories quickly and, soon afterwards, the police dog training area.

Under the A48(T) bridge is a second, slightly bigger but playable, and usually safe, weir. The old and attractive Ewenny Priory appears on the left and the river meanders its way through beautiful countryside to Ogmore Castle - good egress on left. If you leave vehicles in the car park *beware of high tides*! Visit the castle - fine views may be had as the sun sinks its way westwards.

One word of warning: there is a man, who looks like a gamekeeper, on this lower section who can be particularly aggressive. He once let a shotgun off over my head and was desperate for a fight! I discovered who this particular chap was, and don't advise taking up his kind offers for a shindig.

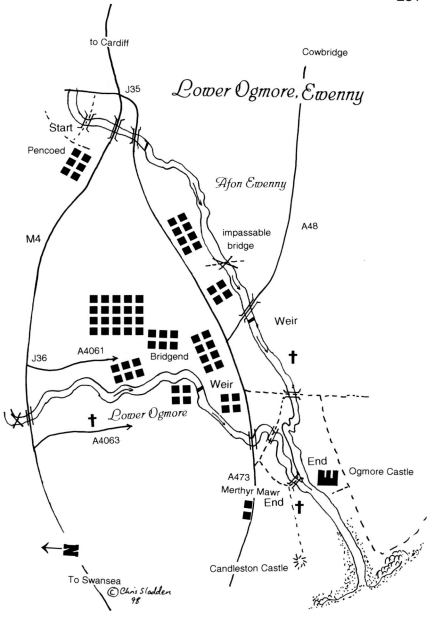

to Cardiff

Cowbridge

J35

Lower Ogmore, Ewenny

Start

Pencoed

Afon Ewenny

impassable
bridge

A48

M4

Weir

J36

A4061

Bridgend

Weir

Lower Ogmore

A4063

End

Ogmore Castle

A473
Merthyr Mawr
End

Candleston Castle

To Swansea

© Chris Sladden
98

Afon Afan

Map: Vale of Glamorgan and Rhondda area, no. 170
Grade: III; and III to IV
Length: 23 km
Access: A4107 and B4286 Port Talbot to Treorchy roads
Notes: two pipes below Cymmer require great care; weirs need to be portaged
Quality: ***

An excellent, fast run especially in high flows. It is now well-used locally and is even often run at night by a few of the far more keen of individuals. This section can be added on to the upper Afan, the Pelenna, or done as a run in its own right. There are some excellent waves to surf and stoppers to play in. A few of the weirs are particularly nasty in big water and so medium levels are probably the best conditions to run this section.

Blaengwynfi/Cymmer to Pontrhydyfen: 11 km grade III; possible portages ***

In high water, the run down from the bridge in Blaengwynfi to Cymmer is an excellent grade II to III. It is fast and steep but nowhere desperate. Alternatively, put in from the left bank of the Afon Corrwg, a short distance up the Cymmer to Glyncorrwg road GR962966 (at higher levels it is possible to put in higher up). Once on the Afan, the river is fast and bouncy and fun. However, beware, for above and below an obvious football pitch are two pipes spanning the river. Although it is possible to pass these obstructions at certain water levels, there is always a danger of being strained underneath if mistakes are made. In flood, these pipes are covered. Portage if in doubt.

From here down through the Afon Argoed Park is an excellent run at a good grade III level. Egress in Pontrhydyfen just below the road bridge GR795942. A weir just below this is **very dangerous in flood** though can easily be shot in medium flows.

Pontrhydyfen to Aberavon: 8 km grade III to IV; weirs to portage ***

Take the B4286 from Aberavon up to Pontrhydyfen. It is worth inspecting the Velindre weirs on the drive up where the road sweeps right next to the river and there is a convenient layby. Just before Pontrhydyfen is a convenient layby where access onto the viaduct rapids can be made GR793940.

If you decide to run down from the upper Afan, the weir in Pontrhydyfen should be portaged on the right along the road. Although runnable at medium flows it forms a particularly *nasty holding stopper in flood*. The viaduct rapids are excellent at grade III to IV. About a half kilometre below the viaduct is a slight left hand sweep of the river and a footbridge crosses over. Immediately under the footbridge is a horseshoe-shaped weir. This is runnable far left in low to medium flows. However, in flood the towback reaches **over 20 feet and should on no account be shot - portage left** before the footbridge. This is easily inspected on the drive up.

The river meanders towards the sea with the occasional surfing wave to shred. As Pontdu is neared, a series of man-made bouldery drops lead down to the box-like weir at Velindre. Although this can be shot when quite high, if in any doubt **portage**

Passing through Port Talbot, Slaughterhouse Falls (or Weir) is reached, which is a huge broken drop of about 12 feet. This is runnable with care middle to right, but beware of any spikes in the weir. This is a suitable place to end the trip GR760897.

Afon Corrwg

Map:	Vale of Glamorgan and Rhondda area, no. 170
Grade:	II to III; rapid grade III to IV above town
Length:	5 km
Access:	A4107 Port Talbot to Treorchy road
Notes:	an alternative run to the upper Afan
Quality:	*

Though I have driven up the Corrwg valley a few times and inspected the river, I have never run it. Locals recommend it as a good alternative to the upper Afan.

<u>Glyncorrwg to Cymmer</u>: 5 km of grade II to III, with one rapid of IV*

Take the small road from Cymmer over the Afan and up to Glyncorrwg. Turn off right before the road bridge in town and follow the main left hand fork for a few hundred metres. Access can be had above a long grade IV run into the town GR877993.

Care needs to be taken halfway down this, where the river is forced between two concrete blocks, through which a kayak will just squeeze. From here the river is fast grade II to III until it joins the Afan in Cymmer. Although apparently clear of obstacles, I have not done the river - so keep the eyes peeled!

Afon Pelenna

Map: Vale of Glamorgan and Rhondda area, no.170
Grade: II to III
Length: 6 km
Access: B4287 Pontrhydyfen to Neath road
Notes: a great spate run
Quality: ***

The time to run the Pelenna is when the skies are opening. This is a great run, especially so to those new to stream paddling. Once hooked on this type of paddling, then you will be looking for excitement every time the rain comes. As you race down the twists and turns, everything else is forgotten as you try to reach the sea before the spate itself.

Cwm Blaenpelenna to Pontrhydyfen: 6 km grade II to III***

Take the A4107 or B4286 Port Talbot to Pontrhydyfen road. Turn up the B4281 road to Neath, past the sign celebrating the birthplace of the great Richard Burton and, just before the little road bridge, turn right up to Tonmawr. Cross the river, and take the small track on the right of the hairpin bend up to the access point by a small bridge GR816973.

The higher the water the better. There is a fall under the first little bridge that people new to this side of the sport should relish. There are two low fences that require care to squeeze under. The rapids keep on going, never desperate, but always exciting. The scaffolding that used to prop up the bridge in Efail-Fach has thankfully long gone. Egress is best made just below the confluence with the Afan, though this feels like hitting a freight train after the Pelenna GR793940.

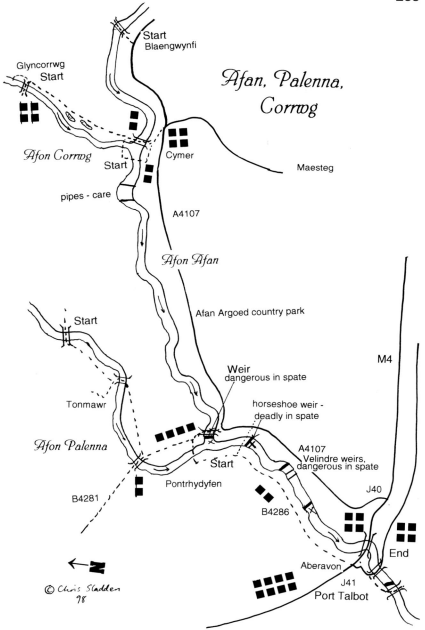

Start
Blaengwynfi

Glyncorrwg
Start

Afan, Palenna,
Corrwg

Afon Corrwg

Start

Cymer

Maesteg

pipes - care

A4107

Afon Afan

Afan Argoed country park

Start

M4

Weir
dangerous in spate

Tonmawr

horseshoe weir -
deadly in spate

Afon Palenna

A4107
Velindre weirs,
dangerous in spate

Start

J40

B4281

Pontrhydyfen

B4286

End

© Chris Sladden
98

Aberavon

J41

Port Talbot

The Neath River

Map: The Vale of Glamorgan and Rhondda area, no. 170
Brecon Beacons, no. 160
Grade: II to III including runnable weirs
Length: 20 km
Access: A465(T) Neath to Merthyr road
Notes: weirs need some caution
Quality: ** and ***

An excellent section of river which, when in flood, has a big volume feel with numerous playspots.

Dinas Rock to Resolven: 12 km grade II to III ***

When I did this section, I got on in Glyn Neath from the main road bridge. A far better access point is from Dinas Rock car park in Pontneddfechan which adds two kilometres of bouncy grade II to III water GR911079. However, Dinas Rock is a car theft blackspot. **Don't leave valuables in the car**.

The Neath runs in a beautiful valley, which is recovering from the ravages of the mining era. During a big flood the camouflaged slag heaps give up their secrets and the river can run a coal-black colour. Normal floods run brown which clear when dropping and make the abundant kingfishers flash even more as they lead the paddler downstream.

In the first couple of kilometres below the Glyn Neath bridge are a series of seven or eight weirs. All can be shot or played in, depending on water levels. If in any doubt, **portage**. There is an old stone bridge with various arches to choose from. If you are unsure of your judgment, inspect the other side as the weir stoppers below may give an *unwelcome surprise*! Some of the holes are superb for honing stopper skills. The river eases off, running fast and flat to the egress point at Resolven, GR826032. There is a public right of way along much of the river bank here. An alternative for a longer trip is to continue to Aberdulais.

Resolven to Aberdulais: 8 km grade II; one weir requires caution **

Access as above at the Resolven bridge carrying the B4434 from the main road into town. A small footbridge is reached below which is a small horseshoe weir step with good waves. Further down is a more formal weir with classic weir buildings on the right. Shootable at most water levels but, if you decide to portage, **go left**. The river slows down and passes through Wenallt woods on its way to Aberdulais. A good egress point is where the river bends right up to the road, before sweeping left and over the large weir by the confluence with the Dulais GR773994. Parking can be found in Aberdulais car park.

Cwm Gwrelych

Map:	Brecon Beacons, no. 160
Grade:	V
Length:	2.5 km
Access:	A465(T) Merthyr to Neath road
Notes:	various portages
Quality:	**for novelty value

An outrageous little run.

Rhigos slag heap to Glyn Neath: 2.5 km grade V; various portages**

Take the little road up from Pont Walby towards Rhigos then bear off right back towards Blaengwrach. Some way along, the road crosses over a small road bridge with the stream passing steeply below through the guts of the slag heap. This is pure adventure at an extreme level for those into this type of run: don't expect play-boating!

Inspect and protect as you go. There is one, narrow drop into a shallow pool that most will portage. As the mother tributary is reached, there is a 20-foot fall onto rock - *portage*.

Further down the main stream are three amphitheatre-shaped falls. A poor man's Travo! The first is a bit shallow. The others are fine. Further still is another mandatory portage of 20 or so feet of water into trees. Finish the run with grade IV rapids and a run down the Pont Walby tunnel. Egress at the first road bridge over the Neath or continue down this river described elsewhere in the book, GR885066.

Afon Sychryd

Map:	Brecon Beacons, no. 160
Grade:	IV to V
Length:	2 km
Access:	off A465 Merthyr to Neath road
Notes:	one definite portage - two trees at time of writing; and one possible portage of fall
Quality:	*

A strange little river - best done in high water. I have received many letters over the years commenting on rivers. One of these recommended the above and asked why I hadn't paddled it. So, here it is, though I'm not sure I can really recommend it - perhaps I had a bad day, so please keep those ideas coming in.

.

Trebanog Isaf to Mellte confluence Dinas Rock: 2 km grade IV to V; portages*

Eastbound on the Heads of the Valleys road, a little way past Pontneddfechan, are a series of laybys. One is conveniently right above the river at GR924073. Scramble down to where you can launch below the tunnel immediately above a little class III fall. The adventurous may try the tunnel itself though I haven't done this. The water is grade II as it rushes along by staked and walled-up supports to the banks above - two trees needed portaging. A vertical ten-foot drop is reached which is probably **best portaged** as it drops into a shallow pool, though it has certainly been done. A section of class II to III leads under a wooden footbridge to the best falls on the river: IV to V, which end through a ten metre-long gorge. The river flattens out and an enormous cave is seen on the right. Time to portage the horrible boulder choke immediately downstream. This is best done on left *with the use of a rope.* The right hand path seemed unduly dangerous. Just below is a class IV and accompanying debris that you may want to shoot before the final section leading down below the bridge and into the Mellte. You'll remember it if nothing else.

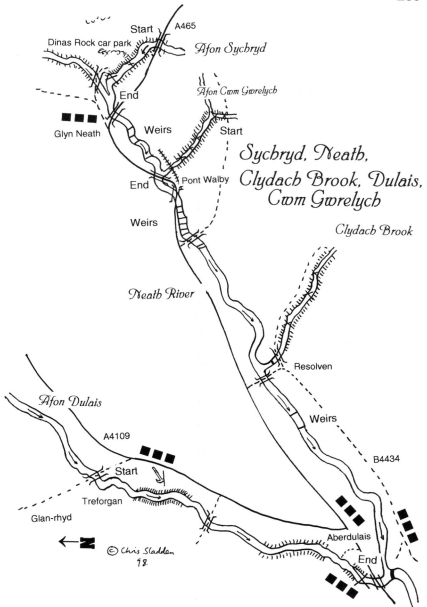

Start
A465
Dinas Rock car park
Afon Sychryd

End
Afon Cwm Gwrelych

Weirs
Start
Glyn Neath

End
Pont Walby

Weirs

Sychryd, Neath,
Clydach Brook, Dulais,
Cwm Gwrelych

Clydach Brook

Neath River

Resolven

Afon Dulais

Weirs

A4109

Start

B4434

Treforgan

Glan-rhyd

Aberdulais

© Chris Sladden
98.

End

Afon Hepste

Map:	Brecon Beacons, no. 160
Grade:	IV to V
Length:	3 km, plus 3 km on Mellte
Access:	A4059 Hirwaun to Brecon road
Notes:	portages around waterfalls; underwater sumps
Quality:	***

The Hepste is an alternative start to the Mellte run, but requires some effort to get to. It is an exciting grade IV to V run, but is **not for inexperienced people surviving at this grade**. Due to its bedrock nature, this river is potentially very dangerous.

Bryn Cul farm to Dinas Rock: 6 km grade IV to V***

There are various ways to walk in to the Afon Hepste. From Penderyn, a footpath allows access to above the gorge at GR937098. Or, continuing through Penderyn on the A4059, there is a footpath just past the cattle grid that allows access to the river. Although the farmer here is friendly enough, he isn't keen on people walking down his private road, so please stick to the footpath. This reaches the river at GR941104, below a small bridge. It is even possible, in big flood, to put on at the normally dry river bed at the Ty Mawr bridge GR945112. However, in these conditions, the gorge below is frightening and outrageous.

The river falls away at continually rocky grade IV until its character changes and a true gorge is entered. There is one 15-foot fall that is easily runnable but with the possibility of severe consequences if things went wrong. Kim Jones has some horror stories about this one. Just looking at low water will show a cave behind which is jammed full of logs - ooh, horrible. Here, the water often doubles in volume as underwater sumps add their flow. Below the drop, totally invisible at high water, is an underwater 50 metre sump - not the place to go swimming. In fact it is quite enlightening to walk the gorge in summer low conditions - a beautiful walk and very interesting.

Excellent ledge stoppers lead down to the thundering Sgwd yr Eira Falls. Although these have been shot on various occasions, it is sensible to portage right and take a walk down to the falls. The scene of many poems and various films, it is possible to walk behind these "falls of snow" as is the English name. In flood, this is totally awe-inspiring, as you stand there with the ground itself trembling. There is nothing anti-climactic about portaging Sgwd yr Eira. The gorge below is only thinkable when the water is low. Even then, to miss the break out above the last of the four drops will mean the end of your paddling career. It is best to carry on with the portage, on the right bank, until it is possible to drop back down to the river (unless choosing a level to do the falls).

A few hundred metres on and past a fallen tree, the Mellte is entered. This is described in its own right but, in short, is as follows: there are two playful stoppers just below the confluence. A great gorge is entered. One fall, onto rock, is easily shot if your back will take it. One weir after is best portaged before the now well-known looping pool is reached. This partially man-made shoot is the best place in the world for pop-outs and multiple loops. Finish the run past another weir reaching Dinas Rock car park GR912079.

Afon Mellte

Map:	Brecon Beacons, no. 160
Grade:	IV to V
Length:	6 km
Access:	off the A465 Hirwaun to Neath road
Notes:	various portages
Quality:	****

The Mellte is one of the most popular white water rivers in South Wales. It holds its water at a canoeable level for a few days after rain, giving class IV water. In flood, it is a much harder and serious class V paddle. Prudent portages are a small price to pay for isolation in this outstanding gorge. It is best not to leave valuables in the car at either the access or egress points - a sad reflection of the times.

Sgwd Clun-gwyn falls to Dinas Rock: 5 km IV to V; various portages****

Just off the A46T Hirwaun to Neath road is the village of Pontneddfechan, which adjoins Glyn Neath. Taking the steep road out of the village towards Ystradfellte, a cattle grid plus rough parking is reached after about five kilometres. Here, by setting off down the public footpaths, access is possible to the river below a major waterfall, Sgwd Clun-gwyn. Originally, and with some novelty value, I used to access the river below Porth yr Ogof. This gave an extra kilometre or so of class III with a difficult portage around the above fall. Now we always walk in to below the drop - it's easier. The fall has been run (by Shaun Baker, Alun Barrett *et al*) but is **generally portaged**.

An easy stretch takes the paddler to Sgwd Isaf Clun Gwyn, a huge waterfall that is found just around a right hand bend. Again, this has been run both on purpose and by accident. The message is clear: if you are not sure where it is have a quick look from the bank! *Portage*.
Immediately below is a 15-foot class V slot, or class V+ powerful fall, depending upon water level. This has been run many times. Immediately below are some excellent Corsica-like drops (see photos S W Wales guide). One of these contained a tree during my last paddles, Autumn '97. Easier water leads down to Sgwd y Pannwr, a large, vertical waterfall found on a left to right slant across the river. This is runnable at around class V or so in the right water levels - ie. high-ish.

Portage along the left bank. Below, are some good drops before the Hepste thunders in from the left. Immediately below are two good stoppers which became a bit sticky in high water. Below here the river passes through several beautiful gorges containing some good class IV or V rapids. All are runnable depending upon water levels on the day, tree damage and keenness. One you may remember as it falls directly onto rock and is preceded by a tricky little slot quite capable of some significant back loops! Also along this section is the now well-known **Paul Howells' Tree rapid** - an easy rapid with an almost-invisible tree responsible for sucking the old man of the Wye out of his boat (Owd Butt). A moral lies here somewhere, for he is a strong and able boater.

The river straightens and the water eases off until the presence of a man-made, vertical weir. This has had various descents but, when low, the landing is suspect and, when high, the stopper has dealt out some severe thrashings. It is generally portaged on the left using the little overflow channel.

Below here is the excellent gunpowder works weir slot or the looping pool. In high flows, one survives the stopper but in medium levels **it is brilliant for pulling all kinds of stunts**. Further down is another, more chossy but runnable weir before the egress point at Dinas rock car park   GR912079.

Afon Llia

Map:	Brecon Beacons, no. 160
Grade:	III to IV
Length:	3 km
Access:	Ystradfellte to Sennybridge road
Notes:	fences need to be avoided; one fall is usually portaged; possible trees
Quality:	**

A fast mountain stream requiring caution because of low trees and fences. One fall is best portaged. Paddled with the Dringarth, it makes for an excellent day out. In early 1998, Nick Eaves told me that the run is snaggled with trees at present but that he had met a farmer who was planning to remove a few for firewood.

Forestry parking place to Afon Mellte: grade III to IV; one waterfall*

Start the run at a parking place just off the Sennybridge road GR928165. Put on below a fence crossing the river. When the river is in flood, the paddler quickly passes down through a forested area. Inspection for trees is required. About halfway down on a left hand bend is a major 18-foot vertical drop into a shallow pool. This has been shot but is **best portaged**. Some of the drops below reach grade IV. Care is required as the confluence is reached because of trees across the river. One required portaging at the time of writing.

Afon Dringarth

Map:	Brecon Beacons, no. 160
Grade:	III to IV; one fall V-
Length:	4 km
Access:	Ystradfellte to Sennybridge road
Notes:	few fences
Quality:	**

The river runs out of Ystradfellte reservoir and relies on dam spill plus stream top-up to be running. Combined with one of the other trips in the area the river makes for a good day out.

Reservoir to Shoni's Farm: 4 km III to IV; one large drop**

There is a small road that crosses at the confluence of the Llia and Dringarth. This can be reached either by continuing up the Mellte, or turning off over the Hepste river north of Penderyn. Both roads end up just north of the village of Ystradfellte, and a public footpath can be followed upstream between the two rivers on the true right-hand of the Dringarth.

Put on via the right bank well **below the reservoir**. In big spate, the river is a serious grade IV but at normal high levels (bouncy grade II water at confluence with Afon Llia) it is a good grade III. About a kilometre down, there is a sloping fall with a fence stretched across the bottom of it. At grade III levels this can just about be sneaked under. From all accounts this may now have gone, but I haven't been down here for a little while.

The banks close in and a large, vertical fall blocks the river. This grade V- fall can be run middle to left or via the left hand chicken shoot, but the landing is a bit suspect. In flood, it produces an enormous stopper, which produces some spectacular back-enders! Below this, two fences needed to be portaged **on the right**.

Otherwise, enjoy a beautiful river in tremendous surroundings. Egress at start of walk-in. One word of note: don't leave boats lying about - they have a habit of being pinched. If they do, ring the police who, from experience, will know the culprits! A moral tale lies hidden here somewhere! It is best on this river to always keep on the right hand bank. This belongs to Shoni and family - very good friends of mine who are happy to see young people enjoying themselves. Unfortunately, the same cannot be said surrounding the circumstances of the left hand bank (disappearing boats).

Nant y Gwair

Map: Brecon Beacons, no. 160
Grade: IV (one fall V)
Length: 2.5 km
Access: Ystradfellte to Sennybridge road
Notes: fences
Quality: ***

An expedition in the making! When Mark Crick and I first ran this river, we had walked in about a month before and buried a boat under a heap of soil and stones. This was to make the walk-in during the rain much easier. We were keen in those days.

Rhos Dringarth to Ystradfellte Reservoir: 2.5 km grade IV***

It is only possible to recommend this short stretch to the highly adventurous. The walk-in with the boat takes about one and a half hours and it needs to be heavily raining at the time. It is possible to walk in from the old Roman Road skirting around Fan Dringarth GR935204. Alternatively, and probably better, is to carry on from the walk-in to the Afon Dringarth, described below. This is via the footpath on river right of the Afon Dringarth, starting just before the confluence with the Llia GR936144.

All these rivers are only big enough for three or four paddlers so please use common sense. The family on the farm through which the footpath runs are true gems so please treat them as such! They are quite happy with small groups paddling the rivers and allow landing on the right hand banks. Shoni and Betty exemplify the real spirit of true Welsh hill farming.

Start the run as high up as the boat will float. In spate the paddling is grade IV, with one fall of V just before the confluence with the Nant y Gaseg.

A strainer prevents the paddler entering the reservoir, which is probably a prudent move. You could either run back up for more goes down, or walk along to the Afon Dringarth for another brilliant run.

The Nedd Fechan

Map:	Brecon Beacons, no. 160
Grade:	IV to V
Length:	3.5 km
Access:	off A465(T) Hirwaun to Neath road
Notes:	two waterfalls - portages
Quality:	****

The Nedd Fechan is a superb white water river, falling steeply through a beautiful and rugged gorge in the heart of the South Wales mountains. During the haecceity of my youth, when I was trying to push and explore as much as possible, I launched on the Nedd Fechan well above the starting point described in the first South Wales book. The river was in big flood, and I took a sharp break out above a steep rapid with an ominous roar. Inspection revealed the whole river turning into an awesome maelstrom before it disappeared down a sump. You may wish to stick to the suggested access point rather than risk a first and last descent of Pwll y Rhyd.

Pont Melin-Fach: 3.5 km class IV to V; two portages ****

Take the first turn off left from the steep Pontneddfechan to Ystradfellte road. This crosses the river at Pont Melin Fach where there is a convenient car park by the river GR908105. The paddler sets off on easy water in a beautifully wooded gorge. Some few 100 metres on is a three-metre double drop. There should be ample water over this if the run is to be worthwhile. A short distance further, around a right hand bend, is the **first portage**. This 20-foot vertical drop (known as Wondre's Wonder) is too shallow to run! Since the first book's publication, there have been a succession of paddlers running Wondre's Wonder, **a fair number of whom have ended up with broken ankles!** *Be warned*. Beautiful though it is, the landing is shallow on the Upper Ddwli Falls. It is worthwhile inspecting the following 200 metres of river as, tagged on the bottom, is a far more serious drop. This is the Lower Ddwli Falls where the water tumbles over a millstone grit edge onto a fronting pavement. I know of no one who has run the fall - *Portage*.

Using throw ropes for security whilst lowering down, the paddler can continue from almost the plunge pool itself. This next section down until the confluence with the Pyrddin contains some excellent falls IV to V. Easy enough in low to medium levels, they become a real challenge in spate and you are forced to take some bold lines through major stoppers.

Below here the gorge is still pleasant, but the grade drops to II to III as the river makes its final journey towards the Neath. Egress at the bridge in Pontneddfechan, conveniently situated next to the Angel Inn GR901077.

Afon Pyrddin

Map:	Brecon Beacons, no. 160
Grade:	IV to IV+
Length:	4 km
Access:	A5109 Glyn Neath to Abercraf road
Notes:	Two waterfalls, one a definite and the other nearly always portaged
Quality:	**** for the expedition value

One of the hidden expeditions of South Wales. One I've only just paddled but a brilliant trip (winter of '96/'97). It is only paddleable in flood and, if you get big water and sunshine, don't forget your camera because the scenery is remarkable. It is best to take a full day *to avoid scrambling round the big edges in the dark! - to be avoided! The river is for experienced adventurers only.*

Forestry bridge to Angel Inn: 4 km IV to IV+; two portages****

Driving up the steep A4109 Glyn Neath to Abercraf road a mining reclamation area is passed on the left and, shortly afterwards, there is a forestry road on the right, usually closed, with a green gate. Access can be made at a bridge 500 metres down this good track (it helps to have a key). There is 500 metres of grade III and IV drops down to a new wooden footbridge. After this the river enters a gorge with grade III water - great care is needed as a few hundred metres down is an awesome waterfall deep in the Pyrddin gorge - *a definite and tricky portage.* Scwd Einion Gam (the fall of the Crooked Anvil) falls over **25 metres** of vertical cliff. This is *directly* at the end of a steep and closed-in grade IV rapid and is portaged with difficulty - scrambling with rope protection well below the fall on the left. Putting on at the foot of the falls allows the running of a grade IV+ drop, at the bottom of this spectacular gorge. Easier water leads to the lip of Gladys (or Lady-) Fall - another nearly always **portaged drop**. One look at the plunge pool in low water will put off most intrepid sky divers. However, this has been run - I have seen video of Tim Davies running this in high flows, and, no, he didn't break his leg doing this but by playing rugby in South Wales - a dangerous occupation.

Below the falls is a final U-shaped grade IV, plus a couple of smaller drops, before the confluence of the Nedd Fechan. Continue down this until the Angel Inn.

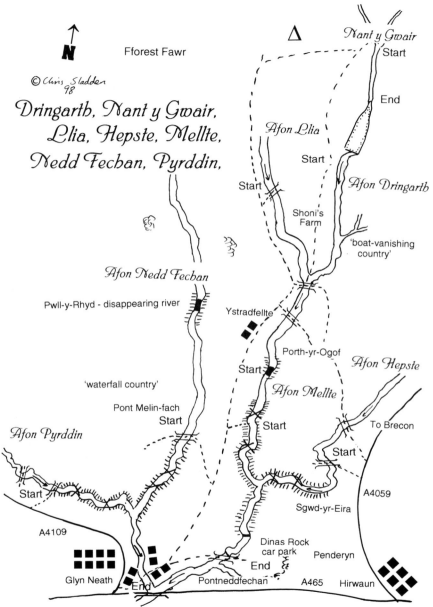

N

Fforest Fawr

© Chris Sladden
98

Dringarth, Nant y Gwair,
Llia, Hepste, Mellte,
Nedd Fechan, Pyrddin,

Nant y Gwair
Start

Δ

End

Afon Llia

Start

Start

Afon Dringarth

Shoni's
Farm

'boat-vanishing
country'

Afon Nedd Fechan

Pwll-y-Rhyd - disappearing river

Ystradfellte

Porth-yr-Ogof

Afon Hepste

Start

Afon Mellte

'waterfall country'

Pont Melin-fach
Start

Start

To Brecon

Afon Pyrddin

Start

Start

A4059

Sgwd-yr-Eira

Start

Dinas Rock
car park

Penderyn

End

Glyn Neath

End

Pontneddfechan

A465

Hirwaun

A4109

Afon Dulais

Map:	Brecon Beacons, no. 160
	Vale of Glamorgan and Rhondda area, no. 170
Grade:	III; one fall grade IV to V
Length:	9 km
Access:	A4109 Aberdulais to Merthyr road
Notes:	there is one hard fall of grade IV (V in very big flows); Aberdulais Falls is a *portage* - best to egress well above
Quality:	***

An excellent though dirty river.

Crynant to Aberdulais: 9 km grade III***

Driving along the A4109 the village of Crynant is reached and there is a small road going off to Glan Rhyd. This crosses the river where access is easy on the true left bank GR793063. The colour of the water may fool you into thinking the water is at a good canoeing level. It is always brown or grey; a constant reminder of the upheaval of the earth in days gone by. The search for coal is one matter, but short-sighted locals and farmers using the rivers as a dumping ground for rubbish is a sad sign of present day attitudes. The local kids have always been very friendly towards me and I find it sad that they have to learn to fish, an important part of growing up, in such surroundings. Enough said: if the shingle banks are covered the paddling is great. A few miles down, and you enter an excellent grade III mini-gorge. At the right water level there are some great play spots here.

Further down, an old railway bridge is passed and some way below a 200-metre, steep grade IV rapid is reached. This can be quite hard and reach grade V in massive flood. Some further rapids take the paddler under an old arched footbridge. Egress is just along here on the left bank and up to the nearby housing estate in Aberdulais GR774996. This is found by taking the second turning on the left past Aberdulais, from the main road to Glyn Neath. Then, turn down into the road signposted Ger yr Afon ("by the river"). Further on is Aberdulais Falls, which is a definite portage. The only feasible portage route is to clamber through the fenced-off National Trust territory - not a good idea as they don't like it. **Egress above.**

Clydach Brook

Map:	Vale of Glamorgan and Rhondda area, no. 170
Grade:	IV to V with harder falls best portaged
Length:	2.5 km
Access:	A465(T) Neath to Merthyr road
Notes:	some of the harder falls are *portaged*. In flood, the portages become desperate
Quality:	***

A hard-hitting, exciting adventure for those paddling at a good grade IV standard and above. This has seen various descents since the publication of the first book and seems to hold a morbid fascination for paddlers. So go there, if you will, and find paddling like no other.

Old footbridge to Resolven: 2.5 km grade IV to V, plus portages***

Take the B4434 into Resolven (off main A465(T)) and bear off in town across the little bridge and up the little road on the true right bank of the stream. By keeping right you will end up in a rough gravel area where there is ample parking. A small track leads off directly down to an old footbridge spanning the stream GR846021. The stream should have a good flow but not be in major flood, when the portaging will be desperate!

At the time of writing, where the stream steepens some trees required portaging. Further on, there is an excellent blast to under a second footbridge. The next fall had a tree in it. Just below is an old water-diverting channel to the right where higher flows offer an alternative to trees. When lower this is obstructed by an old motor car 'thoughtfully' left by the locals.

A new mini-gorge is entered. The entrance fall is grade V to VI and reminiscent of Corsica but, at time of writing, had a tree blocking the line (luckily). This would be easily removed by an interested group (Kimberley Jones was heard to mutter something about a good task for the local scouts during Bob-A-Job Week!).

The next but one fall is also grade V+ to VI, which was normally portaged left - though it apparently has seen a few descents by now. There are a few excellent drops to do before the stream opens out as it enters Resolven. One sloping weir is left before the stream enters the Neath. Egress on the left just before the footbridge GR826032.

Nant Tywynni

Map:	Brecon Beacons, no. 160
Grade:	IV
Length:	4 km
Access:	A4067 Abercraf to Sennybridge road
Notes:	barbed wire, low bridges and one fall generally portaged
Quality:	**

A second tributary of the Tawe, this can only be run when in full spate. Entertaining in its own way, it is perhaps a worthwhile alternative when the upper Tawe is too high!

Tower to confluence: 4 km grade IV**

On a very wet day, it is possible to launch onto the stream where the main road crosses the river GR867193. The stream is less wide than the length of a boat but is entertaining enough in its own right. Some way down is a steep fall onto rock that is best portaged, especially if using your own boat! In fact it is easily run but has split three boats to my knowledge alone. Various barbed wires are slung across the river on the section below this drop - these need to be portaged. As the river flattens out, a low footbridge requires portaging. It is a relief to see that there is no massive stopper guarding the exit to the A4067 road tunnel as you hurl through unable to stop. Continue down to egress at the Glyntawe bridge. Better still, continue down the fabulous Tawe, one of the top few rivers in Wales.

Afon Tawe

Map:	Brecon Beacons, no. 160
	Vale of Glamorgan and Rhondda area, no. 170
Grade:	sections of II,III, IV to V and V to VI
Length:	34 km
Access:	off A4067 Swansea to Sennybridge road
Notes:	certain falls or weirs may require portaging depending upon water levels
Quality:	** and *** and *****

The upper sections of the Afon Tawe gives some of the finest high grade runs in the country. The river rises and falls remarkably quickly but, in the right conditions, gives some outstanding wild water sections through rugged scenery - not that you have much time to observe this. The river is jealously guarded by local fishermen, though attempts have been made to try and find agreement.

The Upper Tawe gorge: Stone Circle to Glyntawe: 6 km V to VI; some tree portages*****

Turn off from the A4069 just north of Glyntawe towards Trecastle. The road climbs steeply before following the river as they both skirt the eastern flanks of Mynydd Ddu. Some way along here the road comes very close to some respectable drops which can be clearly seen GR852213. There is good access above these. In high water we have paddled from the source of the Tawe some three kilometres higher, but this is more of an adventure than good canoeing.

The river needs to be in a reasonable spate to be worth doing. If you don't like these first drops, forget the gorge. As an indication, if you scrape a little at the access point, the gorge below will be IV, and if the drops start back-looping significantly it will be V+ to VI. A good level is somewhere in between.

Exciting water takes the paddler down some excellent steep and bouncy slabs before the walls start closing in and the gorge is entered. A small slot, similar to the Mellte's looping pool, is passed, plus some fast and exciting narrows before a major, 15-foot drop is reached. Unfortunately, for the last couple of years, this has been blocked with a major fallen tree. At present there is no route through.

Below this are some brilliant falls as the Tawe forces its way through its attractively-sculptured upper gorge. Sadly, at the end of '97, there were a further three, huge, fallen trees all requiring portages. However, I know one of the farmers who lives along here fairly well, and I'm going to pitch up with a bottle of whisky and see what can be done.

A footbridge appears (offers escape on the left bank) and the river drops over a brilliant set of squirts and slides into a pool, before plunging over a final sharp fall with a seemingly difficult rock obstruction to miss (and with a water pipe overhead). This is top-notch boating. Below these falls is one of the trees mentioned above - the original one which has been present for a number of years. The water eases off to grade III and IV before the banks open out and the best is over. Carry on down past the confluence of the Nant Tywynni to the bridge at Glyntawe where egress can be made just above onto the right hand **footpath** GR846166.

Glyntawe to Abercraf: 7 km of IV to V to V+*****

Access as above, GR846168, for this second superb section. The grade can easily vary by two at different water levels. Grade II to III water takes the adventurer through the Craig y Nos Country Park to the bridge at Rhongyr Isaf GR845145. If the water is flowing through the trees right over the banks en-route, then the run below this bridge is a serious undertaking. Egress if in doubt. This bridge, signposted to Penwyllt, allows an escape route, or a shorter trip should you not wish for a warm up!

An excellent grade IV run through large waves and holes takes the paddler down to the Pen y Cae bridge. In full spate, this section rises to a serious grade V with some enormous almost river wide stoppers forming. Just before the printing of this book I received a letter from a respected South Wales paddler saying: *"I didn't really think that South Wales could give big water class V until I paddled the Tawe in the high spate of Christmas '97. This is serious, mind-blowing but exciting stuff".* Since the publication of the first book, there have been some major epics during descents of the Tawe, with boats being chased by police helicopters!

There are some large falls over sloping slabs just below the Pen y Cae bridge, which become a very serious undertaking in high water. Enormous stoppers are a very frightening prospect V (VI occasionally!). If in any doubt, portage left.

Some hundreds of metres further on is a large, natural, vertical fall. The route must be left for you to decide - right is the safest but avoid an undercut slot left of centre! The river rushes through a narrow gorge at a good grade IV or V until easing off before the main road bridge before Abercraf. Egress is on the left GR826127.

Abercraf to Twrch confluence: 10 km grade III; one weir portaged in spate***

There is a footpath by the main road bridge upstream of Abercraf that allows access onto the water. This is the egress point for the above run GR827127.

In between the next small bridge and the next main road bridge is Abercraf weir. At low to medium water, the best time to do this run, this is possible with speed. *In a flood it is deadly* and must be approached with great caution and portaged on the right. It can be inspected by walking through the children's playground in the village. It is best portaged from at least 30 metres above! This weir has been swum, the paddler surviving but having a religious experience. It is angled on a left-hand bend and if you approach it from this side you can easily get flushed over. **Approach with care on the right!**

The gorge below is superb, especially so for those relatively new to the sport and this is what it is all about. There are plenty of waves to play in on of the way down to Ystradgynlais. The Giedd river enters from the right. Just below and under a small road bridge is a double weir. This is a okay if taken fast at medium levels. However, in a flood the stopper becomes dangerous. It is worth driving into town to inspect this prior to paddling as it is a little difficult to stop above. A few more broken weirs lead the paddler down to the Twrch river confluence where good egress may be had on the right hand bank GR770084.

Twrch confluence to Swansea: 20 km II; various weirs**

Turn off left at the roundabout on the A4067 into lower Ystradgynlais which leads to the Twrch confluence GR770084. Good access to the river may be made here. At the right levels there is a superb surfing wave just below. This section of the river can get into an angry flood when all the side streams, of which there are many, are full to the brim. At these levels it is probably best to leave the lower Tawe until another day. There is one railway bridge halfway down that sticks in the mind, as it had half the trees of the Swansea Valley rammed through its girders by a tremendous force. This was six feet above the level I have done it at. In big flood I suspect that there would be, probably, just enough room for one or two stray paddlers to fit - Beware!

About one kilometre below the Twrch confluence there is *an enormous sloping weir*. Although straightforward at medium flows this should be scouted and, if necessary, portaged on the right. From here down to the get-off point there is fast flow, with the occasional wave to play in.

Egress is above or below the three broken weirs, which are good for playing in, near Morriston. Turn off junction 45 of the M4 where, a little way past the first roundabout in town, a road goes off down to waste ground near the river GR672974.

It should be noted that there is a new weir on the river just below Pontardawe. I haven't been back to do this, but it is, apparently, canoeable with care at medium levels. Be cautious though.

The Haffes

Map:	Brecon Beacons, no. 160
Grade:	V to VI
Length:	2.5 km
Access:	A4067 Abercraf to Sennybridge road
Notes:	two fences a little way above egress point; one just below
Quality:	*****

"Wild", "outrageous" and "once in a lifetime" are words and expressions to describe the Haffes. In its own way it is one of the hardest runs in Wales. Just writing these notes is enough to set the heart racing! For the walker in the paddler, the Horns of Mynydd Ddu is one of the best walks in South Wales. These rise above the source of the Haffes. Since the publication of the original notes of the Haffes, I have been asked many times why I think it such a hard run. This is because of the following: on most of the rivers that are graded V to VI it is possible, and indeed imperative to pick the ideal water level to run the section. With the Haffes this is simply not an option: it only goes in a major floods - you pays your money and you takes your chances!

Scwd Ddu to Glyntawe: 2.5 km grade V to VI*****

The Haffes is an outstanding run. Only possible *after very heavy rain*, it rises and falls incredibly quickly. At Glyntawe, take the footpath on the true left hand bank of the river GR846166 and start walking. If you don't like the sight of things in the first 100 metres, then it is far better to return another day! The river is followed up the true left bank all the way.

The brave will put in on the plunge pool of the large waterfall a little way below Scwd Ddu (The Black Waterfall). The first few hundred metres is a bedrock slide with a monstrous rapid tumbling out of the pool for the next 500 metres. This makes for one of the wildest descents in the country! Things ease off to Grade V! A swim would be disastrous. There are two fences a few hundred metres above the main road bridge that need portaging. It is essential to egress before the small bridge in Glyntawe as a lethal fence is hung from below. You won't have the adrenalin for another run.

One of my more enthusiastic of boating friends has been desperate to do the Haffes for some time now, but it so rarely comes up. On Christmas Eve 1997 it was pumping, but Tim's leg was in plaster. Not that this stopped him paddling but it stopped him doing the arduous two and a half kilometres of uphill walking. He was demoted (wrapped with a fertilizer bag) to doing the mighty Tawe instead!

Stopping for coffee with some good friends during a trip down the Gwili. Huw, Robert and D4 of White Water Consultancy and myself take some time out. Photo Linda Coote

Shaun Baker - pioneer of Welsh rivers during the '80s shreds a
wave on The Bitches. Photo: Heather Gunn
Reproduction sponsored by Huw Evans of *White Water Consultancy International Ltd.*

Dropping off a summer storm on the Clydach Gorge (tributary of
the Usk), Dick Renshaw leads the way. Photo: Chris Sladden
collection
If the Haffes is 'on' then the walk-in will almost be canoeable.
Photo: Chris Sladden collection

Illegal but allegedly entertaining - Llyn Brianne's spillway

Dropping into one kilometre of continual raging rapid on the
Pontardawe Clydach.
Reproduction for both illus. sponsored by Huw Evans of *White Water Consultancy International Ltd.*

The Author takes the 'General Belgrano' down the falls at Betws y
Garmon on the Gwyrfai. Photo: Chris Sladden collection.

Fun in the sun on the Machno. Photo: Chris Sladden collection

The stunning North Wales Llyfni. Photo: Chris Sladden collection

Reproduction for both illus. sponsored by Huw Evans of *White Water Consultancy International Ltd.*

River Wye at Symonds Yat - a little way before it passes back into
Wales again. Photo: Foxy
Reproduction for illus. sponsored by Huw Evans of *White Water Consultancy International Ltd.*

The top drop on Pont Cyfyng, Afon Llugwy. Photo: Foxy

Reproduction for illus. sponsored by Huw Evans of *White Water Consultancy International Ltd.*

Afon Giedd

Map:	Brecon Beacons, no. 160
Grade:	upper IV to V; lower II
Length:	5 km
Access:	A4067
Notes:	one tree at the top of the gorge required careful negotiation
Quality:	***

Combined with the Nant Cyw, this is a great day out for the thrill-seeker.

Dorwen ar Giedd to Tawe confluence: 5 km grade IV to V***

There are two reasonable approaches into the Giedd river. One is from the Nant Gwys put-on - see relevant page. From here it is possible to head north-easterly over the mountain until you reach the Giedd. The other way is to drive up the small road through Cwm Giedd to the car park and picnic site at GR792128 and then walk up the steep footpath on the true R bank of the river. The river needs to be in spate to run, with the bigger the spate, the harder the gorge.

Get on where you like. The moorland run above the gorge is a refreshing grade II to III run. There was one tree at the top of the gorge that required negotiating at time of writing. Soon a fantastic gorge is entered. There is one kilometre of continually increasing difficulties, involving falls, squirts and pot holes to be negotiated. The gorge finishes off at the picnic site. The two and a half kilometres of grade II water down to the Tawe confluence is well worth doing. Egress above the bridge on the right GR789110, or further down the Tawe.

Nant Cyw

Map:	Brecon Beacons, no. 160
Grade:	IV
Length:	1 km
Access:	A4067 Swansea to Sennybridge road
Notes:	inspect for trees in the gorge.
Quality:	***when combined with the Giedd

Though a bit of a one-hit wonder, because of its unique nature the gorge is well worth combining with the Giedd.

Nant Cyw gorge to Giedd confluence: 1 km grade IV***

Drive to the picnic site mentioned in the Giedd write-up. Walk upstream on the true left bank of the Nant Cyw and get on above the gorge. The gorge itself is so narrow that it is imperative to inspect for trees before paddling. Some small drops lead into this fantastic six foot-wide gorge which goes at a hard grade IV. The last time we ran this, we had to haul a tree out of the entrance drop, but then proceeded to do the gorge 4 or 5 times. A great day out.

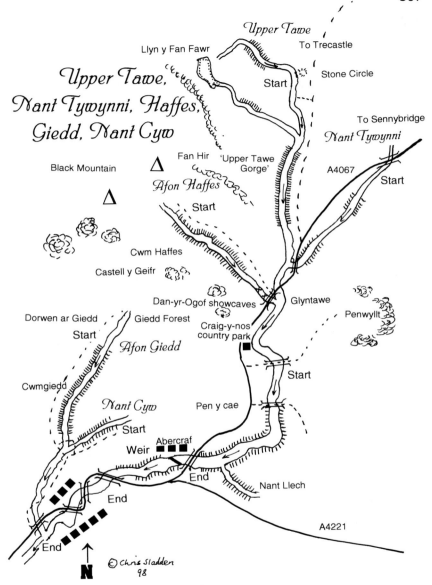

Upper Tawe

To Trecastle

Llyn y Fan Fawr

Stone Circle

Start

To Sennybridge

Nant Tywynni

Upper Tawe,
Nant Tywynni, Haffes,
Giedd, Nant Cyw

Fan Hir   'Upper Tawe
Gorge'

A4067

Start

Black Mountain

△

Afon Haffes

△

Start

Cwm Haffes

Castell y Geifr

Dan-yr-Ogof showcaves

Glyntawe

Penwyllt

Dorwen ar Giedd   Giedd Forest

Craig-y-nos
country park

Start

Afon Giedd

Cwmgiedd

Start

Nant Cyw

Pen y cae

Start

Abercraf

Weir

End

Nant Llech

End

End

A4221

End

© Chris Sladden
98

N

Nant Gwys

Map:	Brecon Beacons, no. 160
Grade:	II to III
Length:	4.5 km
Access:	A4067
Notes:	trees and one fence needed careful negotiating
Quality:	★★★

Stream canoeing *par excellence*.

Minerva Centre to Twrch confluence: 4.5 km grade II to III[**]

Take the Pelleg road by turning off into Gurnos from the A4067. Take the right hand fork, a couple of kilometres along which allows access onto the river by the Minerva centre GR783130.

The river needs to be up enough to float a boat without hitting rocks, but not enough to be obviously fearsome. One barbed wire fence on the upper half of the river *required careful* negotiating at time of writing. Below the little road bridge is an excellent play stopper on a little weir.

The gorges that follow will give the paddler a taste of the real thing and, after tasting this, will almost certainly get you hooked to stream paddling. For the unusually broad-minded paddler, the shale sides here are excellent for fossils. Egress at the first of the two bridges 50 metres above the Twrch GR757114.

Afon Twrch

Map:	Brecon Beacons, no. 160
Grade:	III to IV and IV to V
Length:	12 km
Access:	A4068 Gurnos to Brynamman road
Notes:	weirs require caution and possible portage; two class VI falls in the upper section.
Quality:	***and****

The upper section of the river is a classic expedition type run, which has become a bit more problematical to get up to since the re-development of the open cast mine workings. At the right levels it provides a variety of testing water. Depending on water levels the lower Twrch is a great, bouncy grade III to IV. Caution needs to be exercised at various weirs.

<u>Dorwen to Ystradowen</u>: 5 km grade IV to V; two major class VI falls****

Take the small road to Ystradowen off the A4068 down to where the bridge crosses the river at GR755126. If the rapid below the bridge is well covered, giving a bouncy grade II, then you are in for an extremely exciting run upstream. Any higher and the tight gorges become hectic, though they have certainly been done in full flood by now. Unfortunately, it is now somewhat problematic to work your way upstream via the farms on the true left hand bank of the river. This is because of the redevelopment of an open cast coal mine. Ambrose Hearne did his best to persuade the company to let him through but, in his words, he "was escorted from the premises smartly". The alternatives are to head up the true right-hand bank of the river via the rough but drivable track. Providing the gates are unlocked it is possible to drive to within sight of the large chimney or, if you are lucky, possibly further. But, from here, it is a long hard walk up the, albeit-beautiful, valley.

Assuming you've, hopefully, not been put off by the walk-in, the place to aim for is the large 20-foot waterfall found north of the Dorwen. The walk is beautiful and is even better without the boat. This big drop has now been done on many occasions. Usually this is when the river is quite low. In flood it produces a huge whirlpool which presses everything underneath the left hand undercut. It is quite an awesome spectacle.

Below the falls, bouncy rapids take the paddler down to a sharp left-hand corner; a little way downstream from this is a good rapid with a big stopper at the bottom end. The river narrows as it enters a superbly-carved short gorge. This should be inspected before entering. There is one, very tight, drop at the bottom which is serious and awkward, especially so when the river is high. This is Grade V paddling at its best.

The river opens out before bending to the right. Inspection is necessary as, lurking around one of the corners, is a very dangerous grade VI fall. This has seen only a few descents over the years, especially so as it requires just the right water level and plenty of protection. In addition there is a right hand pot hole, and a left side sump and undercut, all of which make a very serious proposition. The sump itself has been dived to over a depth of 20 metres - not the place to be in a canoe! It is best portaged along the slippery ledge on the right.

Below this the river eases off, but the narrows near the old quarry workings are of interest. Some sloping weir-like drops just above the egress at the bridge can provide some entertainment. In high flows the stoppers are quite capable of doing battle: an excellent run.

Ystradowen to Tawe confluence: 7 km grade III to IV***

Drive up the A4068 towards Ammanford and turn off right on the sharp bend in Ystradowen. Drive down this small road to where it crosses the river and where the upper Twrch, a brilliant paddle, finishes.

In big water, the run is a fast, bouncy grade III to IV ride, including a few broken weirs down to the Nant Gwys confluence. Some larger broken weirs with larger stoppers lead to the two weirs in Cwm-Twrch Uchaf. In most conditions, these can be run after carefully scouting your line. I know of people who run these in the biggest of floods and, occasionally, in the dark but don't be misled by this. Both of these weirs are potentially *dangerous* - if in any doubt, *portage*. There are more rapids until the weir under the road bridge in Cwm-Twrch Isaf. This is best taken right but, if in any doubt, portage.

A diagonal step above the A4067 bridge can loop in high flows. 50 metres further on is the bridge in Ystalyfera, under which there is an enormous weir. This has been shot left many times, but has had recent repair work done to it. Repair work always gives the possibility of debris being thrown in the river. The message is clear - if in doubt, *portage*. This is a good egress point GR773093.

Alternatively, continue, and get off at the Tawe confluence.

Afon Cwm Du

Map:	Brecon Beacons, no. 160
Grade:	IV
Length:	1 km
Access:	off A4067 Swansea to Ystradgynlais road
Notes:	large waterfall above access
Quality:	**

The Cwm Du is a short but sweet *spate* tributary of the Tawe: good if you have an extra hour, plus the energy, after a Tawe trip.

Cwm Du Falls to Canal: 1 km grade IV; possible tree portages**

Turn off the A4067 a few miles north of Pontardawe into the village of Cilmaengwyn. It is possible to work your way up through the estate, where there is a track that leads up to an old mine. It is possible to walk upstream for about ten minutes or so until a large 20-foot fall is reached GR738068. This has been run but falls into a very dubious plunge pool. The river basically consists of a few sharp drops with a wild, sloping ramp about halfway down. Finish the run immediately below a little weir but **before the river sumps** under the canal bridge at GR742059.

Upper Clydach River

Map: Vale of Glamorgan and Rhondda area, no. 170
             Brecon Beacons, no. 160
Grade: (III to IV) to IV+
Length: 3 km
Access: A474 Pontardawe to Ammanford road
Notes: one grade VI fall; one weir - in flood becomes very dangerous
Quality: *****

In big flood, this gives about one and a half kilometres of continually exciting, hard paddling: not to be missed. It is a brilliant paddle

Rhyd y Fro to Pontardawe: 3 km grade (III to IV) to IV+; one VI and one weir *****

Take the A474 Pontardawe to Ammanford road. About three kilometres up the hill on the outskirts of Rhyd y Fro is a road going off left over the river. Access may be had here GR713058. An alternative is to make your way higher up the Afon Egel for a few kilometres of fast grade II to III water.

At the access point it is best to get on **below** the barbed wire fence that is slung from the bridge. If the stream looks brown and angry you are in for a brilliant ride. Lower water and a side-shoot tunnel on the left downstream is an entertaining alternative to the main flow.

Some way on and a bridge crosses the stream. A little way below this is a major grade **VI fall** which is only feasible in big flood. "It is yet to be done - *portage left*", I wrote in my 1994 book (the second in the series). Rumours abound that it has now had a few descents and it probably has: **even so it is an extremely dangerous undertaking**

In spate, the one and a half kilometres below the fall down to Pontardawe is a grade IV+ masterblaster. It is effectively just one continual rapid. There is a box weir as you near the town which, although easy at medium floods, looks **exceptionally dangerous** in big water conditions. Paddlers out of their depth at these flows could go straight over - so beware!! - **portage right**. It is best to egress just above the tunnel in town as I understand that canalization and a new weir are now just below, **so beware**!

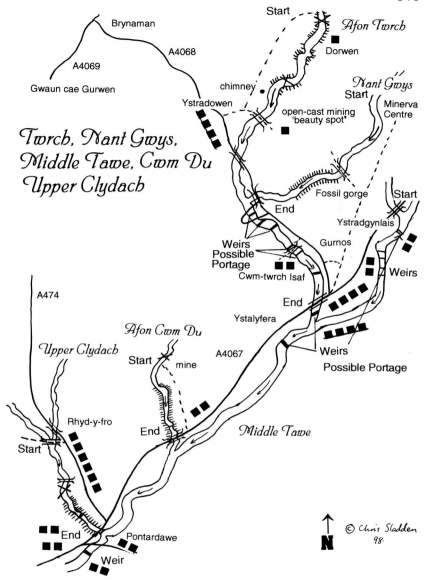

Brynaman

A4069

A4068

Gwaun cae Gurwen

Afon Torch

Start

Dorwen

chimney

Nant Gwys
Start

Ystradowen

Minerva
Centre

open-cast mining
'beauty spot'

*Torch, Nant Gwys,
Middle Tawe, Cwm Du
Upper Clydach*

Fossil gorge

Start

End

Ystradgynlais

Weirs
Possible
Portage

Gurnos

Cwm-twrch Isaf

Weirs

A474

End

Ystalyfera

Weirs

Afon Cwm Du

Start

mine

A4067

Possible Portage

Upper Clydach

Rhyd-y-fro

End

Middle Tawe

Start

End

Pontardawe

Weir

N

© Chris Sladden
98.

Lower Clydach River

Map: Swansea Gower & surrounding area, no. 159
Grade: II to III; one fall IV to V
Length: 10 km
Access: main A4067 Swansea to Sennybridge road
Notes: one fence and a couple of trees require easy portages; one small weir; one pipe needs portaging in high floods; one grade IV to V fall in town
Quality: ***

Starting in the wilds of the Lliw district, the lower Clydach is an excellent run at an easy grade. There is a harder fall in Clydach town for the brave.

Penlanau to Tawe confluence: 10 km grade II to III***

Using a map is the best way to find the starting point for the lower Clydach River. Failing that, turn off into Clydach town from the A4067 and head upstream, keeping the river on your right. When you hit a T junction turn towards Rhyd y Fro, and you will cross the stream at Penanau GR676089. Access can be made here. There should be enough water to float down without hitting rocks.

Near the tract to Nant Moel a footbridge spans the river and a super mini-gorge is reached. For those new to the sport, you will want to take pictures here. In the following wooded section, one fence and two trees required portaging at time of writing.

The small road bridge, just north of Glyn Loch, has a small, boxed-in weir underneath it. So long as one of the locals hasn't dumped a car into midstream, run this straight down the middle.

As you near Clydach, the next proper road bridge has a pipe below that needs portaging if the river is very high. Otherwise, it is easy to squeeze under.

Just above the Tawe is an obvious horizon line and an excellent IV to V fall below. As one floats under the curtain of water (which, somehow, managed to suck Ambrose from his boat) falling from the canal above, the Tawe proper is entered and egress can be made GR689012.

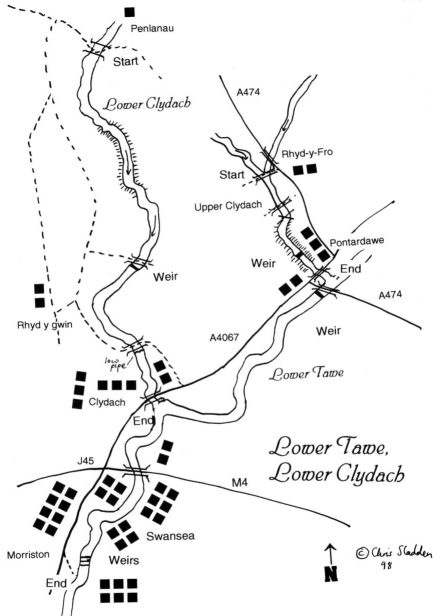

Penlanau

Start

Lower Clydach

A474

Rhyd-y-Fro

Start

Upper Clydach

Pontardawe

Weir

End

A474

Weir

Rhyd y gwin

A4067

Lower Tawe

low pipe

Clydach

End

J45

M4

Lower Tawe,
Lower Clydach

Morriston

Swansea

Weirs

End

N

© Chris Sladden
98

Afon Sawdde

Map: Brecon Beacons, no. 160
Grade: III to IV; one fall IV to IV+; upper section class V
Length: 11 km
Access: A4099 Llangadog to Brynamman road
Notes: one hard fall grade IV-IV+ on the upper river; one fence on
upper stretch. There are low wires across the lower stretch.
Quality: ****

The Sawdde is a beautiful river containing a lovely gorge on the lower section, with many excellent play waves. The gauge on the egress weir should read 6-9 for a good level and grade III in the lower gorge. Any higher and it becomes a continual grade IV with long swim possibilities. The upper section in big flood gives a run similar, but easier to the Haffes - itself found just the other side of the hill.

Llyn y Fan Fach to Blaenau: 2 km Grade V****

If you are lucky, and the small tracks are open, it is possible to work your way upstream to below the lake and launch onto the torrent downstream of the spill system or dam workings. It is possible to recce the whole run on the way up, which is sensible, as the last time I was there, there was a suggestion of some construction going on in the river bed about halfway down the run. Like the Haffes, this section is only possible after exceptionally heavy rain. Egress where things ease off and quickly head back off upstream for another blast down.

Llwynfron to Cefn Coed Common: 9 km grade III to IV; one fall IV to V****

The access point is fairly awkward to locate and so you are advised to use an OS map. Take the small roads up to Twynllanan and turn off right back towards the river. The next on the right leads you down to a small bridge that crosses the river GR757238. At levels greater than 6 on the lower scale, there is usually enough water to put on here by the right bank. Trees and one fence are the only problem for about a kilometre or so. The walls then begin to close in and a short gorge awaits on a right-angled bend. The narrow entrance rapid and following stretch rushing through sculptured red rock are grade IV or IV+ at very high level. Unfortunately at the end of '97 there was an enormous tree, causing a portage, here. Passing under a green pipe the confluence and main A4069 are reached. The rapids begin to build up and Pont ar Llechau is reached (Three Horseshoes pub). An excellent grade III (or IV) gorge follows. Savour this, for it is the very best of the Sawdde.

It is very difficult to pull a swimmer out of this gorge, or to know what to do with one when you have. The rock walls are very rounded, making climbing out very difficult. It is best to inspect this section before you run it. At high flows a pipe and wire crossing the river a little way down may need to be portaged. A good egress point is on the right bank just before the measuring weir next to the main A4069 road GR712266: a superb run. It is possible to continue down to the common or, indeed, the Tywi if you so wish, the only problem being a few broken weirs. However, in big water the aforementioned measuring weir starts to turn nasty and may need to be portaged

Afon Clydach

Map: Brecon Beacons, no. 160
Grade: IV to V
Length: 3 km
Access: A4069 Brynamman to Llangadog road
Notes: fences; trees can be a problem
Quality: ★★★★

Stream paddling *par excllence*. The Clydach is one of the tributaries of the Sawdde.

Pont Clydach to Church Road bridge: 3 km grade IV to V★★★★

Take the A4069 Brynamman to Llangadog road which crosses this raging stream at Pont Clydach GR739196. It is possible to access here or, by walking in via the Foel Fawr (Herbert) Quarries, get upstream without too much effort. The higher you go, the harder it is. The river, like so many others of its genre, rises and falls incredibly quickly with rain. It is continuous and incredibly fast down to the first wooded section, where egress is possible up the footpath to the road at GR733203. One fence needed portaging at time of writing but, with a bit of luck, may since have been washed away. Though I haven't done it, the run down to the Church road bridge is, apparently, a fast and furious grade III with the occasional tree to dodge. Egress at footpath GR727218.

Nant Garw

Map:	Brecon Beacons, no. 160
Grade:	II to III; two falls grade IV
Length:	2 km
Access:	A4069 Brynamman to Llangadog road
Notes:	two hard grade IV falls. Below egress are low wires and bridges
Quality:	*****

A brilliant stream run at the grade with two hard falls to contemplate. Needs to be in a high spate to be run.

Garreg Lwyd to Upper Brynamman: 2 km grade II to III, with two falls of IV*****

Drive up the A4069 north from Brynamman. The river can be seen raging down the mountainside to the right. Use one of the convenient parking spaces and walk down the steep grassy hillside to the river. Access as high as you wish GR724170.

The river is very fast with a few tenuous eddies to make. Where the river steepens off into a right hand bend, with an obvious gorge, it is time to inspect. A hard grade IV drop guards the entrance to this mini-gorge. Beware its right-sided undercut. About 200 metres below is another superb grade IV blast. This time it is a triple drop. One of the many rivers descending from Mynydd Ddu, the Garw is a fantastic run.

Egress is made at the third footbridge up the public footpath on the right. There is convenient parking by the Welsh Water buildings on the outskirts of Brynamman GR721152.

Afon Cennen

Map: Swansea, Gower and surrounding area, no. 159
Grade: II
Length: 9 km
Access: A483 Ammanford to Llandeilo road
Notes: trees and fences are a problem

Quality: * for bottom half only!

In the shadows of the brooding Carreg Cennen Castle, perched high on its crag, the Cennen winds its way to the Tywi. Far better to spend the day with the kids exploring the fantastic monument!

Carreg Cennen Castle to Tywi confluence: 9 km grade II*

Follow the signs to Trapp and the Castle, which are off the A483 Ammanford to Llandeilo road. A small road leads off right before the castle in the direction of the river. Access may be made below a small bridge, GR672190, which crosses the stream.

This could be the longest river in Wales or, at least, that is how it might feel if paddling during summer on a quickly disappearing flood. A pity, really, as the access onto the river below the mighty stronghold of the last Prince of Wales is excellent - for those canoeists whose hopes and expectations exceed waves and stoppers.

In the height of summer, the paddler is quickly battling through branches and fences. The water is never more than grade II. It may well be better to gain access at the little bridge above the A483 road and thus miss out much of the hassle of trees GR627181. The paddling below is of much better quality.

Egress above the bridge in Ffairfach into the convenient car park on the right GR632215.

320

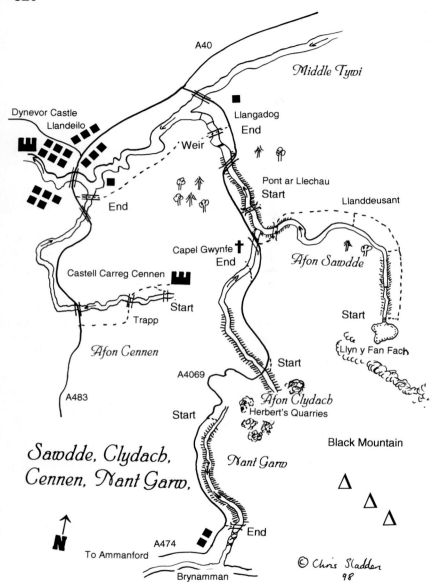

A40

Middle Tywi

Dynevor Castle
Llandeilo

Llangadog
End

Weir

Pont ar Llechau
Start

End

Llanddeusant

Afon Sawdde

Capel Gwynfe
End

Castell Carreg Cennen

Start

Trapp

Start

Afon Cennen

Start

Llyn y Fan Fach

A483

A4069

Start

Afon Clydach
Herbert's Quarries

Black Mountain

Sawdde, Clydach,
Cennen, Nant Garw,

Nant Garw

N

A474

End

To Ammanford

Brynamman

© Chris Sladden
98

Afon Aman

Map:	Brecon Beacons, no. 160
	Swansea, Gower and surrounding area, no. 159
Grade:	III
Length:	10 km
Access:	A474 Ammanford to Brynamman road
Notes:	the weir in Ammanford, though easy in low to medium flow, becomes *lethal* at high water. Other weirs require caution.
Quality:	**

In a run-down mining valley flows the Aman. A strange river to my mind, but it is a popular run with local paddlers. The little stream of no name that flows into the Aman through Gwaun-Cae-Gurwen has a series of large class V falls that are exciting to run (see photos in S W Wales book).

Cwm Aman to Pantyffynnon: 10 km grade III; weirs **

Take the A474 Ammanford to Brynamman road where, about a kilometre before Gwaun Cae Gurwen, is a turn-off left leading to Cwm Aman. Access onto the river may be made downstream right of the bridge GR693134. The river is essentially grade II to III rapids, with stoppers and waves at higher levels, interspersed with broken weirs. One of the weirs, an angled affair found after about four kilometres, has a powerful stopper in flood.

It is as well to inspect the weirs in Ammanford, found by the bridge leading to the village of Betws, prior to paddling GR632120. Although these are easy in medium water, the one immediately under the bridge forms *a terminal holding stopper in high water and under such conditions needs to be portaged*. Ambrose Hearne tells a few horror stories about this one.

Egress at the sports ground in Pantyffynnon; found by turning left off the A483(T) leading towards Pont Abraham from Ammanford town centre GR6245108.

This is a good access point for the Loughor river, thus avoiding the tree-choked upper section of river. The first weir just below the confluence becomes dangerous in flood.

River Loughor

Map:	Swansea, Gower and surrounding area, no. 159
Grade:	II; one waterfall portage
Length:	19 km
Access:	A483(T) Ammanford to Llandeilo road
Notes:	the upper section is tree-infested. One waterfall needs portaging, one friendly pig
Quality:	***

The upper Loughor, though beautiful in its own right, is spoilt by being over-grown with trees. The lower section is a pleasant touring stretch paddled through wildly meandering turns of river. This is classic geography in the making. It may be better to put on at one of the little road bridges on the outskirts of Ammanford, or at the egress point to the Aman River.

Capel Dewi bridge to Pontardulais: 19 km grade II; one waterfall***

Take the A483(T) Ammanford to Llandeilo road and turn off right one kilometre past the first river bridge. Head upstream where access may be made at the bridge near Capel Dewi GR660171 (best to use the OS sheet). The stream is fast flowing and you are immediately entangled with various branches and trunks. This is a pity as, with some gardening, this could be an excellent trip. At Glynhir Mansion GR642152, there is a friendly black and white pig which is well worth stopping to watch as it roams up and down a little footpath (is he still alive?). Whilst you are there it is wise, also, to inspect the 25-foot waterfall at the bottom of this footpath, just below a small bridge over the river. Although this has been done, most people will walk around taking time to pat the friendly pig's head en-route. There is an amazing little gorge, below which inspires to bigger things. Grade II tree-dodging leads the paddler down to the confluence with the Rivers Lash and Marlas.

There are a few broken weirs and small rapids over the next few kilometres, before the river undergoes a classic change in its descent to the sea. The remainder of the trip is history in the making as you weave and wind your way around the numerous bends and soon-to-be oxbow lakes, on the way to Pontardulais. Egress at the main road bridge, in Pontardulais GR588038, though it is possible to run the tidal stretch down to Loughor itself. Just below here the super little Gwili river joins.

Afon Gwili

Map:	Swansea, Gower and surrounding area, no. 159
Grade:	I to II
Length:	8 km
Access:	from M4 and A483
Notes:	a beautiful little river - no portages
Quality:	****

A surprisingly beautiful little river with superb narrow gorges containing myriad bird life.

Plas Newydd Ford to Hendy: 8 km grade I to II****

Turn off at the first small road past the M4 Pont Abraham junction, down to a ford by a caravan site at GR577087. There should be enough water to be able to get on at the ford without hitting any rocks for a good run. The river passes through numerous mini-gorges with small grade II rapids. The bird life is superb. The second motorway crossing is a long, echoing tunnel but holds no unpleasant surprises.

Finish the run at the Hendy Rugby Club bridge GR587039.

324

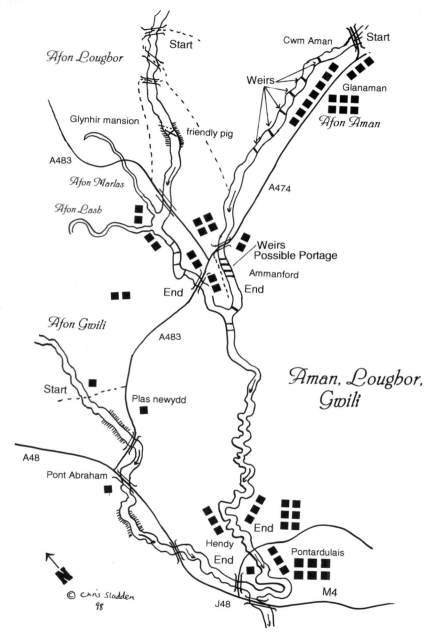

Afon Loughor

Start

Cwm Aman

Start

Weirs

Glanaman

Glynhir mansion

friendly pig

Afon Aman

A483

Afon Marlas

Afon Lash

A474

Weirs
Possible Portage

Ammanford

End

End

End

Afon Gwili

A483

Aman, Loughor,
Gwili

Start

Plas newydd

A48

Pont Abraham

End

End

Hendy

Pontardulais

End

M4

N

© Chris Sladden
98

J48

Gwendraeth Fach

Map: Swansea, Gower and surrounding area, no. 159
Grade: I to II
Length: 11 km
Access: off main A48(T) Swansea to Carmarthen road
Notes: one double weir near end
Quality: ***

This beautiful river can be paddled at most water levels, but is best avoided in flood. The fishermen are happy with paddlers, so please keep off during fishing season!!

Llangendeirne to Mynyddygarreg bridge: 11 km grade I to II***

This is a beautiful, flat river, excellent for beginners or an evening drift with a close friend. Turn off the A48(T) in Cross Hands, and make your way via Tumble to Pontybarem where, crossing the Gwendraeth Fawr and following the B4306, you reach the access point. Either here, or at the little bridge one kilometre down at Alltycadno, is suitable for putting-on GR453137. Heron, dipper and kingfisher hunt as you drift lazily towards Kidwelly. At an obvious right hand bend in the river above a little bridge in Mynyddygarreg is a small double weir which is straightforward at most levels. Egress is about one kilometre down at the little Llangadog bridge GR420078.

Gwendraeth Fawr

Map:	Swansea, Gower and surrounding area, no. 159
Grade:	I to II
Length:	8 km
Access:	off A48(T)
Notes:	low bridge and very low bridges
Quality:	***

A fine, fast river, excellent for training on.

Pontybarem to Pont-Newydd: 8 km grade I to II***

Turn off at Cross Hands and head for Pontybarem on the B4317. Turning right along the B4306 towards Carmarthen, the river is reached and access may be had from the car park upstream left GR502112. The river should have reasonable flow, enabling the paddler to clear any rocks in the channel. Occasionally, after heavy rain, the river rages down and during these conditions is best avoided. The gauge, just after the first footbridge on river left, reads slightly under one metre at a near-perfect level.

There are excellent small rapids and well-defined eddies as the river meanders its way past Pont Henri and Pontyates. There are two low footbridges which need ducking under.

As the paddler approaches Pont Newydd, there is a low railway bridge that poses some problem. Apparently, the line is still occasionally active, though privatisation may put paid to that, no doubt. You will have to tackle the problem yourselves - it is possible to **swim under** or **walk around**. Egress is at Pont-Newydd, only 100 metres downstream, which is another **impossibly low bridge** GR448073.

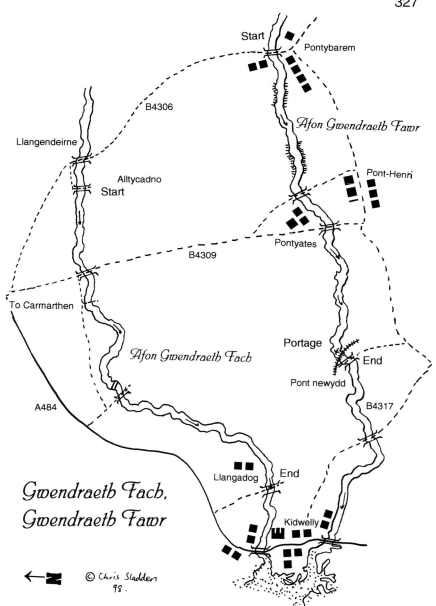

Start

Pontybarem

Afon Gwendraeth Fawr

B4306

Llangendeirne

Pont-Henri

Alltycadno

Start

Pontyates

B4309

To Carmarthen

Portage

Afon Gwendraeth Fach

End

Pont newydd

B4317

A484

Llangadog

End

Gwendraeth Fach,
Gwendraeth Fawr

Kidwelly

← N

© Chris Sladden
98.

Afon Gwili

Map:	Cardigan and surrounding area, no. 145
	Lampeter, Llandovery and surrounding area, no. 146
	Swansea, Gower and surrounding area, no. 159
Grade:	II to III
Length:	8 km
Access:	off the A484 Carmarthen to Newcastle Emlyn road
Notes:	occasional tree problems
Quality:	***

The Gwili is an excellent little river, giving good quality grade II and III rapids in the right water conditions. It also runs past one of the country's foremost canoeing shops, where you can pick up any piece of outdoor equipment you can think of.

Rock and Fountain to Carmarthen: 8 km grade II to III***

Head out from Carmarthen on the A484 Newcastle Emlyn road until you come across the small pub called _The Rock and Fountain_ GR389258. Here access can be made. It runs for quite a few days after heavy rain, but you will have better sport if you get it in a spate condition. There is one small weir a little way down the run which is safe to play in and, indeed, excellent for learning stopper skills. Further still, and one or two drops reach grade III and have superb waves for shredding.

As you pass through Bronwydd Arms, you will pass just behind **White Water Consultancy.** This is one of the (if not _the_) best canoeing shops in Britain. If you need any equipment, you can get it here. As for me, I always stop and blag a coffee and a cake off Huw.

I have known Huwie for a considerable number of years now, but I often picture him after a trip down the South Wales Twrch:

We had been in to get a photograph for my first South Wales book, which involved a long trek in and out of the river. When we were getting changed, there was this funny, bleeping noise that occurred. Back in those days, there weren't many mobile phones around, but Huw had one. Much to my amazement, he proceeded to sell a sea kayak whilst his trousers and towel were around his ankles - quite a frightening sight - but, surely, the ultimate salesman.

The egress point, as stated on the lower Tywi section, is a little bit 'up in the air' at the moment because of the building of the new bypass. It may be necessary to get out on the A40 or in Carmarthen itself. Up-to-date details are available from Huw on 01267 223555.

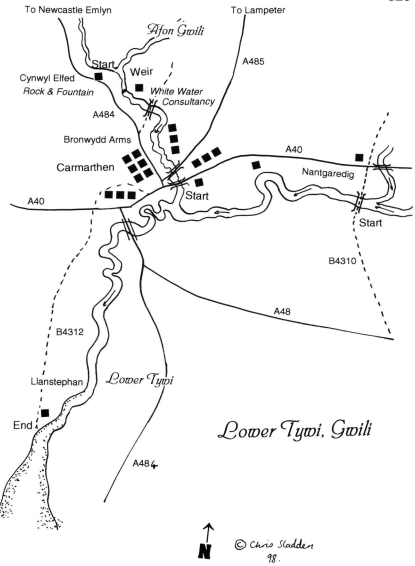

To Newcastle Emlyn

To Lampeter

Afon Gwili

Start

A485

Weir

Cynwyl Elfed
Rock & Fountain

*White Water
Consultancy*

A484

Bronwydd Arms

A40

Carmarthen

Nantgaredig

A40

Start

Start

A40

B4310

A48

B4312

Llanstephan

Lower Tywi

End

A484

N

Lower Tywi, Gwili

© Chris Sladden
98.

Afon Cynin

Map: Tenby and surrounding area, no. 158
Grade: I to II
Length: 10 km
Access: off A40(T) Carmarthen to Haverfordwest road
Notes: trees require respect
Quality: ***

A delightful touring river through beautiful rolling countryside.

Gellywen to St Clears: 10 km grade I to II***

Take the B4299 in St Clears northwards through the village of Meidrum and turn off to Gellywen. Turn off right down the steep road (past the sign to Felindre) and drive up by the river. About a kilometre up here is a house named "Passby" right by the banks of the stream. The pleasant couple who live here will allow access onto the stream GR277243.

If there is enough water to float the boat, then there is enough to paddle; but the river should **not be in flood**. A little way down is a small weir above Gellywen. The surroundings are superb with clear, blue water flowing through wooded banks. If you pick your season, towards late April and May, then myriad bluebells adorn the river banks. There are a couple of weirs further on which pose no problems.

One tree required portaging at time of writing but this is an excellent trip for canoeists at this grade, or those who want to explore this type of water. As you pass under the obvious railway crossing, the character of the stream abruptly changes, and the grip of the sea on the fresh water is evident. Egress at St Clears' boat house, which is reached by turning off left just before the bridge on the A4066 to Laugharne, GR281153.

Afon Taf

Map:	Tenby and surrounding area, no. 158
	Swansea, Gower and surrounding area, no. 159
Grade:	I to II
Length:	Login to Whitland 14 km
Access:	off the A40(T)
Notes:	trees require respect; care required in Laugharne estuary; an experienced leader is sensible here!
Quality:	****

A wonderful touring river bubbling through Dylan Thomas country.

Login to Laugharne: 32 km grade I to II****

By turning off north in Whitland, it is possible to follow the small roads up to the village of Login. There are so many twists and turns that a map is necessary. Here, access can be made onto the river via the left bank just below a weir. It is possible to get in upstream. The gauge at the access point should read 2-3 on the lower scale at the ideal level GR166234.

Nowhere does the stream exceed grade II as you set off down glistening water. A few trees had to be carefully negotiated but none required portaging. The Llanfallteg bends appear to be a popular place for shooting with the local gentry though, hopefully, a large piece of bright yellow won't be mistaken for a duck.

The old bridge in Whitland provides an alternative access or egress point, which allows shortening of a trip. On the way to St Clears, a footbridge and an old broken-down stone bridge are passed after which the river begins to change in character. On reaching St Clears, the water is well and truly tidal. You may wish to time the tide to help you on the last stretch to Laugharne.

When the mists are down you can almost hear the voice of **Captain Cat** calling to you during the eerie paddle to Laugharne. If the mists are down, it is best to hug the right bank, passing the numerous ghost-like fishermen until you reach the little jetty in Laugharne where egress can be made GR306112. From the road this can be reached by passing through Laugharne beach holiday park above Dylan Thomas' boathouse.

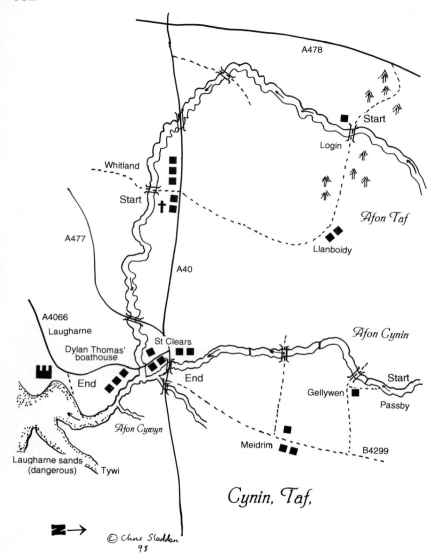

A478

Start

Login

Whitland

Start

†

A477

A40

Afon Taf

Llanboidy

A4066
Laugharne

Dylan Thomas'
boathouse

St Clears

Afon Cynin

Afon Cywyn

End

End

Gellywen

Start

Passby

Meidrim

B4299

Laugharne sands
(dangerous)   Tywi

Cynin, Taf,

N→

© Chris Sladden
95

Western Cleddau

Map:	Tenby and surrounding area, no. 158
Grade:	II
Length:	19 km
Access:	A40(T) Haverfordwest to Fishguard road
Notes:	two weirs; low trees
Quality:	***

A great touring river through beautiful countryside.

Welsh Hook to Haverfordwest: 19 km grade II; probable weir portage at egress ***

Turn off into Wolfs Castle from the A40(T) Haverfordwest to Fishguard road and make the short journey off left up to Welsh Hook. Crossing the river towards Hayscastle Cross the first right allows access to the river by a tiny side stream GR933277.

From here down to Treffgarne the river is exceptionally beautiful. You should pick a day or so after rain when there is an obvious good flow but the water is clear and the sun is out. *In flood the trees become dangerous*.

Below the second major road bridge the river widens out and meanders down towards Haverfordwest. There is one small weir at Withybush that is generally easy to shoot. As the town is entered, various bridges are passed under and a large weir is reached. This is obvious from the river due to, firstly, its classic horizon line and, secondly, the large sign saying 'weir'. I always egress left into the convenient car park above the weir and, therefore, have not shot it. People do shoot it, but in flood it becomes *very dangerous* and since the printing of the first book there have been a few epics in here - *beware!* GR956156. When I was working in Haverfordwest hospital I couldn't resist checking out the attractively named Merlin's Brook but, sadly, it is pretty well uncanoeable - this enters a little way below the weir.

Eastern Cleddau

Map:	Tenby and surrounding area, no. 158
Grade:	II
Length:	20 km
Access:	A478 Tenby to Cardigan road
Notes:	The weir at Canasten is dangerous in flood. Trees and occasional low wires.
Quality:	****

The rolling hills and valleys overlooked by the Preseli Range are some of the most beautiful in Wales. Both Cleddau are superb touring rivers. The wildlife is outstanding and the estuaries breathtaking. The river is best done in the week or so after floods have dropped.

Llangwm Ford to Landshipping: 20 km grade II****

Turning off the A40(T) (Carmarthen to Haverfordwest) on the A478 Cardigan road, the village of Llandissilo is reached. The third turning off left leads down to the ford at Llangwm where access may be had GR106224. The gauge at the bridge is at one and a half to two foot at a near perfect level.

The river tinkles along at around grade II, with the occasional small drop and wave. A few of the bridges have wires slung from them so keep the eyes peeled. Just after the railway bridge, the Afon Syfynwy enters from the right to swell proceedings.

Llawhaden is a convenient place to stop for lunch or to shorten the trip if desired. There is a beautiful church and remains of a castle here for the more cultured of paddlers. Just below the main Canasten bridge is Canasten pumping station and weir. Although easy, this can produce a nasty stopper in flood. Both portage routes are slightly tricky so take your choice. A few boulder shoots take the paddler to the Black Pool Mill. The river becomes tidal and visions of Colditz spring to mind as you sit dwarfed by the austere disused mill. Black Pool Mill is aptly named as you gaze into the swirls, trying to penetrate its mysterious depths.

It is well worth avoiding low tide as the estuary is shallow over the next kilometre but it is difficult to find more flourishing wildlife than on the journey to Landshipping. If the Lord of the Manor, or whoever he is, isn't blasting willy nilly with his shotgun, then you'll never beat the tranquillity of drifting into the setting sun and the slipway just below the Stanley Arms pub, GR012117 - wonderful!

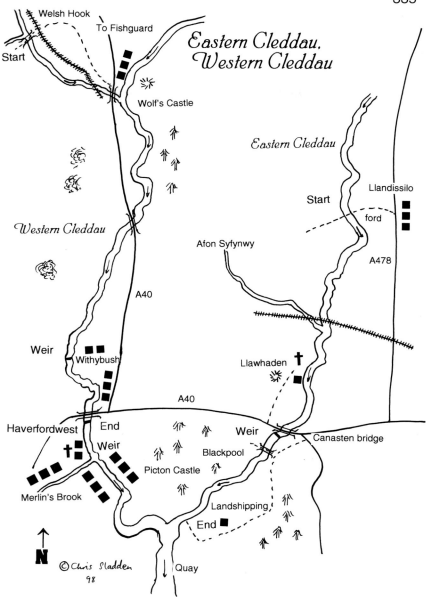

Eastern Cleddau,
Western Cleddau

Welsh Hook

To Fishguard

Start

Wolf's Castle

Eastern Cleddau

Western Cleddau

Start

Llandissilo

ford

Afon Syfynwy

A478

A40

Weir

Withybush

Llawhaden

A40

Haverfordwest

End

Weir

Weir

Canasten bridge

Blackpool

Picton Castle

Merlin's Brook

Landshipping

End

© Chris Sladden
98

N

Quay

Afon Gwaun

Map:	St David's and Haverfordwest area, no. 157
Grade:	II to III
Length:	4 km
Access:	off A487 in Fishguard
Notes:	low trees
Quality:	***

A good low-grade spate run well worth doing if in the area at time of spate. Can easily be combined with a trip to the Bitches. Although I have done the upper five kilometres, it is the worst section ever for fallen trees, so don't bother. The lower needed no portages at time of writing. A few people have since tried the upper section and all have agreed - dreadful for trees!

Llanychaer to Fishguard: 4 km grade II to III***

Take the B4313 out of upper Fishguard up the Gwaun valley. Access may be made at the bridge in Llanychaer, GR987354. The river needs to be in a medium spate to run, and is an excellent blast for those paddling competently at the grade. Trees are the only hazard, but none required portaging at time of writing. The small broken weir towards the town forms an excellent play stopper in big water. The finish into Fishguard harbour is one of the most spectacular in Wales. Egress on the right up the slipway into the car park GR963373.

Afon Nyfer

Map: Cardigan & surrounding area, no. 145
Grade: II to III
Length: 8 km
Access: A487 Cardigan to Fishguard (Abergwaun) road
Notes: one large weir
Quality: ****

The Nyfer is a beautiful little river that tumbles gently out of the Preseli Mountains, returning its waters to the sea in Newport Bay. The kilometre above my get-in goes through an impressive gorge, running at about IV+ with possible portages. I haven't paddled this but would be pleased to hear from anybody who has. I used to fish this stretch as a boy but failed to catch even one elusive salmon - not for want of trying!

Castell Clwyd to Newport: 8 km grade II to III; one weir ****

About 15 kilometres south of Cardigan is the little hamlet of Eglwyswrw and a kilometre after this is the B4329 turning. Follow this until you cross the river, and then take the first right, signposted Newport. Following this for about a kilometre, a very steep section of road is reached which drops to the river. Access can be made on a little side stream (Afon Brynberian) which joins the main river a little below this steep incline GR103374.

From here on down is an excellent kilometre of grade II+ to III, running through delightful gorges. A good level is probably just dropping off the flood as, in full spate, the trees may be a bit of a fright to paddlers at this grade. None needed portaging at time of writing, though there was a bit of negotiation required.

Just as the main road comes into sight on the right hand side is a large, sloping weir. This should be obvious from the river, as it slows the water down quite noticeably. Avoiding the central salmon steps, which have nasty stoppers, it can be run in medium spate far left or right. If in doubt, then portage.

The main A487 road bridge with the visible Salutation Inn is next, followed after a couple of kilometres by the beautiful village of Nevern. Here, found in the local churchyard, if you believe legend, is "the bleeding tree", so-called because of the red-coloured sap that drips down an old, gnarled yew tree.

The water, by now, is grade I with the odd manmade, bouldery step to shoot, but these don't amount to much. The gorge below, though flat, is beautiful. A caravan park, something of a blot on the landscape, is passed before suitable egress at the next road bridge on the outskirts of Newport GR062395. This is on the Moylgrove road. If you like, and if the tide is right, you can continue down to the Parog - about another kilometre. On the ebb, this fairly races out to sea, and you will need to take care. When we were boys, my brother and I used to dare each other to swim out across the current - looking back, I'm probably lucky to have been able to write these lines!

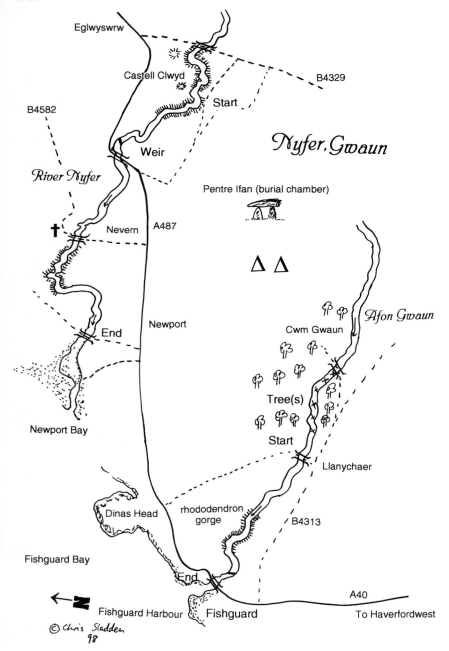

Eglwyswrw

Castell Clwyd

Start

B4329

Nyfer, Gwaun

B4582

Weir

River Nyfer

Pentre Ifan (burial chamber)

Nevern A487

△ △

Afon Gwaun

Newport

Cwm Gwaun

End

Tree(s)

Newport Bay

Start

Llanychaer

Dinas Head

rhododendron gorge

B4313

Fishguard Bay

End

Fishguard Harbour   Fishguard

A40

To Haverfordwest

© Chris Sladden
98

The Bitches - guide by John-Paul Eatock

Introduction

The Bitches and Whelps are not a pack of fierce female dogs, but a line of rocks that juts out into Ramsey Sound, between Ramsey Island (RSPB-owned) and the Welsh mainland. Throughout their history they have, without doubt, earned their name!

For kayakers, they offer some of the most reliable and exciting white water around the whole of the British Isles, and have becomes a well-known feature within the sea kayaking and rodeo world for their uniqueness, character and inherent beauty.

Be aware of the warning:

Paddling the Bitches is a serious undertaking, and safety equipment (flares, strobes, whistles etc.) should be worn by all persons at all times.

Access:

In the heart of the Pembrokeshire National Park is the sleepy cathedral town of St David's, reached by the A478 main road. From here, it is possible to drive westward to the access point of St Justinian GR724252.

Height of tide:

Less than 5.7 m at Milford Haven - Introduction to white water
Between 5.7 m and 6.2 m - Excellent for improver level
Between 6.2 m and 7 m - Intermediate to advanced and rodeo coaching
Above 7.1 m - Hold onto your hats - experts only

On a flood tide the sea flows from the South to the North, producing a rush of white water over the Bitches - comparable to a grade IV river - able to take you, without paddling, one mile in less than ten minutes.

The flood tide starts to flow North about three hours before high water at Milford Haven, until about three hours after high water at Milford Haven.

For a good Bitches session it is best to go out three hours before high water and warm up with the increasing flow of the tide. Remember to add an hour for British Summer Time.

The South-flowing tide runs three hours after high water to three hours before the following high water. The flow it produces is very useful for beginners to practise white water techniques such as breaking-in or out and ferry-gliding.

Routes which are the safest to use are mapped on the diagram and it should be remembered not to underestimate your own or the group's paddling strength and stamina, as it takes an average of 25 minutes constant paddling to get there are 20 minutes to return to St Justinians. This will seem like a lifetime to a novice.

Always get the weather report before attempting the journey, from the local Coastguard - available on 01646 690909 - asking for the forecast for south of St David's Head. Watch out for the effects of wind against tide, which can produce 8-10 foot-high standing waves in the main channel. Horse Rock, at certain tide states, produces a large whirlpool and is a definite no-go area.

Twr-y-Felin Outdoor Centre has produced this information for your safety. We would also like to take this opportunity to ask you to give considered respect to the RSPB Reserve of Ramsey Island. Please do not disturb any of the native inhabitants of the Island, whether they be winged or on the hoof, and keep well clear of seals around beaches and caves as they mate and pup throughout late spring, the summer and early autumn.

If you wish to tell someone that you are going out and your estimated time of arrival back, Twr-y-Felin welcome you to 'sign in' and 'sign out' at their new restaurant and shop, the "Coastal Trader", located on the Cross Square in the centre of St David's.

If you have any queries, want information about annual rodeos, wish to hire a guide or want rodeo coaching from some of the best paddlers in Britain, don't hesitate to contact Twr-y-Felin at:

Twr-y-Felin, St David's, Dyfed SA62 6QS
Tel: 01437 721611   Fax: 01437 721838

THE BITCHES

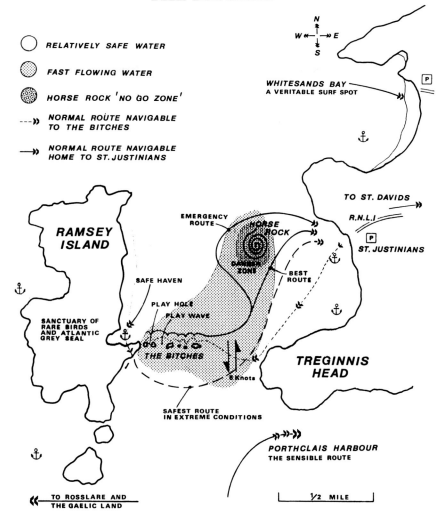

○ RELATIVELY SAFE WATER

◌ FAST FLOWING WATER

◍ HORSE ROCK 'NO GO ZONE'

--->> NORMAL ROUTE NAVIGABLE
      TO THE BITCHES

—>> NORMAL ROUTE NAVIGABLE
    HOME TO ST. JUSTINIANS

N
W ←—|—→ E
S

WHITESANDS BAY —
A VERITABLE SURF SPOT

P

TO ST. DAVIDS

R.N.L.I

P

ST. JUSTINIANS

RAMSEY
ISLAND

EMERGENCY
ROUTE

HORSE
ROCK

DANGER
ZONE

BEST
ROUTE

SAFE HAVEN

PLAY HOLE
PLAY WAVE

SANCTUARY OF
RARE BIRDS
AND ATLANTIC
GREY SEAL

THE BITCHES

TREGINNIS
HEAD

8 Knots

SAFEST ROUTE
IN EXTREME CONDITIONS

PORTHCLAIS HARBOUR
THE SENSIBLE ROUTE

TO ROSSLARE AND
THE GAELIC LAND

½ MILE

BIBLIOGRAPHY

The following list offers other sources of information and inspiration for paddling on Welsh rivers:

Stooke, E, *Stookes' Tourist Map of the River Wye*, London 1892

Cash, J, *The River Wye*, Chapman & Hall, London 1952

Hargreaves, J, Storry, T, *North Wales White Water*, Cascade Press 1981

Fox, A, *Run River Run*, Diadem Books 1990

Sladden, C S, *White Water Runs and Touring Rivers of South Wales*, Chris Sladden 1990

Storry, T, *British White Water*, Constable 1991

Sladden, C S, *White Water Runs and Touring Rivers of South West Wales*, M J Sladden 1994

STAR RATING AND GRADE INDEX

The following is a checklist of rivers by star rating and gradings divided into North, Mid and South Wales sections. It is intended to provide a quick visual guide to what is available in each area.

Please note, however, that a number of rivers appear in more than one category. For example, in North Wales, under the grading section, the Ogwen is found in each of the class III to IV, and IV to V listings. This means that on the Ogwen, there are sections at each of these grades. In terms of star quality this means, for example, in South Wales, the Tawe is listed under five, three and two-star ratings. This means there are separate sections of five, three and two stars to be found on the Tawe river.

NORTH WALES

STAR RATINGS:

***** *Five star rivers:*
Arddu, Colwyn, Conwy, Dee, Gain, Glaslyn Gorge, Lower Glaslyn, Goedal, Llyfni, Mawddach, Ogwen, Prysor, Twrch (Bala), Wnion

**** *Four star rivers:*
Anafon, Artro, Conwy, Dee, Dwryd, Dwyfor (lower gorge), Eden, Elwy, Gamlan, Upper Glaslyn, Llugwy, Machno, Mawddach, Nantygwryd, Nant Peris, Ogwen, Seiont, Tryweryn, Wnion

*** *Three star rivers:*
Aled, Alun, Caseg, Ceidiog, Ceiriog, Ceirw, Clwyd, Clywedog (Ruthin), Conwy, Croesor, Dee, Gwyrfai, Llafar (Bala), Llafar (Ogwen), Lledr, Lliw, Llugwy, Marchlyn Mawr, Nantmor, Ogwen, Rhaeadr Fawr

** *Two star rivers:*
Alwen, Ceiriog, Cledwen, Dwyfach, Rhaeadr Fawr, Tegel, Wen

* *One star rivers:*
Clywedog (Torrent Walk)

'Star-less' rivers:
Crafnant, Hilnant, Clywedog (Wrexham)

344

GRADINGS:

Class I:
Clwyd, Dee, Lower Glaslyn, Machno

Class I to II:
Lower Conwy, Dwryd

Class II:
Ceidiog, Clywedog (Wrexham), Conwy, Dee, Dwyfach, Upper Glaslyn, Llafar (Bala), Lower Mawddach, Lower Wnion

Class II to III:
Aled, Alun, Ceiriog, Ceirw, Cledwen, Clywedog (Ruthin), Llugwy, Llyfni, Prysor

Class III:
Alwen, Artro, Ceiriog, Elwy, Gwyrfai, Seiont, Tryweryn

Class III to IV:
Conwy, Dee, Dwyfor, Eden, Lledr, Ogwen, Rhaeadr Fawr

Class IV:
Colwyn, Conwy, Hilnant, Llugwy, Mawddach, Nantmor, Wen, Wnion, Ysgethin

Class IV to V:
Anafon, Arddu, Caseg, Crafnant, Gain, Glaslyn Gorge, Gwynant, Llafar (Ogwen), Lliw, Ogwen, Rhaeadr Fawr, Twrch (Bala)

Class V:
Conwy, Mawddach, Nant Peris

Class V to VI:
Clywedog (Torrent), Croesor, Cwm Mynach, Cwm Nantcol, Cynfal, Gamlan, Goedal, Llugwy, Lower Prysor, Rhaeadr Fawr, Tegel

MID WALES

STAR RATINGS:

***** *Five star rivers:*
Banwy, Diliw, Ystwyth

**** *Four star rivers:*
Camlad, Claerwen, Clywedog (Llanidloes), Dulas (Forge), Dulas (Llanidloes), Dyfi, Dysynni, Einion, Elan, L'eri, Irfon, Rheidol, Tanat, Twymyn, Vyrnwy, Wye

*** *Three star rivers:*
Angell, Banwy, Cammarch, Chwerfri, Dugoed, Dulas (Corris), Dyfi, Edw, Gam, Ithon, Marteg, Mule, Rhiw, Severn, Sgithwen Brook, Twrch (Banwy), Vyrnwy, Wye

** *Two star rivers:*
Cadair, Carno, Clywedog Brook, Dulas (Builth), Eunant Fawr, Iwrch, Lugg, Severn

* *One star rivers:*
Severn

'Star-less' rivers:
Cain, Llynfi (Talgarth), Rhayader

GRADINGS:

Class I:
Cain, Camlad, Lugg, Severn, Wye

Class I to II:
Banwy, Cammarch, Dyfi, Llynfi, Severn

Class II:
Carno, Clywedog Brook, Chwerfri, Dulas (Builth), Dysynni, Ithon, L'eri, Rhiw, Tanat, Vyrnwy, Wye

Class II to III:
Clywedog (Llanidloes), Gam, Irfon (lower), Ithon, Iwrch, Mule, Severn

Class III:
Cadair, Dulas (Forge), Dugoed, Marteg, Twrch (Banwy), Wye

Class III to IV:
Claerwen, Dulas (Corris), Dyfi, Edw, Twymyn, Vyrnwy, Wye

Class IV:
Dulas (Corris), Dulas (Llanidloes), Rhaeadr

Class IV to V:
Angell, Diliw, Dugoed, Irfon, Sgithwen Brook, Ystwyth

Class V to VI:
Einion, Eunant Fawr, Rheidol

SOUTH WALES

STAR RATINGS:

***** *Five star rivers:*
Clydach (upper), Haffes, Nant Garw, Tawe, Tywi

**** *Four star rivers:*
Cleddau (Eastern), Clydach (Sawdde), Gwili (Aman), Mellte, Monnow, Nant Clydach, Nedd Fechan, Nyfer, Pyrddin, Sawdde, Taf, Teifi, Twrch (South Wales), Tywi, Usk

*** *Three star rivers:*
Aeron, Afan, Cilieni, Cleddau (Western), Clydach Brook, Cothi, Lower Clydach, Clydach (River), Crai, Cynin, Doethie, Dulais (Llanwrda), Dulais (Neath), Ewenny, Giedd, Grwyne, Gwendraeth Fach, Gwendraeth Fawr, Gwili (Tywi), Gwaun, Hepste, Loughor, Nant Cwy, Nant Gwys, Nantygwair, Ogwr Fawr, Palenna, Pysgotwr, Rhondda Fach, Rhondda Fawr, Senni, Taf Fechan, Taff, Tarell, Tawe, Teifi, Twrch (South Wales), Tywi, Usk

** *Two star rivers:*
Aman, Bran (Llandovery), Cwm Du, Cwm Gwrelych, Dringarth, Dulais (Halfway), Ebbw, Ely, Garw, Gwydderig, Honddu (Brecon), Llia, Lwyd, Nant Bran, Nant Twymyn, Neath, Ogwr Fawr, Rhymney, Tawe, Ysgir

* *One star rivers:*
Arth, Cennen, Corrwg, Caerfanell, Cynon, Dore, Sirhowy, Sychryd

'Star-less' rivers:
Taf Fawr, Honddu (Monnow)

GRADINGS:

Class I:
Bran (Llandovery), Dore, Dulais (Halfway), Garw, Usk

Class I to II:
Aeron, Cynin, Ewenny, Gwendraeth Fach, Gwendraeth Fawr, Gwili (Aman), Monnow, Sirhowy, Taf, Taff, Teifi

Class II:
Cennen, Cynon, Eastern Cleddau, Western Cleddau, Ebbw, Ely, Giedd, Honddu (Monnow), Llynfi (Bridgend), Loughor, Lwyd, Monnow, Rhondda Fach, Rhymney, Tawe, Usk

Class II to III:
Aeron, Caerfanell, Corrwg, Cothi, Crai, Clydach (lower), Grwyne, Gwaun, Gwydderig, Gwili (Tywi), Nant Garw, Nant Gwys, Neath, Nyfer, Ogwr Fawr, Palenna, Rhondda Fawr, Senni, Taf Fawr, Taff, Tywi

Class III:
Afan, Aman, Cilieni, Dulais (Neath), Dulais (Llanwrda), Honddu (Brecon), Ogwr Fach, Tawe, Tarell, Teifi, Usk, Ysgir

Class III to IV:
Afan, Dringarth, Llia, Nant Bran, Rhondda Fawr, Rhymney, Sawdde, Twrch (South Wales)

Class IV:
Arth, Clydach (upper), Cwm Du, Doethie, Nant Clydach, Nant Cwy, Nant y Gwair, Nant Tywynni, Pyrddin, Taf Fechan, Teifi

Class IV to V:
Clydach (River), Clydach Brook, Clydach (Sawdde), Giedd, Hepste, Mellte, Nedd Fechan, Sychryd, Tawe, Twrch (South Wales), Tywi

Class V:
Cwm Gwrelych, Sawdde

Class V to VI:
Haffes, Pysgotwr, Tawe

INDEX